The Pen Is Ours

THE SCHOMBURG LIBRARY OF
NINETEENTH-CENTURY BLACK WOMEN WRITERS

Henry Louis Gates, Jr.
General Editor

Titles are listed chronologically; collections that
include works published over a span of years are listed according to
the publication date of their initial work.

The Pen Is Ours

A Listing of Writings by and about
African-American Women before 1910
With Secondary Bibliography
to the Present

Compiled by
JEAN FAGAN YELLIN
CYNTHIA D. BOND

New York   Oxford
OXFORD UNIVERSITY PRESS
1991

Oxford University Press

Oxford   New York
Athens   Auckland   Bangkok   Bombay
Calcutta   Cape Town   Dar es Salaam   Delhi
Florence   Hong Kong   Istanbul   Karachi
Kuala Lumpur   Madras   Madrid   Melbourne
Mexico City   Nairobi   Paris   Singapore
Taipei   Tokyo   Toronto

and associated companies in
Berlin   Ibadan

Copyright © 1991 by Jean Fagan Yellin and Cynthia D. Bond

Published by Oxford University Press, Inc.,
198 Madison Avenue, New York, New York 10016

Oxford is a registered trademark of Oxford University Press

Library of Congress Cataloging-in-Publication Data
Yellin, Jean Fagan.
The pen is ours : a listing of writings by and about African-American
women before 1910 with secondary bibliography to the present /
compiled by Jean Fagan Yellin and Cynthia D. Bond.
p.   cm.—(The Schomburg library of nineteenth-century Black women writers)
Includes bibliographical references and index.
ISBN 0-19-506203-5
1. American literature—Afro-American authors—History and criticism—
Bibliography. 2. American literature—Women authors—History and
criticism—Bibliography. 3. American literature—19th century—
History and criticism—Bibliography. 4. American literature—
Afro-American authors—Bibliography. 5. Afro-American women—History—
19th century—Bibliography. 6. Afro-American women authors—Biography—
Bibliography. 7. Women and literature—United States—Bibliography.
8. American literature—Women authors—Bibliography. 9. Afro-American
women in literature—Bibliography. 10. Afro-Americans in literature—
Bibliography. I. Bond, Cynthia D. II. Title. III. Series.
Z1229.N39Y44   1991
[PS153.N5]   016.8108'09287—dc20   90-41447

6 8 10 9 7 5

Printed in the United States of America on acid-free paper

The
Schomburg Library
of
Nineteenth-Century
Black Women Writers
Is
Dedicated
in Memory
of
PAULINE AUGUSTA COLEMAN GATES

1916–1987

PUBLISHER'S NOTE

FOREWORD TO THE SCHOMBURG SUPPLEMENT

Henry Louis Gates, Jr.

The enthusiastic reception by students, scholars, and the general public to the 1988 publication of the Schomburg Library of Nineteenth-Century Black Women Writers more than justified the efforts of twenty-five scholars and the staff of the Black Periodical Literature Project to piece together the fragments of knowledge about the writings of African-American women between 1773 and 1910. The Library's republication of those writings in thirty volumes—ranging from the poetry of Phillis Wheatley to the enormous body of work that emerged out of the "Black Woman's Era" at the turn of this century—was a *beginning* for the restoration of the written sensibilities of a group of writers who confronted the twin barriers of racism and sexism in America. Through their poetry, diaries, speeches, biographies, essays, fictional narratives, and autobiographies, these writers transcended the boundaries of racial prejudice and sexual discrimination by recording the thoughts and feelings of Americans who were, at once, black *and* female. Taken together, these works configure into a literary tradition because their authors read, critiqued, and revised each other's words, in textual groundings with their sisters.

Indeed, by publishing these texts together as a "library," and by presenting them as part of a larger discourse on race and gender, we hoped to enable readers to chart the formal specificities of this tradition and to trace its origins. As a whole, the works in the Schomburg Library demonstrate that the contemporary literary movement of African-American women writers is heir to a legacy that was born in 1773, when Phillis Wheatley's *Poems on Various Subjects, Religious and Moral* first unveiled the mind of a black woman to the world. The fact that the Wheatley volume has proven to be the most popular in the Schomburg set is a testament to her role as the "founder" of both the black American's and the black woman's literary tradition.

Even before the Library was published, however, I began to receive queries about producing a supplement that would incorporate works that had not been included initially. Often these exchanges were quite dramatic. For instance, shortly before a lecture I was about to deliver at the University of Cincinnati, Professor Sharon Dean asked me if the Library would be reprinting the 1859 autobiography of Eliza Potter, a black hairdresser who had lived and worked in Cincinnati. I had never heard of Potter, I replied. Did Dean have a copy of her book? No, but there *was* a copy at the Cincinnati Historical Society. As I delivered my lecture, I could not help thinking about this "lost" text and its great significance. In fact, after the lecture, Dean and I rushed from the building and drove to the Historical Society, arriving just a few moments before closing time. A patient librarian brought us the book, and as I leafed through it, I was once again confronted with the realization that so often accompanied the research behind the Library's first thirty volumes—the exciting, yet poignant awareness that there probably exist *dozens* of works like Potter's, buried in research libraries, waiting only to be uncovered through an accident of contiguity like that which placed Sharon Dean in Cincinnati, roaming the shelves of its Historical Society. Another scholar wrote to me about work being done on the poet Effie Waller Smith. Several other scholars also wrote to share their research on other authors and their works. A supplement to the Library clearly was necessary.

Thus we have now added ten volumes, among them Potter's autobiography and Smith's collected poetry, as well as a narrative by Sojourner Truth, several pamphlets by Ida B. Wells-Barnett, and two biographies by Josephine Brown and Frances Rollin. Also included are books consisting of various essays, stories, poems, and plays whose authors did not, or could not, collect their writings into a full-length volume. The works of Olivia Ward Bush-Banks, Angelina Weld Grimké, and Katherine Davis Chapman Tillman are in this category. A related volume is an anthology of short fiction published by black women in the *Colored American Magazine* and *Crisis* magazine—a collection that reveals the shaping influence which certain periodicals had upon the generation of specific genres within the black women's literary tradition. Both types of collected books are intended to kindle an interest in still another series of works that bring together for the first time either the complete *oeuvre* of one writer or that of one genre within the periodical press. Indeed, there are several authors whose collected works will establish them as major forces in the nineteenth- and early twentieth-century black women's intellectual community. Compiling, editing, and publishing these volumes will be as important a factor in constructing the black women's literary tradition as has been the republication of books long out of print.

Finally, the Library now includes a detailed bibliography of the writings of black women in the nineteenth and early twentieth centuries. Prepared by Jean Fagan Yellin and Cynthia Bond, this bibliography is the result of years of research and will serve as an indispensable resource in future investigations of black women writers, particularly those whose works appeared frequently throughout the nineteenth century in the principal conduit of writing for black women *or* men, the African-American periodical press.

The publication of this ten-volume supplement, we hope, will make a sound contribution toward reestablishing the importance of the creative works of African-American women and reevaluating the relation of these works not only to each other but also to African-American *and* American literature and history as a whole. These works are invaluable sources for readers intent upon understanding the complex interplay of ethnicity and gender, of racism and sexism—of how "race" becomes gendered and how gender becomes racialized—in American society.

FOREWORD
In Her Own Write

Henry Louis Gates, Jr.

One muffled strain in the Silent South, a jarring chord and a vague and uncomprehended cadenza has been and still is the Negro. And of that muffled chord, the one mute and voiceless note has been the sadly expectant Black Women, ...

The "other side" has not been represented by one who "lives there." And not many can more sensibly realize and more accurately tell the weight and the fret of the "long dull pain" than the open-eyed but hitherto voiceless Black Woman of America.

. . . as our Caucasian barristers are not to blame if they cannot *quite* put themselves in the dark man's place, neither should the dark man be wholly expected fully and adequately to reproduce the exact Voice of the Black Woman.

—Anna Julia Cooper
A Voice From the South (1892)

The birth of the African-American literary tradition occurred in 1773, when Phillis Wheatley published a book of poetry. Despite the fact that her book garnered for her a remarkable amount of attention, Wheatley's journey to the printer had been a most arduous one. Sometime in 1772, a young African girl walked demurely into a room in Boston to undergo an oral examination, the results of which would determine the direction of her life and work. Perhaps she was shocked upon entering the appointed room. For there, perhaps gathered in a semicircle, sat eighteen of Boston's most notable citizens. Among them were John Erving, a prominent Boston merchant; the Reverend Charles Chauncy, pastor of the Tenth Congregational Church; and John Hancock, who would later gain fame for his signature on the Declaration of Independence. At the center of this group was His Excellency, Thomas Hutchinson, governor of Massachusetts, with Andrew Oliver, his lieutenant governor, close by his side.

Why had this august group been assembled? Why had it seen fit to summon this young African girl, scarcely eighteen years old, before it? This group of "the most respectable Characters in *Boston*," as it would define itself, had assembled to question closely the African adolescent on the slender sheaf of poems that she claimed to have "written by herself." We can only speculate on the nature of the questions posed to the fledgling poet. Perhaps they asked her to identify and explain—for all to hear—exactly who were the Greek and Latin gods and poets alluded to so frequently in her work. Perhaps they asked her to conjugate a verb in Latin or even to translate randomly selected passages from the Latin, which she and her master, John Wheatley, claimed that she "had made some Progress in." Or perhaps they asked her to recite from memory key passages from the texts of John Milton and Alexander Pope, the two poets by whom the African claimed to be most directly influenced. We do not know.

We do know, however, that the African poet's responses were more than sufficient to prompt the eighteen august gentlemen to compose, sign, and publish a two-paragraph "Attestation," an open letter "To the Publick" that prefaces Phillis Wheatley's book and that reads in part:

> We whose Names are under-written, do assure the World, that the Poems specified in the following Page, were (as we

verily believe) written by Phillis, a young Negro Girl, who was but a few Years since, brought an uncultivated Barbarian from *Africa,* and has ever since been, and now is, under the Disadvantage of serving as a Slave in a Family in this Town. She has been examined by some of the best Judges, and is thought qualified to write them.

So important was this document in securing a publisher for Wheatley's poems that it forms the signal element in the prefatory matter preceding her *Poems on Various Subjects, Religious and Moral,* published in London in 1773.

Without the published "Attestation," Wheatley's publisher claimed, few would believe that an African could possibly have written poetry all by herself. As the eighteen put the matter clearly in their letter, "Numbers would be ready to suspect they were not really the Writings of Phillis." Wheatley and her master, John Wheatley, had attempted to publish a similar volume in 1772 in Boston, but Boston publishers had been incredulous. One year later, "Attestation" in hand, Phillis Wheatley and her master's son, Nathaniel Wheatley, sailed for England, where they completed arrangements for the publication of a volume of her poems with the aid of the Countess of Huntington and the Earl of Dartmouth.

This curious anecdote, surely one of the oddest oral examinations on record, is only a tiny part of a larger, and even more curious, episode in the Enlightenment. Since the beginning of the sixteenth century, Europeans had wondered aloud whether or not the African "species of men," as they were most commonly called, *could* ever create formal literature, could ever master "the arts and sciences." If they could, the argument ran, then the African variety of humanity was fundamentally related to the European variety. If not, then it seemed clear that the African was destined by nature to be a slave. This was the burden shouldered by Phillis Wheatley when she successfully defended herself and the authorship of her book against counterclaims and doubts.

Indeed, with her successful defense, Wheatley launched two traditions at once—the black American literary tradition *and* the black woman's literary tradition. If it is extraordinary that not just one but both of these traditions were founded simultaneously by a black woman—certainly an event unique in the history of literature—it is also ironic that this important fact of common, coterminous literary origins seems to have escaped most scholars.

That the progenitor of the black literary tradition was a woman means, in the most strictly literal sense, that all subsequent black writers have evolved in a matrilinear line of descent, and that each, consciously or unconsciously, has extended and revised a canon whose foundation was the poetry of a black woman. Early black writers seem to have been keenly aware of Wheatley's founding role, even if most of her white reviewers were more concerned with the implications of her race than her gender. Jupiter Hammon, for example, whose 1760 broadside "An Evening Thought. Salvation by Christ, With Penitential Cries" was the first individual poem published by a black American, acknowledged Wheatley's influence by selecting her as the subject of his second broadside, "An Address to Miss Phillis Wheatly [*sic*], Ethiopian Poetess, in Boston," which was published in Hartford in 1778. And George Moses Horton, the second African American to publish a book of poetry in English (1829), brought out in 1838 an edition of his *Poems By A Slave* bound together with Wheatley's work. Indeed, for fifty-six years, between 1773 and 1829, when Horton published *The Hope of Liberty*, Wheatley was the *only* black person to have published a book of imaginative literature in English. So central was this black woman's role in the shaping of the

African-American literary tradition that, as one historian has maintained, the history of the reception of Phillis Wheatley's poetry *is* the history of African-American literary criticism. Well into the nineteenth century, Wheatley and the black literary tradition were the same entity.

But Wheatley is not the only black woman writer who stands as a pioneering figure in African-American literature. Just as Wheatley gave birth to the genre of black poetry, Ann Plato was the first African American to publish a book of essays (1841) and Harriet E. Wilson was the first black person to publish a novel in the United States (1859).

Despite this pioneering role of black women in the tradition, however, many of their contributions before this century have been all but lost or unrecognized. As Hortense Spillers observed as recently as 1983,

> With the exception of a handful of autobiographical narratives from the nineteenth century, the black woman's realities are virtually suppressed until the period of the Harlem Renaissance and later. Essentially the black woman as artist, as intellectual spokesperson for her own cultural apprenticeship, has not existed before, for anyone. At the source of [their] own symbol-making task, [the community of black women writers] confronts, therefore, a tradition of work that is quite recent, its continuities, broken and sporadic.

Until now, it has been extraordinarily difficult to establish the formal connections between early black women's writing and that of the present, precisely because our knowledge of their work has been broken and sporadic. Phillis Wheatley, for example, while certainly the most reprinted and discussed poet in the tradition, is also one of the least understood. Ann Plato's seminal work, *Essays* (which includes biographies and poems), has not been reprinted since it was published a century and a half ago. And Harriet Wilson's *Our Nig*, her compelling novel of a black woman's expanding consciousness in a racist Northern antebellum environment, never received even *one* review or comment at a time when virtually *all* works written by black people were heralded by abolitionists as salient arguments against the existence of human slavery. Many of the books reprinted in this set experienced a similar fate, the most dreadful fate for an author: that of being ignored then relegated to the obscurity of the rare book section of a university library. We can only wonder how many other texts in the black woman's tradition have been lost to this generation of readers or remain unclassified or uncatalogued and, hence, unread.

This was not always so, however. Black women writers dominated the final decade of the nineteenth century, perhaps spurred to publish by an 1886 essay entitled "The Coming American Novelist," which was published in *Lippincott's Monthly Magazine* and written by "A Lady From Philadelphia." This pseudonymous essay argued that the "Great American Novel" would be written by a black person. Her argument is so curious that it deserves to be repeated:

> When we come to formulate our demands of the Coming American Novelist, we will agree that he must be native-born. His ancestors may come from where they will, but we must give him a birthplace and have the raising of him. Still, the longer his family has been here the better he will represent us. Suppose he should have no country but ours, no traditions but those he has learned here, no longings apart from us, no future except in our future—the orphan of the world, he finds with us his home. And with all this, suppose he refuses to be fused into that grand conglomerate we call the "American type." With us, he is not of us. He is original, he has humor, he is tender, he is passive and fiery, he has been taught what we call justice, and he has his own opinion about it. He has suffered everything a poet, a dra-

matist, a novelist need suffer before he comes to have his lips anointed. And with it all he is in one sense a spectator, a little out of the race. How would these conditions go towards forming an original development? In a word, suppose the coming novelist is of African origin? When one comes to consider the subject, there is no improbability in it. One thing is certain,—our great novel will not be written by the typical American.

An atypical American, indeed. Not only would the great American novel be written by an African American, it would be written by an African-American *woman:*

> Yet farther: I have used the generic masculine pronoun because it is convenient; but Fate keeps revenge in store. It was a woman who, taking the wrongs of the African as her theme, wrote the novel that awakened the world to their reality, and why should not the coming novelist be a woman as well as an African? She—the woman of that race—has some claims on Fate which are not yet paid up.

It is these claims on fate that we seek to pay by publishing The Schomburg Library of Nineteenth-Century Black Women Writers.

This theme would be repeated by several black women authors, most notably by Anna Julia Cooper, a prototypical black feminist whose 1892 *A Voice From the South* can be considered to be one of the original texts of the black feminist movement. It was Cooper who first analyzed the fallacy of referring to "the Black man" when speaking of black people and who argued that just as white men cannot speak through the consciousness of black men, neither can black *men* "fully and adequately . . . reproduce the exact Voice of the Black Woman." Gender and race, she argues, cannot be conflated, except in the instance of a black woman's voice, and it is this voice which must be uttered and to which we must listen. As Cooper puts the matter so compellingly:

It is not the intelligent woman vs. the ignorant woman; nor the white woman vs. the black, the brown, and the red,—it is not even the cause of woman vs. man. Nay, 'tis woman's strongest vindication for speaking that *the world needs to hear her voice*. It would be subversive of every human interest that the cry of one-half the human family be stifled. Woman in stepping from the pedestal of statue-like inactivity in the domestic shrine, and daring to think and move and speak,—to undertake to help shape, mold, and direct the thought of her age, is merely completing the circle of the world's vision. Hers is every interest that has lacked an interpreter and a defender. Her cause is linked with that of every agony that has been dumb—every wrong that needs a voice.

It is no fault of man's that he has not been able to see truth from her standpoint. It does credit both to his head and heart that no greater mistakes have been committed or even wrongs perpetrated while she sat making tatting and snipping paper flowers. Man's own innate chivalry and the mutual interdependence of their interests have insured his treating her cause, in the main at least, as his own. And he is pardonably surprised and even a little chagrined, perhaps, to find his legislation not considered "perfectly lovely" in every respect. But in any case his work is only impoverished by her remaining dumb. The world has had to limp along with the wobbling gait and one-sided hesitancy of a man with one eye. Suddenly the bandage is removed from the other eye and the whole body is filled with light. It sees a circle where before it saw a segment. The darkened eye restored, every member rejoices with it.

The myopic sight of the darkened eye can only be restored when the full range of the black woman's voice, with its own special timbres and shadings, remains mute no longer.

Similarly, Victoria Earle Matthews, an author of short stories and essays, and a cofounder in 1896 of the National Association of Colored Women, wrote in her stunning essay,

"The Value of Race Literature" (1895), that "when the literature of our race is developed, it will of necessity be different in all essential points of greatness, true heroism and real Christianity from what we may at the present time, for convenience, call American literature." Matthews argued that this great tradition of African-American literature would be the textual outlet "for the unnaturally suppressed inner lives which our people have been compelled to lead." Once these "unnaturally suppressed inner lives" of black people are unveiled, no "grander diffusion of mental light" will shine more brightly, she concludes, than that of the articulate African-American woman:

> And now comes the question, What part shall we women play in the Race Literature of the future? . . . within the compass of one small journal ["Woman's Era"] we have struck out a new line of departure—a journal, a record of Race interests gathered from all parts of the United States, carefully selected, moistened, winnowed and garnered by the ablest intellects of educated colored women, shrinking at no lofty theme, shirking no serious duty, aiming at every possible excellence, and determined to do their part in the future uplifting of the race.
>
> If twenty women, by their concentrated efforts in one literary movement, can meet with such success as has engendered, planned out, and so successfully consummated this convention, what much more glorious results, what wider spread success, what grander diffusion of mental light will not come forth at the bidding of the enlarged hosts of women writers, already called into being by the stimulus of your efforts?
>
> And here let me speak one word for my journalistic sisters who have already entered the broad arena of journalism. Before the "Woman's Era" had come into existence, no one except themselves can appreciate the bitter experience and sore

disappointments under which they have at all times been compelled to pursue their chosen vocations.

If their brothers of the press have had their difficulties to contend with, I am here as a sister journalist to state, from the fullness of knowledge, that their task has been an easy one compared with that of the colored woman in journalism.

Woman's part in Race Literature, as in Race building, is the most important part and has been so in all ages. . . . All through the most remote epochs she has done her share in literature. . . .

One of the most important aspects of this set is the republication of the salient texts from 1890 to 1910, which literary historians could well call the "Black Woman's Era." In addition to Mary Helen Washington's definitive edition of Cooper's *A Voice From the South*, we have reprinted two novels by Amelia Johnson, Frances Harper's *Iola Leroy*, two novels by Emma Dunham Kelley, Alice Dunbar-Nelson's two impressive collections of short stories, and Pauline Hopkins's three serialized novels as well as her monumental novel, *Contending Forces*—all published between 1890 and 1910. Indeed, black women published more works of fiction in these two decades than black men had published in the previous half century. Nevertheless, this great achievement has been ignored.

Moreover, the writings of nineteenth-century African-American women in general have remained buried in obscurity, accessible only in research libraries or in overpriced and poorly edited reprints. Many of these books have never been reprinted at all; in some instances only one or two copies are extant. In these works of fiction, poetry, autobiography, biography, essays, and journalism resides the mind of the nineteenth-century African-American woman. Until these works are made readily available to teachers and their students, a significant segment of the black tradition will remain silent.

Oxford University Press, in collaboration with the Schomburg Center for Research in Black Culture, is publishing thirty volumes of these compelling works, each of which contains an introduction by an expert in the field. The set includes such rare texts as Johnson's *The Hazeley Family* and *Clarence and Corinne*, Plato's *Essays,* the most complete edition of Phillis Wheatley's poems and letters, Emma Dunham Kelley's pioneering novel *Megda,* several previously unpublished stories and a novel by Alice Dunbar-Nelson, and the first collected volumes of Pauline Hopkins's three serialized novels and Frances Harper's poetry. We also present four volumes of poetry by such women as Henrietta Cordelia Ray, Adah Menken, Josephine Heard, and Maggie Johnson. Numerous slave and spiritual narratives, a newly discovered novel—*Four Girls at Cottage City*—by Emma Dunham Kelley (-Hawkins), and the first American edition of *Wonderful Adventures of Mrs. Seacole in Many Lands* are also among the texts included.

In addition to resurrecting the works of black women authors, it is our hope that this set will facilitate the resurrection of the African-American woman's literary tradition itself by unearthing its nineteenth-century roots. In the works of Nella Larsen and Jessie Fauset, Zora Neale Hurston and Ann Petry, Lorraine Hansberry and Gwendolyn Brooks, Paule Marshall and Toni Cade Bambara, Audre Lorde and Rita Dove, Toni Morrison and Alice Walker, Gloria Naylor and Jamaica Kincaid, these roots have branched luxuriantly. The eighteenth- and nineteenth-century authors whose works are presented in this set founded and nurtured the black women's literary tradition, which must be revived, explicated, analyzed, and debated before we can understand more completely the formal shaping of this tradition within a tradition, a coded literary universe through which, regrettably, we are only just beginning to navigate our way. As Anna Cooper said nearly one hundred years ago, we have been blinded by the loss of sight in one eye and have therefore been unable to detect the full *shape* of the African-American literary tradition.

Literary works configure into a tradition not because of some mystical collective unconscious determined by the biology of race or gender, but because writers read other writers and *ground* their representations of experience in models of language provided largely by other writers to whom they feel akin. It is through this mode of literary revision, amply evident in the *texts* themselves—in formal echoes, recast metaphors, even in parody—that a "tradition" emerges and defines itself.

This is formal bonding, and it is only through formal bonding that we can know a literary tradition. The collective publication of these works by black women now, for the first time, makes it possible for scholars and critics, male and female, black and white, to *demonstrate* that black women writers read, and revised, other black women writers. To demonstrate this set of formal literary relations is to demonstrate that sexuality, race, and gender are both the condition and the basis of *tradition*—but tradition as found in discrete acts of language use.

A word is in order about the history of this set. For the past decade, I have taught a course, first at Yale and then at Cornell, entitled "Black Woman and Their Fictions," a course that I inherited from Toni Morrison, who developed it in the mid-1970s for Yale's Program in Afro-American Studies. Although the course was inspired by the remarkable accomplishments of black women novelists since 1970, I gradually extended its beginning date to the late nineteenth century, studying Frances Harper's *Iola Leroy* and Anna Julia Cooper's *A Voice From the South,* both published in 1892. With the discovery of Harriet E. Wilson's seminal novel, *Our Nig* (1859), and Jean Yellin's authentication of Harriet Jacobs's brilliant slave narrative, *Incidents in the Life of a Slave Girl* (1861), a survey course spanning over a century and a quarter emerged.

But the discovery of *Our Nig*, as well as the interest in nineteenth-century black women's writing that this discovery generated, convinced me that even the most curious and diligent scholars knew very little of the extensive history of the creative writings of African-American women before 1900. Indeed, most scholars of African-American literature had never even read most of the books published by black women, simply because these books—of poetry, novels, short stories, essays, and autobiography—were mostly accessible only in rare book sections of university libraries. For reasons unclear to me even today, few of these marvelous renderings of the African-American woman's consciousness were reprinted in the late 1960s and early 1970s, when so many other texts of the African-American literary tradition were resurrected from the dark and silent graveyard of the out-of-print and were reissued in facsimile editions aimed at the hungry readership for canonical texts in the nascent field of black studies.

So, with the help of several superb research assistants—including David Curtis, Nicola Shilliam, Wendy Jones, Sam Otter, Janadas Devan, Suvir Kaul, Cynthia Bond, Elizabeth Alexander, and Adele Alexander—and with the expert advice of scholars such as William Robinson, William Andrews, Mary Helen Washington, Maryemma Graham, Jean Yellin, Houston A. Baker, Jr., Richard Yarborough, Hazel Carby, Joan R. Sherman, Frances Foster, and William French, dozens of bibliographies were used to compile a list of books written or narrated by black women mostly before 1910. Without the assistance provided through this shared experience of scholarship, the scholar's true legacy, this project would not have been conceived. As the list grew, I was struck by how very many of these titles that I, for example, had never even heard of, let alone read, such as Ann Plato's *Essays*, Louisa Picquet's slave narrative, or Amelia Johnson's two novels, *Clarence and Corinne* and *The Hazeley Family*. Through our research with the Black Periodical Fiction and Poetry Project (funded by NEH and the Ford Foundation), I also realized that several novels by black women, including three works of fiction by Pauline Hopkins, had been serialized in black periodicals, but had never been collected and published as books. Nor had the several books of poetry published by black women, such as the prolific Frances E. W. Harper, been collected and edited. When I discovered still another "lost" novel by an African-American woman (*Four Girls at Cottage City*, published in 1898 by Emma Dunham Kelley-Hawkins), I decided to attempt to edit a collection of reprints of these works and to publish them as a "library" of black women's writings, in part so that I could read them myself.

Convincing university and trade publishers to undertake this project proved to be a difficult task. Despite the commercial success of *Our Nig* and of the several reprint series of women's works (such as Virago, the Beacon Black Women Writers Series, and Rutgers' American Women Writers Series), several presses rejected the project as "too large," "too limited," or as "commercially unviable." Only two publishers recognized the viability and the import of the project and, of these, Oxford's commitment to publish the titles simultaneously as a set made the press's offer irresistible.

While attempting to locate original copies of these exceedingly rare books, I discovered that most of the texts were housed at the Schomburg Center for Research in Black Culture, a branch of The New York Public Library, under the direction of Howard Dodson. Dodson's infectious enthusiasm for the project and his generous collaboration, as well as that of his stellar staff (especially Diana Lachatanere, Sharon Howard, Ellis Haizip, Richard Newman, and Betty Gubert), led to a joint publishing initiative that produced this set as part of the Schomburg's major fund-raising campaign. Without Dodson's foresight and generosity of spirit, the set would not have materialized. Without William P. Sisler's masterful editorship at Oxford and his staff's careful attention to detail, the set would have remained just another grand idea that tends to languish in a scholar's file cabinet.

I would also like to thank Dr. Michael Winston and Dr. Thomas C. Battle, Vice-President of Academic Affairs and the Director of the Moorland-Spingarn Research Center (respectively) at Howard University, for their unending encouragement, support, and collaboration in this project, and Esme E. Bhan at Howard for her meticulous research and bibliographical skills. In addition, I would like to acknowledge the aid of the staff at the libraries of Duke University, Cornell University (especially Tom Weissinger and Donald Eddy), the Boston Public Library, the Western Reserve Historical Society, the Library of Congress, and Yale University. Linda Robbins, Marion Osmun, Sarah Flanagan, and Gerard Case, all members of the staff at Oxford, were extraordinarily effective at coordinating, editing, and producing the various segments of each text in the set. Candy Ruck, Nina de Tar, and Phillis Molock expertly typed reams of correspondence and manuscripts connected to the project.

I would also like to express my gratitude to my colleagues who edited and introduced the individual titles in the set. Without their attention to detail, their willingness to meet strict deadlines, and their sheer enthusiasm for this project, the set could not have been published. But finally and ultimately, I would hope that the publication of the set would help to generate even more scholarly interest in the black women authors whose work is presented here. Struggling against the seemingly insurmountable barriers of racism *and* sexism, while often raising families and fulfilling full-time professional obligations, these women managed nevertheless to record their thoughts and feelings and to *testify* to all who dare read them that the will to harness the power of collective endurance and survival is the will to write.

The Schomburg Library of Nineteenth-Century Black Women Writers is dedicated in memory of Pauline Augusta Coleman Gates, who died in the spring of 1987. It was she who inspired in me the love of learning and the love of literature. I have encountered in the books of this set no will more determined, no courage more noble, no mind more sublime, no self more celebratory of the achievements of all African-American women, and indeed of life itself, than her own.

A NOTE FROM
THE SCHOMBURG CENTER

Howard Dodson

The Schomburg Center for Research in Black Culture, The New York Public Library, is pleased to join with Dr. Henry Louis Gates and Oxford University Press in presenting The Schomburg Library of Nineteenth-Century Black Women Writers. This thirty-volume set includes the work of a generation of black women whose writing has only been available previously in rare book collections. The materials reprinted in twenty-four of the thirty volumes are drawn from the unique holdings of the Schomburg Center.

A research unit of The New York Public Library, the Schomburg Center has been in the forefront of those institutions dedicated to collecting, preserving, and providing access to the records of the black past. In the course of its two generations of acquisition and conservation activity, the Center has amassed collections totaling more than 5 million items. They include over 100,000 bound volumes, 85,000 reels and sets of microforms, 300 manuscript collections containing some 3.5 million items, 300,000 photographs and extensive holdings of prints, sound recordings, film and videotape, newspapers, artworks, artifacts, and other book and nonbook materials. Together they vividly document the history and cultural heritages of people of African descent worldwide.

Though established some sixty-two years ago, the Center's book collections date from the sixteenth century. Its oldest item, an Ethiopian Coptic Tunic, dates from the eighth or ninth century. Rare materials, however, are most available for the nineteenth-century African-American experience. It is from these holdings that the majority of the titles selected for inclusion in this set are drawn.

The nineteenth century was a formative period in African-American literary and cultural history. Prior to the Civil War, the majority of black Americans living in the United States were held in bondage. Law and practice forbade teaching them to read or write. Even after the war, many of the impediments to learning and literary productivity remained. Nevertheless, black men and women of the nineteenth century persevered in both areas. Moreover, more African Americans than we yet realize turned their observations, feelings, social viewpoints, and creative impulses into published works. In time, this nineteenth-century printed record included poetry, short stories, histories, novels, autobiographies, social criticism, and theology, as well as economic and philosophical treatises. Unfortunately, much of this body of literature remained, until very recently, relatively inaccessible to twentieth-century scholars, teachers, creative artists, and others interested in black life. Prior to the late 1960s, most Americans (black as well as white) had never heard of these nineteenth-century authors, much less read their works.

The civil rights and black power movements created unprecedented interest in the thought, behavior, and achievements of black people. Publishers responded by revising traditional texts, introducing the American public to a new generation of African-American writers, publishing a variety of thematic anthologies, and reprinting a plethora of "classic texts" in African-American history, literature, and art. The reprints usually appeared as individual titles or in a series of bound volumes or microform formats.

The Schomburg Center, which has a long history of supporting publishing that deals with the history and culture of Africans in diaspora, became an active participant in many of the reprint revivals of the 1960s. Since hard copies of original printed works are the preferred formats for producing facsimile reproductions, publishers frequently turned to the Schomburg Center for copies of these original titles. In addition to providing such material, Schomburg Center staff members offered advice and consultation, wrote introductions, and occasionally entered into formal copublishing arrangements in some projects.

Most of the nineteenth-century titles reprinted during the 1960s, however, were by and about black men. A few black women were included in the longer series, but works by lesser known black women were generally overlooked. The Schomburg Library of Nineteenth-Century Black Women Writers is both a corrective to these previous omissions and an important contribution to African-American literary history in its own right. Through this collection of volumes, the thoughts, perspectives, and creative abilities of nineteenth-century African-American women, as captured in books and pamphlets published in large part before 1910, are again being made available to the general public. The Schomburg Center is pleased to be a part of this historic endeavor.

I would like to thank Professor Gates for initiating this project. Thanks are due both to him and Mr. William P. Sisler of Oxford University Press for giving the Schomburg Center an opportunity to play such a prominent role in the set. Thanks are also due to my colleagues at The New York Public Library and the Schomburg Center, especially Dr. Vartan Gregorian, Richard De Gennaro, Paul Fasana, Betsy Pinover, Richard Newman, Diana Lachatanere, Glenderlyn Johnson, and Harold Anderson for their assistance and support. I can think of no better way of demonstrating than in this set the role the Schomburg Center plays in assuring that the black heritage will be available for future generations.

CONTENTS

The Pen Is Ours

INTRODUCTION

Jean Fagan Yellin
Cynthia D. Bond

One may not "cry loud" as they are bid,
and lift our voices in the *public* ear;
Nor yet be mute. The pen is ours to wield,
The heart to will, and hands to execute.
                                    —SARAH LOUISA FORTEN [1]

With these words, written in 1836, the black poet Sarah Forten inscribed herself a writer. Although rejecting the role of "female orator" pioneered a few years earlier by Maria W. Stewart, Forten expressed her determination to participate in public discourse.

When Forten composed these lines, woman's place was disputed in America. While "true women" were urged to restrict their energies to the "domestic sphere," free antislavery women were boldly pushing into the "public sphere" on behalf both of slaves and of themselves. Like other free black women excluded from white America's true womanhood on grounds of race, Forten had her own ideas. Defining themselves both as true women and as black, these innovative African-American women entered public debate. Some, like Forten, were writers; others, like Sarah Lenox Remond, became platform speakers. They were not working alone. Our bibliography, retracing the network that they created, reconstructs the tradition that they consciously built. In their choices of themes and of tropes, these nineteenth-century African-American women defined themselves and established their own literature. In the process, they articulated a critique of dominant definitions of true womanhood.

3

Working a century and a half after Forten, I was astonished to realize that I could identify eighty black women whose writings were separately published in this country, a dozen more who had been held in slavery and had become the subject of dictated narratives or biographies, and another forty-five who had written for magazines, newspapers, and periodicals—all before the end of 1910. But while amazed by my discovery of the presence, the productions, and the size of this group of writers, I was equally surprised to learn that although I had not known of them, these women knew of each other—as is attested, for example, by Angelina Weld Grimké's "To Keep the Memory of Charlotte Forten Grimké" and by Katherine Davis Chapman Tillman's "Lines to Ida B. Wells."

The African-American women who, a century ago, were writing, compiling, and publishing collective biographies of other African-American women worked both consciously and collectively. Consider: Susan I. Lankford Shorter published *Heroines of African Methodism* in 1891; the next year, probably modeling her article on William J. Simmons's *Men of Mark* (1887), Susan Elizabeth Frazier presented "Some Afro-American Women of Mark" in the *A.M.E. Church Review.* In 1893 two black men, Lawson Andrew Scruggs and Monroe Alphus Majors, brought out collective biographies of African-American women.[2] Then in 1894, Gertrude E. H. Bustill Mossell published *The Work of the Afro-American Woman,* a collective biography naming hundreds of women in essays discussing women's activities. After this, African-American women celebrated themselves in a series of volumes. Some, like Ann Amelia Bustill Smith's *Reminiscences of Colored People of Princeton, New Jersey. 1800–1900* (1913), included men, but most were devoted solely to women—books like Hallie Q. Brown's *Homespun Heroines and Other*

Women of Distinction (1926); Sadie Iola Daniel's *Women Builders* (1931); and Elizabeth Lindsay Davis's *Lifting As They Climb: The National Association of Colored Women* (1934).

In 1894 Mossell voiced the impulse behind these volumes: "that some note of inspiration might be found in these writings for the budding womanhood of the race." Her statement testifies to the presence of a self-aware black women's culture at the turn of the century.[3] Books like Mossell's, in which black women wrote about each other for an audience of their daughters and granddaughters, constitute a self-conscious African-American female literary tradition.

This tradition can be studied in various ways. It can be traced historically, for example, by examining the literary societies the women established in the nineteenth century; it can be understood imaginatively by trying to place ourselves in their situation, by sensing that these writers knew of each other because they needed to feel that they were contributing to an ongoing discourse, that there were other writers, that there were readers, that they were not alone.

This is a working bibliography. We have not succeeded in gathering all citations pertinent to our subject—or even in completing all citations that we have gathered. What we offer is a first effort at providing a list of the writings *by* and *about* African-American women whose earliest publications appeared by the end of 1910—the year that W.E.B. Du Bois founded *Crisis* magazine—and a list of all subsequent works by them as well. This bibliography presents, for the first time, both this extraordinarily large grouping of nineteenth-century African-American women writers and the extraordinarily wide range of their writings, from lyric poetry to memoirs, from a study of mortality to a historical monograph in French.

Our listing is in five parts. The first three present the discourse of nineteenth-century African-American women.

Part I is intended as a serious contribution toward a systematic, comprehensive listing of writings by and about African-American women whose earliest publications appeared before the end of 1910 and who produced separately published writings; as the authors of separate publications, their names can be found in library catalogues. This section lists first all the published writings *by* these women that we have found. (Because microfilm publication has made many of the papers of black abolitionists and many items in a grouping of black and abolitionist periodicals generally accessible, items in *Black Abolitionist Papers, 1830–1865* [New York: Microfilming Corporation of America, 1981], as well as in newspapers like the *Liberator*, which has been microfilmed, are included.) We also present a gathering of anthologies reprinting the authors' writings. This section lists next the selected writings *about* these women and their work. (Where secondary sources include indexes, page numbers may not be listed.) Finally, this section includes pertinent papers and other items in special collections.

Part II is a listing of writings *by* and *about* women who had been held in slavery and whose dictated narratives or biographies were published before the end of 1910. A note about this section: Like all literatures, African-American literature presents genuine anomalies, and bibliographical listings necessarily reflect these. Some items included here are "dictated narratives," texts literally dictated by their subjects for transcription by an amanuensis; others were instead elicited as responses to an interrogator's questions; still others were composed by the subject's relatives, friends, or acquaintances. Of the items grouped in this section, some were obviously substantially shaped by editors; others apparently were not.

As African-American literary and historical scholarship grows, the status of these texts will become clearer. In the interim, for the convenience of the reader, we have chosen to present items traditionally included both in lists of dictated slave narratives and in lists of biographies of former slaves.

For more specialized discussions of the slave narrative, and for guides to scholarly literature on the narratives, we refer our readers to the following: John W. Blassingame, "Introduction," *Slave Testimony: Two Centuries of Letters, Speeches, Interviews, and Autobiographies* (Baton Rouge: Louisiana State University Press, 1977), xvii–lxv; Frances S. Foster, *Witnessing Slavery: The Development of Ante-Bellum Slave Narratives* (Westport, CT: Greenwood Press, 1979); *The Art of Slave Narrative*, John Sekora and Darwin Turner, eds. (Macomb: Western Illinois University, 1982); *The Slave's Narrative*, Charles T. Davis and Henry Louis Gates, Jr., eds. (New York: Oxford University Press, 1985); and William L. Andrews, *To Tell a Free Story: The First Century of Afro-American Autobiography, 1760–1865* (Urbana: University of Illinois Press, 1986).

Part III is a listing of African-American women whose writings appeared in newspapers, magazines, and collections, and whose earliest publications appeared before the end of 1910. This section includes a listing of published writings *by* these women, a listing of writings *about* them and their work, and a listing of pertinent items in special collections. A peculiar problem emerged as we worked on this section. We encountered references to writers whose work we could not locate. Although ultimately we were able to find publications by several of these writers, other authors remain in search of a text. Accordingly, we have omitted the following writers whose works remain unlocated: Lillian Lewis [pseud. Bert Islew], Ida V. Simpson, and A. L. Tilghman.

The final sections of this bibliography present materials in which nineteenth-century black American women are the subject of the writings of others.

Part IV names women prominent in this period who, as far as we know, neither published any writings nor produced any dictated slave narratives; it lists writings about these women and their work. (For an introduction to African-American women distinguished in fields other than literature, we recommend *Notable American Women*, Edward and Janet James, eds. [Cambridge, MA: Harvard University Press, 1971]; and *Dictionary of American Negro Biography*, Rayford W. Logan and Michael R. Winston, eds. [New York: W. W. Norton, 1982].)

Part V, a fragmentary effort, is an attempt to present a topical listing of items that were written *about*, but not *by*, African-American women before the end of 1910.

Reluctantly, we have decided to limit our listing of unpublished materials—letters, documents, diaries—to writings by and about the women included in the first three sections. For an introduction to letters and documents by and about "anonymous" nineteenth-century black women, we refer our readers to Dorothy Sterling, *We Are Your Sisters: Black Women in the Nineteenth Century* (New York: W. W. Norton, 1984); *A Documentary History of the Negro People in the United States*, Herbert Aptheker, ed., 2 vols. (New York: Citadel Press, 1951, 1962); *Slave Testimony*, John S. Blassingame, ed. (Baton Rouge: Louisiana State University Press, 1977); *Black Women in White America: A Documentary History*, Gerda Lerner, ed. (New York: Pantheon Books, 1972); *"Dear Master": Letters of a Slave Family*, Randall M. Miller, ed. (Ithaca, NY: Cornell University Press, 1978); *Blacks in Bondage: Letters of American Slaves*, Robert S. Starobin, ed.

(New York: New Viewpoints, 1974); *Dear Ones at Home: Letters from Contraband Camps,* Henry L. Swint, ed. (Nashville: Vanderbilt University Press, 1966); and Carter G. Woodson's pioneering *The Mind of the Negro as Reflected in Letters Written During the Crisis, 1800–1860* (Washington, DC: Association for the Study of Negro Life and History, 1940).

Nor, unless an author, an editor, or a compiler is named, do we include publications of black women's organizations. For a taste of these materials, see *Early Negro Writing,* Dorothy B. Porter, ed. (Boston: Beacon Press, 1971), and items such as the *Annual Reports* of the National League for the Protection of Colored Women (1910), and *National Notes,* vols. 1–51, no. 5 (Washington, DC, 1899–1933), the official organ of the National Association of Colored Women. We have, in addition, omitted authors known only by their pseudonyms; these, too, can be sampled in Porter, noted above.

This bibliography clarifies the status of a number of authors and texts. For example, verifying that the poet Sarah Forten was the mysterious "Ada" and including her pseudonymously published poems among her writings, we provide a new perspective on Forten as a poet.[4] Another instance involves Julia Ringwood Coston. Although unable to locate a copy of *Ringwood's Afro-American Journal of Fashion,* which she established in 1892, we have at last located an example of Coston's writing. In addition, we made an effort to present a corrected listing of Molly E. Lambert's writings after we learned of Ann A. Shockley's accurate claim that this black writer had been confused with the white poet Mary Eliza (Perrine) Tucker Lambert. Furthermore, after establishing that Margaret Elizabeth M. Sangster and Edith Matilda Thomas were not black, we dropped them from our list.[5]

Like all joint efforts, this bibliography is the result of divided responsibilities. I conceived of the project long ago, upon completing an index of the literary materials in Du Bois' *Crisis* (*CLA Journal* [June 1971, Dec. 1971]). After spending a year and a half in libraries—most often at Pace University, Sarah Lawrence College, and the Schomburg Center of The New York Public Library—I had done all I could do working alone with file cards and a pencil. To complete this project required people, computers, and access to special collections. After repeated, unsuccessful attempts to win the funding necessary, I packed away my file cards, publishing a small revamped segment of my draft manuscript in *But Some of Us Are Brave: Black Women's Studies*, Gloria T. Hull et al., eds. (New York: Feminist Press, 1982). Years passed. Then, learning that Oxford University Press was planning to add more volumes to The Schomburg Library of Nineteenth-Century Black Women Writers, I offered my earlier compilations as the core of a listing of writings by and about nineteenth-century African-American women.

Accordingly, in the spring of 1988, General Editor Henry Louis Gates, Jr., arranged for me to meet Cynthia D. Bond, Research Director of the Black Periodical Literature Project at Cornell University. Cynthia flew down to New Rochelle, and together we worked our way through boxes of file cards, then packed them to be carried to Ithaca. At the Cornell offices of the Black Periodical Literature Project, she established procedures to check my work, to expand it with the research findings of the Project, and to update it. Then, as the bibliography neared completion, I again became deeply involved—trying to conceptualize ways of organizing and presenting these extraordinary materials, rethinking bibliographical categories, and rechecking entries.

We are confident that readers will find this work useful.

We understand, however, that while correcting some errors, we have doubtless created and perpetuated others. This bibliography is thus an early attempt, published among the volumes of the Schomburg Library, to encourage further study of the women whose work the Library presents. Not only have African-American women's writings not yet become "canonized," they have not yet even been completely identified. The mistakes and confusions evident in this volume dramatize the need for more work. Accordingly, we urgently invite comments of all kinds. This is the best we can do today, but we are confident that we will be able to do better tomorrow—when the completion of the Black Periodical Literature Project makes available more information about women's periodical writings, and when readers offer their comments and corrections.

J.F.Y.

* * *

In compiling this bibliography our methods were perhaps more generous than rigorous, more inclusive than definitive. We have sought to gather as many citations pertinent to our subjects as possible, and as part of that effort we offer all sources—from volumes to squibs—with equal emphasis. It has been our experience that disparate pieces of information, once brought together, form an entity of some significance.

When I met with Jean Yellin in the spring of 1988, she showed me the extensive files of materials she had been collecting on nineteenth-century black women in the course of her academic work. We went through the material, along with her drafts and outlines for the bibliography she had been compiling until the late 1970s, and we devised ways to resuscitate lapsed plans and organize past research. I brought her earlier work to Ithaca and the offices of the Black

Periodical Literature Project at Cornell University and began
assessing her research in order to bring it up to date and
augment it with the editorial findings of the Project.

Following the list of nineteenth-century women already
compiled, combined with the women reprinted in the 1988
volumes of The Schomburg Library of Nineteenth-Century
Black Women Writers, the staff and I collected references
from the core of essential source materials presented in the
List of Abbreviations that follows this introduction. We
extended our research to the various reference tools on the
abolitionist and black periodical press compiled in the Project
office (all works surveyed are listed at the end of this book).
We also included any references to secondary works from the
notes and introductions of the thirty initial Oxford volumes.
From this base we expanded our research further by contact-
ing those institutions with renowned collections of black
studies materials. Some institutions regretfully declined our
request because they lacked the necessary time and personnel;
and in the case of some of the larger collections we availed
ourselves of the published dictionary catalogues. To cover
twentieth-century periodical criticism regarding our subjects,
we used the services of the reference department of Cornell's
Olin Library to search the online MLA database and the
American History and Life database.

Compiling material regarding the women listed here, we
searched author and subject headings using as many name
variants as possible to ensure inclusiveness (for example, we
searched not only for "Alice Dunbar-Nelson" but also for
"Alice Ruth Moore," "Alice Ruth Dunbar," and "Alice
Dunbar"). The same procedure was followed in searching the
online databases mentioned above. We catalogued all citations
by author, double-checking for duplicate sources. In the
Bibliography we do list duplicate sources that are special

editions of a cited work (autographed copies in special collections, for example). We have endeavored to make our citations complete and accurate, double-checking publication information whenever possible. After some debate, we agreed to include incomplete citations in the belief that even the slightest information would be useful to scholars.

The resources of the Black Periodical Literature Project were crucial to the completion of this bibliography. Although the Project's work of indexing, cataloguing, and reviewing the poems, stories, and book reviews in the nearly one thousand periodical titles listed in its working bibliography is far from complete, the current index database provided an abundance of pieces by and about the women listed in this volume. Many of these women were documented within the black periodical literary culture of their time but remain largely unread in our century; and many are revealed here for the first time in, I think, real substantiality.

A few remarks about our handling of Project research are in order: We list as "searched" only those periodicals that have been completely indexed for literature, as well as for literary notices and reviews. Several other partially indexed titles were checked but are not listed here, pending future research. In addition, although we picked up some verifiable names of unexamined black authors from our periodical research, we attempted to restrain any expansionist tendencies that would threaten to undercut the thoroughness of our existing research. Those women who received less than complete, systematic scrutiny are indicated by an asterisk in the text. There are undoubtedly many black women writers who escaped our notice and remain to be identified by the Project. For the purposes of this bibliography, we focused much of our attention on the specifically literary journals of the period like the *Colored American Magazine* and the *Voice of the Negro*, as well as periodicals of cultural significance such as the *Christian Recorder*. Assessing these and other periodicals for the purposes of this bibliography underscored our fundamental understanding in our daily work at the Project that the black periodical context of the nineteenth century was profoundly self-conscious and interdiscursive.

Even this relatively small sampling of the Black Periodical Literature Project's ongoing research has yielded impressive results, bringing to light new authors and fleshing out the publication histories of many more. Mary E. Ashe Lee, for instance, receives no real mention in the current critical literature but was recognized as a literary figure in her own day and is revealed in this bibliographic listing as a familiar poet in the periodical context. The Black Periodical Literature Project promises to yield still more prolific returns in the future. We look forward to those results and the benefits they represent for a great range of scholarly concerns.

C.D.B.

NOTES

1. Sarah Louisa Forten, "Lines, Suggested on Reading 'An Appeal to the Christian Women of the South' [by A. E. Grimké]," *Liberator* 6 (29 Oct. 1836): 176.

2. Lawson Andrew Scruggs, *Women of Distinction* (Raleigh, NC: L. A. Scruggs, 1893); Monroe Alphus Majors, *Noted Negro Women: Their Triumphs and Activities* (Chicago: Donohue and Henneberry, 1893).

3. Mrs. N. F. Mossell, *The Work of the Afro-American Woman* (Philadelphia: G. S. Ferguson, 1894; New York: Oxford University Press, 1988), 5.

4. Ibid., 74; *Liberator* (22 Jan. 1831).

5. See Ann A. Shockley, *Afro-American Women Writers, 1746–*

1933 (Boston: G. K. Hall, 1988), 188. This confusion first appeared in Joan R. Sherman, *Invisible Poets* (Urbana: University of Illinois Press, 1974), 241; its consequences include the publication, in The Schomburg Library of Nineteenth-Century Black Women Writers, of two books by the white poet: *Loew's Bridge, A Broadway Idyl* (1867) and *Poems* (1867), both republished in *Collected Black Women's Poetry*, Joan R. Sherman, ed., vol. 1 (New York: Oxford University Press, 1988). For documentation establishing the white "Rebel" Mary Eliza (Perrine) Tucker Lambert as the author of *Loew's Bridge* and *Poems*, see *The Living Female Writers of the South*, Mary T. Tardy (pseud. Ida Raymond), ed. (Philadelphia: Moore Brothers, 1872), 163–71. For Sangster and Thomas, identified as "Occasional Poets" in Sherman, *Invisible Poets*, 245–46, see *Notable American Women*, Edward T. James and Janet W. James, eds. (Cambridge, MA: Harvard University Press, 1971).

LIST OF ABBREVIATIONS

Because of the frequency of their use, the following resources are indicated throughout the bibliography by the abbreviated citations listed here.

BAP

Carter, George, and C. Peter Ripley, eds. *Black Abolitionist Papers, 1830–1865: A Guide to the Microfilm Edition*. New York: Microfilming Corporation of America, 1981.

Brawley, *NBH*

Brawley, Benjamin Griffith. *Negro Builders and Heroes*. Chapel Hill: University of North Carolina Press, 1937.

Brawley, *NG*

Brawley, Benjamin Griffith. *The Negro Genius*. New York: Dodd, Mead, 1937; New York: Biblo and Tannen, 1966.

Brawley, *NLA*

Brawley, Benjamin Griffith. *The Negro in Literature and Art in the United States*. New York: Duffield & Co., 1918.

Brown

Brown, Hallie Q., comp., ed. *Homespun Heroines and Other Women of Distinction*. Xenia, OH.: Aldine Publishing Co., 1926; New York: Oxford University Press, 1988.

Bullock	Bullock, Penelope L. *The Afro-American Periodical Press, 1838–1909*. Baton Rouge and London: Louisiana State University Press, 1981.
Culp	Culp, Daniel Wallace, ed. *Twentieth Century Negro Literature: or, A Cyclopedia of Thought on the Vital Topics Relating to the American Negro by One Hundred of America's Greatest Negroes*. Toronto, Naperville, IL, and Atlanta: J. L. Nichols & Co., [c.1902]; Miami: Mnemosyne Publishing Co., 1969.
DANB	Logan, Rayford W., and Michael R. Winston, eds. *Dictionary of American Negro Biography* (New York: W. W. Norton, 1982.
Daniel	Daniel, Sadie Iola. *Woman Builders*. Washington, DC: The Associated Press, 1931; Associated Publishers, [c.1970].
Dann	Dann, Martin E. *The Black Press 1827–1890: The Quest for National Identity*. New York: G. P. Putnam's Sons, 1971.
Dannett	Dannett, Sylvia. *Profiles of Negro Womanhood*. 2 vols. Yonkers, NY: Educational Heritage, 1964–1966.
Davis	Davis, Elizabeth. *Lifting As They Climb*. Chicago: National Association of Colored Women, 1933.
Loggins	Loggins, Vernon. *The Negro Author: His Development in America*. New York: Columbia University Press, 1931, 1959; Port Washington, NY: Kennikat Press, 1964.

Majors   Majors, Monroe Alphus. *Noted Negro Women, Their Triumphs and Activities.* Chicago: Donohue and Henneberry, 1893.

Mossell   Mossell, Mrs. N. F. [Gertrude Bustill]. *The Work of the Afro-American Woman.* Philadelphia: G. S. Ferguson Co., 1894; New York: Oxford University Press, 1988.

NAW   James, Edward T., and Janet W. James, eds. *Notable American Women, 1607–1950: A Biographical Dictionary.* Cambridge, MA: Harvard University Press, 1971.

Penn   Penn, Irvine Garland. *The Afro-American Press and Its Editors.* Springfield, MA: Wiley and Co., 1891; New York: Arno Press and the *New York Times,* 1969.

Robinson   Robinson, Wilhelmina S. *Historical Negro Biographies.* International Library of Negro Life and History. New York: New York Publishers Co., 1967. 2nd Edition Rev., Washington, DC: New York Publishers Co., 1969.

Rush   Rush, Theressa G., Carol F. Meyers, and Esther S. Arata, eds. *Black American Writers Past and Present: A Biographical and Bibliographical Dictionary.* 2 vols. Metuchen, NJ: Scarecrow Press, 1975.

Scruggs   Scruggs, Lawson A. *Women of Distinction: Remarkable Works and Invincible Character.* Raleigh, NC: L. A. Scruggs, 1893.

Sherman   Sherman, Joan R. *Invisible Poets: Afro-Americans of the Nineteenth Century.* Urbana: University of Illinois Press, 1974.

Shockley   Shockley, Ann Allen. *Afro-American Women Writers, 1746–1933: An Anthology and Critical Guide*. Boston: G. K. Hall, 1988.

Wesley   Wesley, Charles Harris. *The History of the National Association of Colored Women's Clubs: A Legacy of Service*. Washington, DC: National Association of Colored Woman's Clubs, 1984.

PART I

*Writings by and about
African-American Women Who Produced
Separately Published Writings and Whose
Earliest Publications Appeared
before the End of 1910*

Note: Asterisk indicates writers identified in the process of compiling this listing, hence not searched in all the resources listed at the end of this volume.

Octavia Victoria Rogers Albert
(1853–c.1890)

Writings by

The House of Bondage; or Charlotte Brooks and Other Slaves. . . . New York: Hunt and Eaton; Cincinnati: Cranston & Stowe, 1890.

The House of Bondage; or Charlotte Brooks and Other Slaves. . . . (Introduction by Frances Smith Foster. New York: Oxford University Press, 1988.

Writings about

Blassingame, John W. *Slave Testimony: Two Centuries of Letters, Speeches, Interviews and Autobiographies.* Baton Rouge: Louisiana State University Press, 1977. 219.

DANB, 7–8.

Fleming, John E. "Slavery, Civil War and Reconstruction: A Study of Black Women in Microcosm." *Negro History Bulletin* 38.6 (1975): 430–33.

Loggins, 258, 439.

Majors, 219–20, 333.

Christina Moody Briggs

Writings by

The Story of the East St. Louis Riot. N.p.: n.p., [c.1917].

A Tiny Spark. Washington, DC: Murray Brothers Press, 1910.

Writings about
Majors, 48.

Virginia W. Broughton

Writings by
Twenty Year's Experience of A Missionary. Chicago: The Pony Press, 1907.

Anthologies
Twenty Year's Experience of A Missionary. In *Spiritual Narratives*. Introduction by Sue E. Houchins. New York: Oxford University Press, 1988.

Writings about
Haley, James T., comp. *Sparkling Gems of Race Knowledge Worth Reading*. . . . Nashville: J. T. Haley and Co., 1897. 99 [portrait].

Hallie Quinn Brown (1850–1949)

Writings by
Bits and Odds: A Choice Selection of Recitations. Xenia, OH, 1880.
A Dramatization of the Rev. P. A. Nichol's Trouble in Turkeytrot Church. Privately printed, 1917.
First Lessons in Public Speaking. [Xenia, OH?]: Privately printed, 1920.
Homespun Heroines and Other Women of Distinction. Hallie Q. Brown, comp., ed. Xenia, OH: Aldine Publishing Co., 1926; Freeport, NY: Books for Libraries Press, 1971.

Homespun Heroines and Other Women of Distinction. Introduction by Randall K. Burkett. New York: Oxford University Press, 1988.

Our Women Past, Present and Future. Xenia, OH: Eckerle Printing Co., 1940.

Pen Pictures of Pioneers of Wilberforce. Hallie Q. Brown, comp., ed. Xenia, OH: Aldine Publishing Co., 1937.

Tales My Father Told. Wilberforce, OH: Homewood Cottage, 1925.

"Blanket-Making Time—A Fantasy." *Competitor* (March 1920): 58.

"I Am a College Negro Problem." *Colored American Magazine* (July 1909): 30–33.

"Mrs. Mary Church Terrell at Cornell University." *Voice of the Negro* (Aug. 1905): 637.

"On the Wing" [Review]. *Christian Recorder* (3 Apr. 1890): 3.

Letters

Letter to W.E.B. Du Bois. In *The Correspondence of W.E.B. Du Bois.* Herbert Aptheker, ed. Amherst: University of Massachusetts Press, 1973–1978.

Writings about

DANB, 67–68.

Daniel, 289–308.

Dannett, 1: 50, 56, 235.

Davis, 173–76.

Delany, F. S. "Miss Hallie Q. Brown." In *Afro-American Encyclopedia.* . . . James T. Haley, comp. Nashville: Haley & Florida, 1895. 581–83.

———. "Miss Hallie Q. Brown." In *Sparkling Gems of Race*

Knowledge Worth Reading. . . . James T. Haley, comp. Nashville: J. T. Haley and Co., 1897. 91–94.

Dunlap, Mollie E. "A Biographical Sketch of Hallie Quinn Brown." *Central State University Alumni Journal* (June 1963).

Kammen, Carol. "An Outstanding Black Woman, Cornell Class of '08." *Ithaca Journal* (26 Nov. 1988): 15B.

Lee, Mary E. "To Hallie Q. Brown." *Christian Recorder* (24 Apr. 1890): 1.

Majors, 230–36.

McFarlin, Annjeannette S. "Hallie Quinn Brown: Black Woman Elocutionist." *Southern Speech Communication Journal* 46 (1980): 72–82.

"Miss Hallie." *Christian Recorder* (16 Oct. 1890): 6.

"Miss Hallie Q. Brown" [Review]. *Christian Recorder* (14 Aug. 1890): 2; (24 Apr. 1890): 4; (9 Oct. 1890): 4; (12 March 1891): 5.

"Miss Hallie Q. Brown" [Review]. *Philadelphia Tribune.* Reprinted in *Christian Recorder* (15 May 1890): 2.

["Miss Hallie Q. Brown . . ." (Review).] *Woman's Journal* (27 May 1893).

Mossell, 22.

NAW, 1: 253–54.

Neely, Ruth. *Women of Ohio: A Record of Their Achievements in the History of the State.* Chicago: S. J. Clarke, 1939. 1: 237–38.

Norris, J. W. "Miss Hallie Q. Brown." *Christian Recorder* (1 May 1890): 8.

Onque, Alice S. *History of the Hallie Q. Brown Community House.* Minneapolis: University of Minnesota Press, 1959.

Robinson, 168–69.

Robinson, George F. *History of Greene County Ohio.* Chicago: S. J. Clarke, 1902.

Scruggs, 14–22.

Stetson, Erlene. "Black Feminism in Indiana, 1893–1933." *Phylon* 46.4 (1983): 292–98.

Wesley, 9–10, 12–13, 14, 16, 17–28, 31, 34, 60, 71–73, 85, 87, 89–93, 97, 104, 107, 110, 114, 224, 354–55, 357, 387, 396, 412, 416, 487, 507.

Winks, Robin. " 'A Sacred Animosity': Abolition in Canada." In *The Anti-Slavery Vanguard: New Essays on the Abolitionists*. Martin Duberman, ed. Princeton: Princeton University Press, 1965. 301–42.

Wright, A. Augustus. *Who's Who in the Lyceum*. Philadelphia: Pearson Brothers, [c.1906].

Papers in Collections

Hallie Q. Brown Memorial Library of Central State University.

Garrison Collection Biography File, Sophia Smith Collection, Smith College.

McFarlin, Annjeannette Sophie. "Hallie Quinn Brown— Black Woman Elocutionist: 1845(?)–1949." Diss., Washington State University, 1975.

Newsome, Effie Lee. "Miss Hallie Q. Brown, Lecturer and Reciter." Unpublished essay, 17 Apr. 1942.

———. "Significance of Hallie Q. Brown's Closing Days." Unpublished essay, Sept. 1949.

Josephine Brown (1839–?)

Writings by

Biography of an American Bondman, by His Daughter. Boston: R. F. Wallcut, 1856.

Letters

Letter to Mr. May. *Liberator* (26 May 1854): 82.
Letter to Mr. May. *Pennsylvania Freeman* (1 June 1854): 87.
Letter to Rev. May. *Liberator* (20 Oct. 1854).

Anthologies

Biography of an American Bondman, by His Daughter. In *Two Biographies by African-American Women.* Introduction by William L. Andrews. New York: Oxford University Press, 1991.

Writings about

Loggins, 162, 387, 388, 435.
Robinson, William H., Jr., ed. *Early Black American Prose.* Dubuque, IA: William C. Brown Company Publishers, 1971. 193.

Sarah D. Brown (1875–1963)

Writings by

Color Trees and Tracks. Chicago: the Author, [c.1906].
Launching Beyond the Color Line. Chicago: National Purity Association, 1905.

Andasia Kimbrough Bruce
[Mrs. William Liddell Bruce] (1868–?)

Writings by

Uncle Tom's Cabin of To-Day. New York and Washington, DC: Neale Publishing Co., 1906.

Marie Louise Burgess-Ware
[Marie Louise Burgess]

Note: Though we have no adequate critical information to date regarding Marie Louise Burgess-Ware, we have good reason to believe she is Marie Louise Burgess, author of *Ave Maria: A Tale*, listed below. We list citations for both author names here.

Writings by

Ave Maria: A Tale. Boston: Press of the Monthly Review, 1895.

"Bernice, The Octoroon" [Serial]. *Colored American Magazine* (Sept. 1903): 607–16; (Oct. 1903): 652–57.

"The Dixie Hospital and Hampton Training School for Nurses." *Woman's Era* (Aug. 1894): 5–6.

"A Night Watch." *Woman's Era* (Sept. 1894): 2.

"Notes on Nursing." *Woman's Era* (July 1894): 13–14.

"The Nursing of Sick Children." *Woman's Era* (1 June 1894): 3–4.

"Typhoid Fever." *Woman's Era* (Sept. 1894): 2–3.

Anthologies

Ammons, Elizabeth, comp. *Short Fiction by Black Women, 1900–1920*. New York: Oxford University Press, 1991.

Shockley, 243.

Writings about

Colored American Magazine (July 1903).

Rush, 126.

Shockley, 242–43.

Nannie Helen Burroughs (1879–1961)

Writings by

Grow . . . A Handy Guide for Progressive Churchwomen.
Washington, DC, n.d.

Making Their Mark. Washington, DC: The National Training School for Women and Girls, n.d.

A Manual for Sunshine Band Leaders: Methods—Programs.
Washington, DC, n.d.

The Slabtown District Convention, A Comedy in One Act. 11th Edition. Washington, DC, 1942.

"Black Women and Reform." *Crisis* (Aug. 1915).

"The Declaration of 1776 Is the Cause of the Harlem Riot."
Afro-American (13 Apr. 1935).

"Industrial Education—Will It Solve the Negro Problem?"
Colored American Magazine (March 1904): 188–90.

"Miss Burroughs Replies to Mr. Carrington." *Voice of the Negro* (Feb. 1905): 106.

"Nannie Burroughs Says Hound Dogs Are Kicked But Not Bulldogs." *Afro-American* (17 Feb. 1934).

"Not Color But Character." *Voice of the Negro* (July 1904):
277–79.

"With All Thy Getting." *Southern Workman* (July 1927):
301.

Writings about

Barnett, Evelyn Brooks. "Nannie Burroughs and the Education of Black Women." In *The Afro-American Woman: Struggles and Images.* Sharon Harley and Rosalyn Terbourg-Penn, eds. Port Washington, NY: National University Publications, 1978. 97–108.

Boulware, Marcus H. *The Oratory of Negro Leaders: 1900–1968.* Westport, CT: Greenwood Press, 1969.

Brawley, *NBH*, 263.

Bullock, 127.

Colored American Magazine (Jan.–Feb. 1902): 251.

DANB, 81.

Daniel, 111.

Dannett, 1: 239.

"The Great Christian Congress." *Voice of the Negro* (Sept. 1906): 671.

Harrison, Earl L. *The Dream and the Dreamer.* 1956.

Lewis, Cary B. "Louisville and Its Afro-American Citizens." *Colored American Magazine* (Apr. 1906): 261–62, 264.

[Obituaries.] *Washington Post* (21 May 1961): B6; (22 May 1961): B8.

Pickens, William. *Nannie Burroughs and the School of the 3 B's.* New York: n.p., 1921.

"The *Voice of the Negro* for 1905." *Voice of the Negro* (Dec. 1904).

Wesley, 64, 69, 85, 90, 97, 98, 111, 222, 239, 423.

Papers in Collections

Nannie Burroughs Papers, Library of Congress.

Annie L. Burton (1859/1860?–?)

Writings by

Memories of Childhood's Slavery Days. Boston: Ross Publishing Co., 1909.

Anthologies

Loewenberg, Bert J., and Ruth Bogin, eds. *Black Women in Nineteenth-Century American Life: Their Words, Their Thoughts, Their Feelings.* University Park: Pennsylvania State University Press, 1976. 95–103.

Memories of Childhood's Slavery Days. In *Six Women's Slave Narratives*. Introduction by William L. Andrews. New York: Oxford University Press, 1988.

Olivia Ward Bush-Banks
[Olivia Ward Bush] (1869–1944)

Writings by

The Collected Works of Olivia Ward Bush-Banks. Bernice Guillaume, comp., ed. New York: Oxford University Press, 1991.

Driftwood. Cranston, RI: Atlantic Printing Co., 1914.

Memories of Calvary: An Easter Sketch. Philadelphia: A.M.E. Book Concern, c.1917.

Original Poems. Providence, RI: Press of Louis A. Basinet, 1899.

"Echoes from the Cabin Song." *Westchester Record-Courier* (30 Apr. 1932).

[Essay on John Greene.] *Westchester Record-Courier* (21 May 1932).

"Northeastern Federation of Women's Clubs." *Colored American Magazine* (Sept. 1900): 234–35.

"On the Long Island Indian." *Annual Report of the Montauk Tribe of Indians for the Year 1916* (31 Aug. 1916), at The Library of Anthropology, Nassau County Museum, Sands Point Preserve, Port Washington, NY.

"A Picture." *Colored American Magazine* (June 1900): 77–78.

"Regret." *Voice of the Negro* (June 1905): 400.

"Undercurrents of Social Life." *Colored American Magazine* (Dec. 1900): 155–56.

"Voices." *Voice of the Negro* (Dec. 1905): 866.

Anthologies
Shockley, 344–45.

Writings about

Bullock, 112, 133.

Daniels, John. *In Freedom's Birthplace: A Study of the Boston Negroes, 1914.* New York: Negro Universities Press, 1968.

"Driftwood and Other Poems" [Review]. *Colored American Magazine* (June 1900): 127.

Guillaume, Bernice F. "Character Names in *Indian Trails* by Olivia Ward Bush (Banks): Clues to Afro Assimilation into Long Island's Native Americans." *Afro-Americans in New York Life and History* 10.2 (1986): 45–53.

———. "The Female as Harlem Sage: The 'Aunt Viney's Sketches' of Olivia Ward Bush-Banks." *Langston Hughes Review* 6.2 (1987): 1–10.

———. "Olivia Ward Bush: Factors Shaping the Social and Cultural Outlook of a Nineteenth-Century Writer." *Negro History Bulletin* (Apr.–June 1980): 32–34.

Hatch, James V., and Omanii Abdullah. *Black Playwrights, 1823–1977: An Annotated Bibliography of Plays.* New York: R. R. Bowker, 1977.

The History and Archaeology of the Montauk Indians. Suffolk County Archaeological Association, Readings in Long Island Archaeology and Ethnohistory 3. Lexington, MA: Ginn, 1979.

Hopkins, Pauline E. "Echoes from the Annual Convention of Northeastern Federation of Colored Women's Clubs." *Colored American Magazine* (Oct. 1903): 709–13.

Matinecoc Longhouse of Long Island, Inc. *Newsletter* 3.9 (1987): 1–2.

Mitchell-Hill, Beulah. "Music and Musicians." *The Light and "Heebie Jeebies"* (26 Nov. 1927): 31.

Robinson, William H., Jr. *Black New England Letters: The Uses of Writings in Black New England.* NEH Learning Library Program, no. 2. Boston: Boston Public Library, 1977.

Sherry, Linda. "Biographical Quest." *East Hampton Star* (9 Aug. 1984): sec. 2, 18.

Shockley, 341–44.

Wortis, Helen Z. *A Woman Named Matilda and Other True Accounts of Old Shelter Island.* New York: Publishing Center for Cultural Resources, 1978.

Papers in Collections

The Olivia Ward Bush-Banks Papers, Amistad Research Center, Tulane University. 2 May 1989.

Guillaume, Bernice Forrest. "The Life and Work of Olivia Ward Bush (Banks), 1869–1944." Diss., Tulane University, 1983.

Selena S. Butler

Writings by

The Chain-Gang System [Read before the National Association of Colored Women, at Nashville, TN, 18 Sept. 1897]. Tuskegee, AL: Normal School Press, 1897.

"Atlanta Woman's Club." *Woman's Era* (June 1896): 6.

Writings about

Davis, 269–70.

Harris, Harvie J., ed. *Founder, the Georgia Congress of Colored Parents and Teachers.* N.p.: n.p., 1971.

Mary Ann Shadd Cary
[Mary Ann Shadd] (1823–1893)

Writings by

Condition of Colored People [Pamphlet]. Wilmington, DE: n.p., 1849.

A Plea for Emigration, or Notes of Canada West. Detroit: G. W. Pattison, 1852.

[Advertisement for the School of M. A. Shadd Cary and Amelia Freeman Shadd.] *Provincial Freeman* (18 June 1859).

[Advertisement for William Still's Boarding House.] *Frederick Douglass' Monthly* (17 Sept. 1858). *(BAP)*.

Agent agreement with Abraham McKinney. 29 Aug. 1861. Mary Ann Shadd Cary Papers, Moorland-Springarn Research Center, Howard University. *(BAP)*.

"The American Anti-Slavery Society." *Provincial Freeman* (30 May 1857). *(BAP)*.

"Anti-Slavery Lecture." *Provincial Freeman* (11 Apr. 1857). *(BAP)*.

"Anti-Slavery Meetings in Chatham." *Provincial Freeman* (18 Apr. 1857). *(BAP)*.

"Anti-Slavery Pamphlets." *Provincial Freeman* (5 July 1856). *(BAP)*.

[Article.] *Provincial Freeman* (12 July 1856; 18 Apr. 1857; 9 May 1857; 13 June 1857; 20 June 1857; 4 July 1857; [8 Aug.] 1857; [?] Sept. 1857). *(BAP)*.

[Article about Windsor Anti-Slavery Society.] *Voice of the Fugitive* (21 Oct. 1852). *(BAP)*.

"Beggars." *Provincial Freeman* (27 Dec. 1856). *(BAP)*.

"Canadian Churches Fellowshipping the Pro-Slavery Religious Bodies of the United States." *Provincial Freeman* (13 Dec. 1856). *(BAP)*.

"A Census List of the Inhabitants of Stratford CW." *Provincial Freeman* (28 March 1857). *(BAP)*.

"Chicago—The White Citizens—Colored Churches—Etc." [Letter to the Editor, William P. Newman]. *Provincial Freeman* (2 Feb. 1856). *(BAP)*.

"The 'Children's Paper.' " *Provincial Freeman* (24 Jan. 1857). *(BAP)*.

"The Cleveland Convention." *Provincial Freeman* (25 Nov. 1856). *(BAP)*.

[Comment on Article from *Liberator*.] *Provincial Freeman* (19 July 1856). *(BAP)*.

[Comment on Article from *Planet*.] *Provincial Freeman* (26 July 1856). *(BAP)*.

"Dr. Barker's View of Kent and Chatham." *Provincial Freeman* (13 June 1857). *(BAP)*.

"Editorial." *Provincial Freeman* (22 Dec. 1855). *(BAP)*.

"Editorials." *Provincial Freeman* (22 Aug. 1855). *(BAP)*.

"The Emigration Convention." *Provincial Freeman* (5 July 1856). *(BAP)*.

"Exposed at Last." *Provincial Freeman* (2 May 1857). *(BAP)*.

"Frederick Douglass' Paper." *Provincial Freeman* (7 Feb. 1857). *(BAP)*.

"A Good Boarding House Greatly Needed by the Colored Citizens." *Provincial Freeman* (6 Dec. 1856). *(BAP)*.

"Grammar School." *Provincial Freeman* (26 July 1856). *(BAP)*.

"Haytian Emigration at a Discount in Chatham." *Weekly Anglo-African* (19 Oct. 1861). *(BAP)*.

"The Hon. Colonel Prince in Parliament." *Provincial Freeman* (4 Apr. 1857).

"The Indignation Meeting, Col. Prince & C." *Provincial Freeman* (4 July 1857). *(BAP)*.

"Insurrections, Underground Railroad, Republican Victory,

Fugitive Slave Case." Nov. 1857. Mary Shadd Cary Papers, Ontario Archives, Toronto. *(BAP)*.

["James Taylor and Mary Ann Shadd."] *Voice of the Fugitive* (29 Jan. 1852).

"The Last Words of Peter Poyas." *Christian Recorder* (5 July 1862): 105.

"Lecture." *Provincial Freeman* (25 Apr. 1857). *(BAP)*.

"The Lecture by Elihu Burritt, Esq." *Provincial Freeman* (7 March 1857). *(BAP)*.

"The Letters from Hiram Wilson." *Provincial Freeman* (10 Jan. 1857). *(BAP)*.

Literary Announcement for *A Plea for Emigration, or Notes of Canada West*. Public Archives, Ottawa. *(BAP)*.

"Local Matters." *Provincial Freeman* (21 Feb. 1857). *(BAP)*.

"Looks Like More Begging!" *Provincial Freeman* (6 June 1857). *(BAP)*.

"Meeting on the African Subject by M. R. Delany." *Chatham Planet* (29 March 1861). [Variant copy, Ullman Papers, Black Medical History File.] *(BAP)*.

"Meetings at Philadelphia." *Provincial Freeman* (18 Apr. 1857). *(BAP)*.

"The Mental Feast on Wednesday Evening." *Provincial Freeman* (10 Jan. 1857). *(BAP)*.

"Miss E. T. Greenfield, 'The Black Swan.' " *Weekly Anglo-African* (9 Feb. 1861). *(BAP)*.

"Monthly Report of the UGRR." *Provincial Freeman* (21 March 1857). *(BAP)*.

"More Begging!" *Provincial Freeman* (30 May 1857). *(BAP)*.

"New Homeopathic Physician in Chatham." *Provincial Freeman* (25 July 1857). *(BAP)*.

"Newspaperdom" [With Isaac D. Shadd and H. Ford Douglass]. *Provincial Freeman* (11 Apr. 1857). *(BAP)*.

"Notice from the Editors: Mary Ann Shadd Cary, Isaac D.

Shadd and H. Ford Douglass." *Provincial Freeman* (9 May 1857). *(BAP)*.

"Obstacles to the Progress of Colored Canadians." *Provincial Freeman* (31 Jan. 1857). *(BAP)*.

"Obstacles to the Progress of Colored Canadians." [1859?] Mary Shadd Cary Papers, Ontario Archives, Toronto. *(BAP)*.

"Old Clothes." *Provincial Freeman* (3 Jan. 1857). *(BAP)*.

"On the Chronicle of a Clay Farm." [1857?] Mary Shadd Cary Papers, Ontario Archives, Toronto. *(BAP)*.

"Our Town and Township Councils and Indigent Colored People." *Provincial Freeman* (14 Feb. 1857). *(BAP)*.

"Out Canvassing." *Provincial Freeman* (25 July 1857). *(BAP)*.

Passport Application. 8 Feb. 1865. Shadd Cary Papers, National Library of Canada, Ottawa. *(BAP)*.

"Pay Us What You Owe." *Provincial Freeman* (28 Feb. 1857). *(BAP)*.

"Plastering & C." *Provincial Freeman* (19 July 1856). *(BAP)*.

"Politics." [1858?] Mary Shadd Cary Papers, Ontario Archives, Toronto. *(BAP)*.

"Politics." *Provincial Freeman* (31 Jan. 1857). *(BAP)*.

"Politics." *Provincial Freeman* (25 July 1857). *(BAP)*.

"The Preachers and the Press." *Provincial Freeman* (9 May 1857). *(BAP)*.

"The Presidential Election in the United States." *Provincial Freeman* (6 Dec. 1856). *(BAP)*.

"Prodigious." *Provincial Freeman* (13 June 1857). *(BAP)*.

"The Proposed High School." *Provincial Freeman* (9 May 1857). *(BAP)*.

"Prospectus of the *Provincial Freeman*." *Provincial Freeman* (25 March 1854). *(BAP)*.

"Prospectus of the *Provincial Freeman and Weekly Advisor*." *Provincial Freeman* (30 June 1855). *(BAP)*.

Provincial Freeman (11 Apr. 1857). *(BAP)*.

"Purely Local—What Shall We Do?" *Provincial Freeman* (18 July 1857). *(BAP)*.

"The Queen's Birth Day." *Provincial Freeman* (30 May 1857). *(BAP)*.

"The 'Raleigh Plains' Lands." *Provincial Freeman* (25 Apr. 1857). *(BAP)*.

"Raleigh Plains, No. 2." *Provincial Freeman* (9 May 1857). *(BAP)*.

"The Reform Alliance." *Provincial Freeman* (24 Jan. 1857). *(BAP)*.

"Refugees in Canada." *Provincial Freeman* (21 Feb. 1857). *(BAP)*.

"Refugees in Canada, No. 2." *Provincial Freeman* (14 March 1857). *(BAP)*.

"Refugee's Home." *Provincial Freeman* (4 July 1857). *(BAP)*.

"Remarks." *Provincial Freeman* (16 June 1855). *(BAP)*.

[Response to Letter from J. S. Campbell.] *Provincial Freeman* (9 June 1855). *(BAP)*.

[Response to Letter to the Editors.] *Provincial Freeman* (14 March 1857). *(BAP)*.

[Response to Letter to the Editors.] *Provincial Freeman* (25 Apr. 1857). *(BAP)*.

"Rowdyism by Three Trustees." *Provincial Freeman* (18 Apr. 1857). *(BAP)*.

"School for All!" *Provincial Freeman* (13 June 1857). *(BAP)*.

"School for All!" [Advertisement for Mary Ann Shadd Cary and Amelia Freeman Shadd's School]. *Provincial Freeman* (28 Jan. 1859). *(BAP)*.

"Sign the Pledge." *Christian Recorder* (30 Aug. 1877): 1.

"Slavery and Humanity" [Circular by Mary Ann Shadd Cary, Isaac D. Shadd, and H. Ford Douglass]. Feb.

1857. Shadd Cary Papers, Public Archives of Canada, Ottawa. *(BAP)*.

"Sunday Evening." 6 Apr. 1858. Mary Shadd Cary Papers, Ontario Archives, Toronto. *(BAP)*.

"To the Patrons of the 'Freeman.' " *Provincial Freeman* (25 Nov. 1856). *(BAP)*.

"The Things Most Needed." *Provincial Freeman* (25 Apr. 1857). *(BAP)*.

"The Toronto Anti-Slavery Society." *Provincial Freeman* (30 May 1857). *(BAP)*.

"Trifles." *Anglo-African Magazine* (Feb. 1859). *(BAP)*.

"Very Small Indeed." *Provincial Freeman* (13 June 1857). *(BAP)*.

"Voice of the Bondsman." *Provincial Freeman* (7 Feb. 1857). *(BAP)*.

"What Colored Men Are Doing in Canada." *Provincial Freeman* (25 July 1857). *(BAP)*.

"Where Are the Colored Ministers of Chatham?" *Provincial Freeman* (9 May 1857). *(BAP)*.

"Why Antoinette Brown's Church Was Closed" [Notice from the Editors, Mary Ann Shadd Cary, Isaac D. Shadd, and H. Ford Douglass]. *Provincial Freeman* (30 May 1857). *(BAP)*.

"The Windsor Herald in a 'Stew.' " *Provincial Freeman* (21 June 1856). *(BAP)*.

Letters

"Condition of the Colored People—Philadelphians, etc." [Letter to Isaac D. Shadd]. *Provincial Freeman* (Feb. 1856). *(BAP)*.

"A Correction, A Fact, and A Batch of Wonders" [Letter to the Editor, Robert Hamilton]. *Weekly Anglo-African* (28 Dec. 1861).

"Haytian Emigration" [Letter to the Editor, Robert Hamilton]. *Weekly Anglo-African* (28 Sept. 1861). *(BAP)*.

"Haytian Emigration" [Letter to the Editor, Robert Hamilton]. *Weekly Anglo-African* (26 Oct. 1861). *(BAP)*.

"Haytian Emigration" [Letter to the Editor, Robert Hamilton]. *Weekly Anglo-African* (9 Nov. 1861). *(BAP)*.

"Haytian Emigration in Canada" [Letter to the Editor, Robert Hamilton]. *Weekly Anglo-African* (19 Oct. 1861). *(BAP)*.

"The Haytian Fever and Its Diagnostics in Canada" [Letter to the Editor, Robert Hamilton]. *Weekly Anglo-African* (14 Dec. 1861). *(BAP)*.

"An Investigation into the Mission School Affairs at Chatham, CW" [Letter to William Lloyd Garrison]. *Liberator* (28 Feb. 1862). *(BAP)*.

Letter. 15 Jan. 1853. AMA Collection, Amistad Research Center, Tulane University. *(BAP)*.

Letter to American Missionary Association. 6 Sept. 1852. AMA Collection, Amistad Research Center, Tulane University. *(BAP)*.

[Letter to C.] *Provincial Freeman* (21 Oct. 1854). *(BAP)*.

Letter to Frederick Douglass. *North Star* (23 March 1849). *(BAP)*.

Letter to the Editor. *Planet* [Chatham Tri-Weekly] (29 May 1860). *(BAP)*.

Letter to Executive Committee, American Missionary Association. 3 Apr. 1852. AMA Collection, Amistad Research Center, Tulane University. *(BAP)*.

Letter to Executive Committee, American Missionary Association. 24 Oct. 1852. AMA Collection, Amistad Research Center, Tulane University. *(BAP)*.

Letter to Charles C. Foote. 5 Jan. 1853. AMA Collection, Amistad Research Center, Tulane University. *(BAP)*.

Letter to Mr. Garrison. *Liberator* (4 March 1853): 36.

Letter to William Lloyd Garrison. 5 Oct. 1852. Anti-Slavery
   Collections, Boston Public Library. *(BAP)*.

Letter to William P. Newman. *Provincial Freeman* (8 Sept.
   1855; 22 Sept. 1855; 6 Oct. 1855; 3 Nov. 1855; 8 Dec.
   1855; 22 Dec. 1855; 29 Dec. 1855; Jan. 1856). *(BAP)*.

Letter to D. W. Richard, R. Jackson, Flemming, Johnson,
   Cornelius Charity and Others. 24 Oct. 1854. Mary
   Shadd Cary Papers, Ontario Archives, Toronto. *(BAP)*.

Letter to Isaac D. Shadd. 16 Sept. [1854?]. Mary Shadd
   Cary Papers, Ontario Archives, Toronto. *(BAP)*.

Letter to Isaac D. Shadd. *Provincial Freeman* (26 Apr. 1856).
   (BAP).

Letter to George Whipple. 27 Oct. 1851; 14 Feb. 1852; 22
   Apr. 1852; 21 June 1852; 21 July 1852; 18 Aug. 1852;
   6 Dec. 1852; 28 Dec. 1852; 7 Feb. 1853; 28 March
   1853; 2 Apr. 1853; 21 June 1859; 3 Nov. 1859; 7 May
   1864; 22 June 1864. AMA Collection, Amistad Research
   Center, Tulane University. *(BAP)*.

["M. A. Shadd et al."] [Letter]. *Provincial Freeman* (22
   Dec. 1855). *(BAP)*.

"Miss Shadd's Pamphlet" [Letter to Frederick Douglass].
   North Star (8 June 1849). *(BAP)*.

"The Mission School at Chatham CW" [Letter to the Editor,
   Robert Hamilton]. *Weekly Anglo-African* (5 Apr. 1862).
   (BAP).

"Our Tour" [Letter to Samuel Ringgold Ward]. *Provincial
   Freeman* (22 July 1854; 5 Aug. 1854). *(BAP)*.

"A Short Letter—Visit to Racine and Rockford—etc." [Letter
   to Isaac D. Shadd]. *Provincial Freeman* (8 March 1856).
   (BAP).

"Success—H. Ford Douglass, etc." [Letter to Isaac D.
   Shadd]. *Provincial Freeman* (9 Feb. 1856). *(BAP)*.

"An Unmitigated Falsehood" [Letter to the Editor, Robert Hamilton]. *Weekly Anglo-African* (15 Feb. 1862). *(BAP)*.

"A Voice of Thanks" [Letter to William Lloyd Garrison]. *Liberator* (29 Nov. 1861). *(BAP)*.

Anthologies

Sterling, Dorothy, ed. *Speak Out in Thunder Tones: Letters and Other Writings by Black Northerners, 1787–1865.* Garden City, NY: Doubleday, 1973. 285, 329–30, 372–73.

———. *The Trouble They Seen: Black People Tell the Story of Reconstruction.* Garden City, NY: Doubleday, 1976.

———. *We Are Your Sisters: Black Women in the Nineteenth Century.* New York: W. W. Norton, 1984. 164–75, 413–14.

Writings about

"American Slavery." *British Banner* (20 Nov. 1855). *(BAP)*.

[Announcement of Donation Party for Mary Ann Shadd.] *Voice of the Fugitive* (19 Nov. 1851). *(BAP)*.

Beardin, Jim, and Linda Jean Butler. *The Life and Times of Mary Shadd Cary.* Toronto: NC Press, 1977.

Blake, Edwin. [Editorial Remarks.] *Provincial Freeman* (3 June 1854). *(BAP)*.

Brown, 92–96.

Brown, William Wells. *The Rising Son; or, the Antecedents and Advancement of the Colored Race.* Boston: A. G. Brown and Co., 1874. 539–40.

Bullock, 21, 61.

DANB, 552–53.

Dann, 347.

Dannett, 1: 150–57.

Davis, 294–95.

Delany, Martin Robinson. *The Condition, Elevation, Immigration, and Destiny of the Colored People of the United States*. Philadelphia: the Author, 1852; New York: Arno Press, 1968. 131.

"Editorial Remarks Upon M. A. Shadd Cary and H. Ford Douglass." *Provincial Freeman* (29 March 1856). *(BAP)*.

Frazier, Susan Elizabeth. "Some Afro-American Women of Mark." *A.M.E. Church Review* (Apr. 1892): 378–86.

Hancock, Harold B. "Mary Ann Shadd: Negro Editor, Educator, and Lawyer." *Delaware History* (Apr. 1973): 187–94.

Johnson, Clifton H. "Mary Ann Shadd: Crusader for the Freedom of Man." *Crisis* (Apr.–May 1971): 89–90.

"The Late Philadelphia Libel Suit." *Weekly Anglo-African* (19 May 1860). *(BAP)*.

Loguen, Jermain Wesley. "J. W. Loguen's Visit to Canada." *Syracuse Daily Standard* (26 May 1856).

Majors, 112–13.

NAW, 1: 300–301.

Newman, William P., and J. B. Lewis. "Meeting to Organize the Provincial Union." *Provincial Freeman* (19 Aug. 1854). *(BAP)*.

Order appointing Mary Ann Shadd Cary a "recruiting officer to enlist colored volunteers." 15 Aug. 1864. Shadd Cary Papers, Moorland-Spingarn Research Center, Howard University. *(BAP)*.

"Our Literary Women." *Lancet* (10 Oct. 1885): 1.

Pease, William H., and Jane H. Pease. *Black Utopia*. Madison: State Historical Society of Wisconsin, 1963.

Penn, 427.

Quarles, Benjamin. *Black Abolitionists*. New York: Oxford University Press, 1969. 79, 88, 178, 217, 218, 231.

Recruiting Certificate for W. G. Shadd. 17 Aug. 1863. Shadd Cary Papers, Moorland–Spingarn Research Center, Howard University. *(BAP)*.

Shadd, Isaac D. "Dull times–Son shot by his father— Weather—State of crops, etc." *Provincial Freeman* (16 June 1855). *(BAP)*.

Stanton, Elizabeth Cady, et al., eds. *History of Woman Suffrage*. New York: Fowler and Wells, 1881. 3: 72.

Stock Certificate. [1858?] Mary Shadd Cary Papers, Ontario Archives, Toronto. *(BAP)*.

Wesley, *5*, 9, 13.

Winks, Robin W. *The Blacks in Canada: A History*. Montreal: McGill-Queen's University Press; New Haven: Yale University Press, 1971.

Letters

Note: Letters to Mary Ann Shadd Cary in her office as editor of the *Provincial Freeman* are not generally personal correspondence.

A. [Letter to the Editor.] *Provincial Freeman* (20 Jan. 1855). *(BAP)*.

An Afro-American. [Letter to the Editor.] *Provincial Freeman* (17 Feb. 1855). *(BAP)*.

Alpha. [Letter to Mary Ann Shadd.] *Provincial Freeman* (9 Sept. 1854). *(BAP)*.

Americus. [Letter to the Editors.] *Provincial Freeman* (25 Apr. 1857). *(BAP)*.

Anderson, Osborne. [Letter to the Editors.] *Provincial Freeman* (8 Aug. 1857). *(BAP)*.

A. S. [Letter to the "Editress."] *Provincial Freeman* (16 June 1855). *(BAP)*.

Brooks, H. J. [Letter to the Editors.] *Provincial Freeman* (21 Feb. 1857). *(BAP)*.

Burns, Robert. [Letter to the Editor.] *Provincial Freeman* (4 Nov. 1854). *(BAP)*.

Campbell, Israel. [Letter to the Editor.] *Provincial Freeman* (23 Dec. 1854). *(BAP)*.

Campbell, J. S. [Letter to the Editor.] *Provincial Freeman* (9 June 1855). *(BAP)*.

Cary, Thomas F. Letter to Mary Ann Shadd Cary. 21 May 1857; 11 June 1857; 17 Dec. 1857; 21 Jan. 1858. Mary Shadd Cary Papers, Ontario Archives, Toronto. *(BAP)*.

Curtis, A. W. *"On Slavery* (by Rev. E. Bibbins)" [Letter to the Editors]. *Provincial Freeman* (27 Dec. 1856). *(BAP)*.

Davidson, James Alexander. "Letter from Mr. Davidson— The Temperance Lecturer, and (Converted Infidel)" [Letter to the Editors]. *Provincial Freeman* (14 March 1857). *(BAP)*.

Delany, Martin R. Letter to Mary Ann Shadd Cary. 7 Dec. 1863. Shadd Cary Papers, Moorland-Spingarn Research Center, Howard University. *(BAP)*.

Depp, C. S. [Letter to Mary Ann Shadd.] *Provincial Freeman* (26 Aug. 1854). *(BAP)*.

Depp, Costus S. [Letter to Mary Ann Shadd.] *Provincial Freeman* (21 Apr. 1855).

A Descendant of the African Race. [Letter to the Editor.] *Provincial Freeman* (17 March 1855; 21 Apr. 1855; 5 May 1855; 12 May 1855; 23 June 1855). *(BAP)*.

Douglass, H. Ford. Letter to Mary Ann Shadd Cary. 15 [Nov.?] [1857?]. Mary Shadd Cary Papers, Ontario Archives, Toronto. *(BAP)*.

———. Letter to Mary Ann Shadd Cary. Mary Shadd Cary Papers, Ontario Archives, Toronto. *(BAP)*.

Fisher, William. [Letter to the Editors.] *Provincial Freeman* (30 May 1857). *(BAP)*.

Foote, Charles C. Letter to Mary Ann Shadd Cary. 1 March 1861. AMA Collection, Amistad Research Center, Tulane University. *(BAP)*.

Foster, Levi. [Letter to Mary Ann Shadd.] *Provincial Freeman* (30 June 1855). *(BAP)*.

Gaines, John I. "Emigration" [Letter to the Editor]. *Provincial Freeman* (20 Jan. 1855). *(BAP)*.

Hannibal. [Letter to the Editors.] *Provincial Freeman* (24 May 1856). *(BAP)*.

Harvey, George D. L. [Letter to the Editor.] *Provincial Freeman* (19 May 1855). *(BAP)*.

Hubert, Samuel G. Letter to Mary Ann Shadd Cary. 29 May 1857. Mary Shadd Cary Papers, Ontario Archives, Toronto. *(BAP)*.

Hull, V. "Sabbath Desecration, its Cure" [Letter to the Editors]. *Provincial Freeman* (19 July 1856). *(BAP)*.

An Inquirer. [Letter to Mary Ann Shadd.] *Provincial Freeman* (21 Oct. 1854). *(BAP)*.

Jones, Jacob. "True Band Society—Refugee's Home—Poor Fugitives?" [Letter to the Editors]. *Provincial Freeman* (16 June 1855). *(BAP)*.

Jones, Thomas. [Letter to the Editor.] *Provincial Freeman* (5 May 1855). *(BAP)*.

L. Letter to Mary Ann Shadd Cary. 17 Dec. 1854. Mary Shadd Cary Papers, Ontario Archives, Toronto. *(BAP)*.

Lawrence, Francis H. [Letter to the Editors.] *Provincial Freeman* (28 March 1857). *(BAP)*.

Linton, J.J.E. [Letter to the Editors.] *Provincial Freeman* (5 July 1856). *(BAP)*.

———. "The Upper Canada Tract Society; Toronto and

Slavery" [Letter to the Editors]. *Provincial Freeman* (19 July 1856). *(BAP)*.

Loguen, Jermain Wesley. "Rev. J. W. Loguen's Visit to Canada" [Letter to Mary Ann Shadd Cary, Isaac D. Shadd, and H. Ford Douglass]. *Provincial Freeman* (24 May 1856).

Lott, John B. [Letter to Mary Ann Shadd.] *Provincial Freeman* (30 June 1855). *(BAP)*.

Lowery, Samuel A. S. "Gains on Submission, or an Anti-Emigrationist Reviewed" [Letter to the Editor]. *Provincial Freeman* (17 Feb. 1855). *(BAP)*.

———. "Gains on Submission, or an Anti-Emigrationist Reviewed, No. 2" [Letter to the Editor]. *Provincial Freeman* (17 March 1855). *(BAP)*.

Many Inquirers. [Letter to Mary Ann Shadd.] *Provincial Freeman* (28 Oct. 1854). *(BAP)*.

McClaughy, William H. Letter to Mary Ann Shadd Cary. [1?] Jan. 1858. Mary Shadd Cary Papers, Ontario Archives, Toronto. *(BAP)*.

A Member of the Convention. [Letter to the Editors.] *Provincial Freeman* (24 Jan. 1857). *(BAP)*.

Miller, George H. A. Letter to Mary Ann Shadd Cary. 12 Feb. 1855. Mary Shadd Cary Papers, Ontario Archives, Toronto. *(BAP)*.

An Observer. [Letter to the Editors.] *Provincial Freeman* (17 May 1856). *(BAP)*.

Pardee, Benjamin S. Letter to Mary Ann Shadd Cary. 3 March 1864. Shadd Cary Papers, Moorland-Spingarn Research Center, Howard University. *(BAP)*.

Payne, John. Letter to Mary Ann Shadd Cary. [1858?] Mary Shadd Cary Papers, Ontario Archives, Toronto. *(BAP)*.

Pryer, Alonzo. [Letter to the Editors.] *Provincial Freeman* (21 March 1857; 13 June 1857). *(BAP)*.

Pugh, Sarah. [Letter to Mary Ann Shadd.] *Provincial Freeman* (25 July 1857). *(BAP)*.

Q. [Letter to the Editors.] *Provincial Freeman* (10 May 1856). *(BAP)*.

R.M.J. "Emigration" [Letter to the Editor]. *Provincial Freeman* (17 March 1855).

S. [Letter to the Editors.] *Provincial Freeman* (14 June 1856). *(BAP)*.

Shadd, Abraham. Letter to Mary Ann Shadd Cary. 8 Dec. 1844. Shadd Cary Papers, Moorland-Spingarn Research Center, Howard University. *(BAP)*.

Shorts, Stephen. [Letter to the Editor.] *Provincial Freeman* (14 March 1857). *(BAP)*.

Sleets, Benjamin C. [Letter to the Editor.] *Provincial Freeman* (16 June 1855). *(BAP)*.

Smallwood, Thomas F. [Letter to the Editor.] *Provincial Freeman* (24 March 1855). *(BAP)*.

Smith, Andrew, and G. W. Brodie. [Letter to the Editors.] *Provincial Freeman* (21 March 1857). *(BAP)*.

Smith, Joshua B. [Letter to the Editors.] *Provincial Freeman* (21 March 1857). *(BAP)*.

Spears, L. G. [Letter to the Editors.] *Provincial Freeman* (7 Feb. 1857). *(BAP)*.

A Spectator. [Letter to the "Editress."] *Provincial Freeman* (30 June 1855). *(BAP)*.

Stevens, Major, et al. [Letter to the Editor.] *Provincial Freeman* (7 Apr. 1855). *(BAP)*.

Still, John N. [Letter to Mary Ann Shadd.] *Provincial Freeman* (9 Sept. 1854; 30 June 1855). *(BAP)*.

———. [Letter to the Editor.] *Provincial Freeman* (23 Dec. 1854). *(BAP)*.

Still, William. "From Our Philadelphia Correspondent" [Letter to the Editors]. *Provincial Freeman* (28 March 1857). *(BAP)*.

Still, William. [Letter to Mary Ann Shadd.] *Provincial Freeman* (2 Sept. 1854). *(BAP)*.

——. [Letter to Mary Ann Shadd.] *Provincial Freeman* (24 March 1855). *(BAP)*.

——. [Letter to Mary Ann Shadd.] *Provincial Freeman* (14 Apr. 1855). *(BAP)*.

——. Letter to Mary Ann Shadd Cary. 8 Jan. 1854; 1 Feb. 1854; 18 Sept. 1857; Jan. [1858?]; 30 Jan. 1858. Mary Shadd Cary Papers, Ontario Archives, Toronto. *(BAP)*.

——. "Miss Frances Ellen Watkins, & c." [Letter to the Editors]. *Provincial Freeman* (7 March 1857). *(BAP)*.

Tanner, Benjamin S. [Letter to the Editors.] *Provincial Freeman* (25 Apr. 1857). *(BAP)*.

Tanner, William C. "Sabbath Desecration" [Letter to the Editors]. *Provincial Freeman* (7 June 1856). *(BAP)*.

Tate, Wesley W. [Letter to Mary Ann Shadd.] *Provincial Freeman* (14 Oct. 1854; 4 Nov. 1854). *(BAP)*.

Temperance. [Letter to the Editor.] *Provincial Freeman* (9 June 1855). *(BAP)*.

Turner, Daniel A. [Letter to the Editors.] *Provincial Freeman* (14 March 1857). *(BAP)*.

Uninitiated. [Letter to the Editors.] *Provincial Freeman* (21 Feb. 1857). *(BAP)*.

Washington, Dennis. [Letter to the Editors.] *Provincial Freeman* (18 Apr. 1857; 25 Apr. 1857). *(BAP)*.

Wentworth, James, Jr. [Letter to Mary Ann Shadd.] *Provincial Freeman* (2 Sept. 1854; 16 Sept. 1854). *(BAP)*.

Wil[?], H. J. Letter to Mary Ann Shadd Cary and Isaac D. Shadd. 23 Apr. 1858. Mary Ann Shadd Cary Papers, Ontario Archives, Toronto. *(BAP)*.

Williams, E. J. Letter to Mary Ann Shadd Cary. 2 Nov.

1858. Mary Shadd Cary Papers, Ontario Archives, Toronto. *(BAP)*.

Williams, E. L. Letter to Mary Ann Shadd Cary. 18 Jan. 1858. Mary Shadd Cary Papers, Ontario Archives, Toronto. *(BAP)*.

Williamson, Amelia C. Shadd[?]. Letter to Mary Ann Shadd. 7 May 1852. Mary Shadd Cary Papers, Ontario Archives, Toronto. *(BAP)*.

Willment, William. Letter to Mary Ann Shadd Cary. 15 June 1857. Mary Shadd Cary Papers, Ontario Archives, Toronto. *(BAP)*.

Wilson, Hiram. [Letter to Mary Ann Shadd.] *Provincial Freeman* (2 Sept. 1854). *(BAP)*.

X.Y.Z. "From our Chatham Correspondent, No. II." *Provincial Freeman* (16 June 1855). *(BAP)*.

———. [Letter to the Editor.] *Provincial Freeman* (26 May 1855; 21 March 1857; 4 Apr. 1857). *(BAP)*.

Z.H.M. [Letter to the Editor.] *Provincial Freeman* (9 June 1855). *(BAP)*.

———. [Letter to Mary Ann Shadd.] *Provincial Freeman* (30 June 1855). *(BAP)*.

Papers in Collections

Mary Ann Shadd Cary Papers, 1844–1884 Manuscript Collection, Moorland-Spingarn Research Center, Howard University.

Citizenship Certificate. 9 Sept. 1862. Shadd Family Papers, National Library of Canada, Ottawa. *(BAP)*.

[J.J.E.L.?] Letter. [12 Nov.?] 1857. Mary Shadd Cary Papers, Ontario Archives, Toronto.

———. Letter. [1 Dec.?] 1857. Mary Ann Shadd Cary Papers, Ontario Archives, Toronto.

Johnson, George. Letter to E. Flexner. 1957. Negro Women
    Collection, Sophia Smith Collection, Smith College.

Arabella Virginia Chase

Writings by

A Peculiar People. Washington, DC: W. C. Chase, Jr.,
    Printer, 1905.
"The Black Heir" [Serial]. *Washington Bee* (1 Sept., 8 Sept.,
    15 Sept., 22 Sept., 29 Sept., 6 Oct. 1902).
"She Kept Her Word" [Serial]. *Washington Bee* (4 Aug., 11
    Aug. 1902).

Writings about

"Our Literary Women." *Lancet* (10 Oct. 1885): 1.
"A Peculiar People" [Review]. *Washington Bee* (28 Jan.
    1905): 1.

Carrie Williams Clifford (1862–1934)

Writings by

Race Rhymes. Washington, DC: Pendleton, 1911.
The Widening Light. Boston: Walter Reid Company, [c.1922];
    New York: Thomas Y. Crowell, 1971.
"America." *Alexander's Magazine* (15 Nov. 1907): 20.
"Atlanta's Shame." *Voice of the Negro* (Nov. 1906): 497.
"Brothers." *Opportunity* (Dec. 1925): 357.
"The Business Career of Mrs. M. E. Williams." *Colored
    American Magazine* (Sept. 1905): 477–81.
"Oh Christmas with Its Memories!" *Alexander's Magazine*
    (15 Dec. 1905): 54–55.
"Cleveland and Its Colored People." *Colored American Mag-
    azine* (July 1905): 365–80.

"An Easter Message." *Crisis* 19 (1920): 336.

"For the New Year." *Crisis* 19 (1920): 193.

"The Great American Question." *Colored American Magazine* (May 1907): 364–73.

"Idealism and Materialism." *Colored American Magazine* (March 1906): 165–67.

"Lines to Garrison." *Alexander's Magazine* (15 Jan. 1906): 8–9.

"Love's Way (A Christmas Story)." *Alexander's Magazine* (15 Jan. 1906): 55–58.

"My Little Son." *Alexander's Magazine* (15 Dec. 1906): 101–2.

"Sorrow Songs." *Crisis* 34 (1927): 123.

"Spring." *Crisis* 10 (1915): 136.

"To My Poet Lover." *Voice of the Negro* (March 1905): 175.

"The Way of Life." *Alexander's Magazine* (15 Feb. 1907): 182.

"The Way of Life." *Colored American Magazine* (Sept. 1907): 212.

"Which Shall It Be?" *Colored American Magazine* (Jan. 1907): 33–34.

Anthologies

Stetson, Erlene, ed. *Black Sister: Poetry by Black American Women, 1746–1980*. Bloomington: Indiana University Press, 1981. 82.

Writings about

Bullock, 115, 133, 140.

Walton, Elizabeth. *"The Widening Light"* [Review]. *Opportunity* (July 1925): 217.

Wesley, 57, 92, 353, 412, 416.

Lucretia H. Newman Coleman

Writings by

Poor Ben: A Story of Real Life. Nashville: A.M.E. Sunday-
school Union, [c.1890].

Writings about

American Baptist (Sept. 1884).

Dann, 62.

Dunnigan, Alice E. "Early History of Negro Women in
Journalism." *Negro History Bulletin* 28 (Summer 1965):
178.

Majors, 197–98.

Meier, August. *Negro Thought in America, 1880–1915: Racial Ideologies in the Age of Booker T. Washington*. Ann
Arbor: University of Michigan Press, 1963. 132.

Mossell, 14.

Penn, 384–86.

Scruggs, 210–11.

Anna Julia Haywood Cooper (1858–1964)

Writings by

*L'Attitude de la France à l'egard de l'esclavage pendant la
revolution*. Paris: Imprimerie de la Cour d'Appel, 1925.

Charlemagne. Voyage à Jerusalem et à Constantinople. Anna
Julia Haywood Cooper, ed. Paris: A. Lahure, 1925.

Christmas Bells, A One Act Play for Children. [No imprint.]

Christ's Church. Atlanta: Atlanta University Press, n.d.

Equality of Races and the Democratic Movement. Washington,
DC: the Author, 1945.

Legislative Measures Concerning Slavery in the United States.
N.p.: n.p., 1942.

Les Idées egalitaires et la mouvement democratique. Paris, 1945.

The Life and Writings of the Grimké Family. Anna Julia Haywood Cooper, ed. 2 vols. N.p.: the Author, 1951.

The Social Settlement: What It Is, and What It Does. Washington, DC: Murray Brothers Press, 1913.

The Third Step. N.p.: n.p., n.d.

A Voice From the South, By a Black Woman of the South. Xenia, OH: Aldine Printing House, 1892; New York: Negro Universities Press, 1969.

A Voice From the South, By a Black Woman of the South. Introduction by Mary Helen Washington. New York: Oxford University Press, 1988.

"Angry Saxons and Negro Education." *Crisis* (May 1938): 148.

"The Higher Education of Women." *Southland* (Apr. 1891): 190–94.

"The Humour of Teaching." *Crisis* (Nov. 1930): 387.

"One of our most interesting . . ." [Review]. *Southern Workman* (Apr. 1894): 54.

Anthologies

Loewenberg, Bert J., and Ruth Bogin, eds. *Black Women in Nineteenth-Century American Life: Their Words, Their Thoughts, Their Feelings.* University Park: Pennsylvania State University Press, 1976. 317–31.

Shockley, 209.

Writings about

Bullock, 79, 102–3.

Carby, Hazel. " 'On the Threshold of Woman's Era': Lynching, Empire, and Sexuality in Black Feminist Theory." *Critical Inquiry* (Autumn 1985): 262–77.

Chitty, Arthur Ben. "Women and Black Education: Three

Profiles." *Historical Magazine of the Protestant Episcopal Church* 52.2 (1983): 153–65.

DANB, 128–29.

Dannett, 1: 245.

Dyson, Zita E. "Biographical Sketch of Anna J. Cooper." *Parent-Teacher Journal* (May–June 1930): 12.

Giddings, Paula. *When and Where I Enter: The Impact of Black Women on Race and Sex in America*. New York: William Morrow, 1984. 13, 54–55, 81, 82, 87–88, 96, 101, 103, 104–5, 108–9, 113, 116, 122–23, 171–81, 210–12.

Harley, Sharon. "Anna J. Cooper: A Voice for Black Women." In *The Afro-American Woman: Struggles and Images*. Sharon Harley and Rosalyn Terborg-Penn, eds. Port Washington, NY: Kennikat Press, 1978. 87–96.

Hatley, Flora J. [Review of *Anna J. Cooper: A Voice from the South*, by Louise Daniel Hutchinson.] *North Carolina Historical Review* (Winter 1982): 80–81.

Hundley, Mary Gibson. *The Dunbar Story (1870–1955)*. New York: Vantage Press, 1965.

Hutchinson, Louise Daniel. *Anna J. Cooper: A Voice from the South*. Washington, DC: Anacostia Neighborhood Museum of the Smithsonian Institution, by the Smithsonian Institution Press, 1981.

Keller, Frances Richardson. "The Perspective of a Black American on Slavery and the French Revolution: Anna Julia Cooper." *Proceedings of the Annual Meeting of the Western Society for French History* 3 (1975): 165–76.

Majors, 284–87.

McClellan, G. M. "The Negro as a Writer." Culp, 279.

Mossell, 11, 13, 14, 60–61.

"Notes." *Woman's Era* (Aug. 1894): 8.

Ploski, Harry A., and Ernest Kaiser. *The Negro Almanac*. 2nd Edition. New York: Bellwether, 1971. 873–74.

Rush, 173–74.

Scruggs, 207–9.

Shockley, 204–9.

Washington, Mary Helen. "Anna Julia Cooper: The Black Feminist Voice of the 1890's." *Legacy* (Fall 1987): 3–15.

"We have received for notice . . ." [Review]. *Southern Workman* (May 1893).

Wesley, 5, 9, 25, 32.

White, Deborah. [Review of *Anna J. Cooper: A Voice from the South*, by Louise Daniel Hutchinson.] *Georgia History Quarterly* (Fall 1983): 415–17.

Yenser, Thomas, ed. *Who's Who in Colored America: Dictionary of Notable Living Persons of African Descent in America, 1938–39–40*. 5th Edition. Brooklyn, NY: Thomas Yenser, 1940. 133.

Papers in Collections

Biographical materials, correspondence, publications. Sophia Smith Collection, Smith College.

Anna Julia Cooper Papers, Manuscript Collection, Moorland-Spingarn Research Center, Howard University.

Cooper, Anna Julia. "L'Attitude de la France à l'egard de l'esclavage pendant la revolution." Thèse pour le doctorat d'Université, Paris, 1925. Sophia Smith Collection, Smith College.

————. "The Attitude of France towards Slavery during the Revolution." Translation (partial) by Leona C. Gabel. [Manuscript and notes, typescript.] Sophia Smith Collection, Smith College.

————. Letter. 1 May 1909. *Class Letters of 1884*. Vol. 5. Oberlin, OH: Oberlin College.

————. *The Third Step*. Anna Julia Cooper Papers, Moorland-Spingarn Research Center, Howard University.

Gabel, Leona Christine. "Anna Julia (Haywood) Cooper."

Notable American Women Collection, 1980. Sophia Smith
Collection, Smith College.

————. *From Slavery to the Sorbonne and Beyond.* . . . Smith
College Studies in History. Sophia Smith Collection,
Smith College.

Frances (Fanny) Jackson Coppin
[Mrs. Levi J. Coppin] (1837–1913)

Writings by

Reminiscences of School Life, and Hints on Teaching. Philadelphia: A.M.E. Book Concern, 1913.

"Christmas Eve Story." *Christian Recorder* (30 Dec. 1880):
2.

"Christmas Eve Story." *Christian Recorder* (29 Dec. 1881).

"A Plea for Industrial Opportunity." In *Masterpieces of Negro
Eloquence.* Alice Moore Dunbar, ed. New York: The
Bookery, 1914. 251–56.

"Women and the Race Question." *Harper's Weekly* (27 Aug.
1904): 1323, 1330–31.

Anthologies

Loewenberg, Bert J., and Ruth Bogin, eds. *Black Women in
Nineteenth-Century American Life: Their Words, Their
Thoughts, Their Feelings.* University Park: Pennsylvania
State University Press, 1976. 317–31.

Writings about

[African Methodist Episcopal Church. Bishop's Council.
Committee on Deaconesses. Abraham Grant, Chairman.]
Deaconess Manual of the African Methodist Episcopal Church.
[N.p.], 1902.

A.M.E. Church Review (Jan. 1901).

Brawley, *NBH*, 142, 273–78.

Brown, 119–26.

Brown, William Wells. *The Rising Son; or, the Antecedents and Advancement of the Colored Race*. Boston: A. G. Brown and Co., 1874.

Bullock, 97.

Burton, Margaret E. *Comrades in Service*. New York: Missionary Education Movement of the United States and Canada, 1915.

Coppin, Bishop Levi J. *Unwritten History: An Autobiography*. Philadelphia: A.M.E. Book Concern, [c.1913]; New York: Negro Universities Press, 1968.

Cromwell, John Wesley. *The Negro in American History; Men and Women Eminent in the Evolution of the American of African Descent*. Washington, DC: The American Negro Academy, [c.1914]. 213–18.

DANB, 130–32.

Daniel, 219.

Dannett, 1: 247.

Davis, 202–3.

Embry, Rev. J. C. "Notes and Observations from the West." *Christian Recorder* (4 Sept. 1890): 1.

Frazier, Susan Elizabeth. "Some Afro-American Women of Mark." *A.M.E. Church Review* (Apr. 1892): 378–86.

Majors, 170.

Mossell, 10–11, 13.

"Mrs. Coppin." *Christian Recorder* (4 Aug. 1890): 4; (4 Sept. 1890): 4.

NAW, 3: 383–85.

Perkins, Linda M. "Heed Life's Demands: The Educational Philosophy of Fanny Jackson Coppin." *Journal of Negro Education* 51.3 (1982): 181–90.

Richings, B. F. *Evidences of Progress among Colored People*.

3rd Edition. Philadelphia: George S. Ferguson Co., 1897. 258.

Robinson, 67.

Scruggs, 75.

Wesley, 8, 13, 20, 21, 36, 38, 43, 66, 493.

Papers in Collections

Perkins, Linda Marie. "Fanny Jackson Coppin and the Institute for Colored Youth: A Model of Nineteenth-Century Black Female Educational and Community Leadership, 1837–1902." Diss., University of Illinois, Urbana-Champaign, 1978.

Lucy A. Berry Delaney

Writings by

From the Darkness Cometh the Light or Struggles for Freedom. St. Louis: J. T. Smith Publishing House, [c.1891].

Anthologies

From the Darkness Cometh the Light or Struggles for Freedom. In *Six Women's Slave Narratives.* Introduction by William L. Andrews. New York: Oxford University Press, 1988.

Charlotte Gilburg Draper

Writings by

For the Presbyterian Female of Color's Enterprising Society in Baltimore. A Freewill Offering. Baltimore: Frederick A. Hanzsche, 1860.

Kate Drumgoold

Writings by

A Slave Girl's Story. Brooklyn, NY: Privately printed, 1898.

Anthologies

A Slave Girl's Story. In *Six Women's Slave Narratives*. Introduction by William L. Andrews. New York: Oxford University Press, 1988.

Alice Ruth Moore Dunbar-Nelson (1875–1935)

Writings by

An Alice Dunbar-Nelson Reader. R. Ora Williams, ed. Washington, DC: University Press of America, 1979.

The Dunbar Speaker and Entertainer: Containing the Best Prose and Poetic Selections by and about the Negro Race. Naperville, IL: J. L. Nichols & Co., 1920.

Give Us Each Day: The Diary of Alice Dunbar-Nelson. Gloria T. Hull, ed. New York: W. W. Norton, 1984.

The Goodness of St. Rocque and Other Stories. New York: Dodd, Mead, 1899; AMS Press, 1975.

Masterpieces of Negro Eloquence: The Best Speeches Delivered By the Negro from the Days of Slavery to the Present Time. Alice Moore Dunbar, ed. New York: The Bookery, 1914; The Basic Afro-American Reprint Library, 1970; Johnson Reprints, 1970.

[With W. S. Scarborough and Rev. C. Ransom.] *Paul Laurence Dunbar, Poet Laureate of the Negro Race*. Philadelphia: A.M.E. Church Review, [191?].

Scott's Official History of the American Negro in the World War. Emmett J. Scott. Chicago: Homewood Press, [c.1919]. Chapter 27.

Violets and Other Tales. Boston: Monthly Review, 1895.

The Works of Alice Dunbar-Nelson. Gloria T. Hull, ed. 3 vols. New York: Oxford University Press, 1988.

"April Is On the Way." *Ebony and Topaz* (1927): 52.

"As In a Looking Glass" [Newspaper Column]. *Washington Eagle* (1926–1930).

"At Bay St. Louis." Mossell, 88–89.

The Author's Evening at Home [Play]. *Smart Set* (Sept. 1900): 105–6.

"The Autobiography of an Ex-Colored Man" [Review]. *Opportunity* (Nov. 1927): 337.

"The Ball Dress." *Leslie's Weekly* (12 Dec. 1901).

"Cano—I Sing." *American Inter-Racial Peace Committee Bulletin* (Oct. 1929).

"Club Notes." *Woman's Era* (Oct.–Nov. 1896): 12..

"Communion." *Opportunity* (July 1925): 216.

"Convention Notes." *Woman's Era* (Aug. 1896): 10.

"Edward." *Southern Workman* (June 1900): 308.

"Esteve, the Soldier Boy." *Southern Workman* (Nov. 1900): 631.

"Forest Fire." *Harlem I* (Nov. 1928): 22.

"From A Woman's Point of View" [Newspaper Column]. *Pittsburgh Courier* (2 Jan. 1926–13 Feb. 1926).

"Harlem John Henry Views the Armada." *Crisis* 39 (1932): 458.

"Hope Deferred." *Crisis* 8 (1914): 238–42.

"Is It Time for the Negro Colleges of the South to Be Put into the Hands of Negro Teachers?" Culp, 139–41.

"Leslie, the Choir Boy." *Southern Workman* (Nov. 1901): 615.

"Little Excursions Week by Week." *The Light and "Heebie Jeebies"* (26 Nov. 1927).

"Little Excursions Week by Week." *Norfolk Journal and Guide* (7 Jan. 1928): 14.

"Little Roads." *Dunbar News* 11.23 (11 March 1931).

"The Locket." *Home Magazine* (n.d.).

"Louisiana." *Woman's Era* (Apr. 1895): 6; (June 1895): 5–6; (July 1895): 13–14; (May 1896): 12–13; (June 1896): 7–8.

Mine Eyes Have Seen [Play]. *Crisis* 15 (1918): 271–75.

"Music." *Opportunity* (July 1925): 216.

"Negro Literature for Negro Pupils." *Southern Workman* (Feb. 1922).

"Of Old St. Augustine." *Opportunity* (July 1925): 216.

"On the Bayou Bridge." *Champion Magazine* (Dec. 1916): 186–89.

"The Pearl in the Oyster." *Southern Workman* (Aug. 1902): 444.

"People of Color in Louisiana." *Journal of Negro History* pt. 1 (Oct. 1916): 361–76; pt. 2 (Jan. 1917): 51–78.

"The Poet and His Song." *A.M.E. Church Review* 13 (1914): 122–35.

"The Proletariat Speaks." *Crisis* 36 (1929): 378.

"Rainy Day." *New York Advertiser* (18 Sept. 1898).

"So It Seems to Alice Dunbar-Nelson" [Newspaper Column]. *Pittsburgh Courier* (Jan.–May 1930).

"A Song of Love." *Munsey's Magazine* (July 1902): 603.

"Sonnet." *Crisis* 18 (1919): 193.

"Summit and Vale." *Lippincott's Magazine* (Dec. 1902): 715.

"To Madame Curie." *Philadelphia Public Ledger* (21 Aug. 1921).

"Tom—An Incident." *Woman's Era* (Jan. 1897): 11–13.

"Violets." *Crisis* (Aug. 1917): 198.

"Women's Clubs at Tuskegee." *Woman's Journal* (5 June 1897).

"Une Femme Dit" [Newspaper Column]. *Pittsburgh Courier* (20 Feb. 1926–18 Sept. 1926).

Anthologies

Ammons, Elizabeth, comp. *Short Fiction by Black Women, 1900–1920*. New York: Oxford University Press, 1991.

Chametzky, Jules, and Sidney Kaplan, eds. *Black and White in American Culture: An Anthology from the Massachusetts Review*. Amherst: University of Massachusetts Press, 1969. 362.

Cromwell, Otelia, Lorenzo D. Turner, and Eva B. Dykes, eds. *Readings form Negro Authors*. New York: Harcourt, Brace, 1931. 32.

Cullen, Countee, ed. *Caroling Dusk: An Anthology of Verse by Negro Poets*. New York: Harper & Brothers, 1927.

Eleazer, Robert B., comp. *Singers in the Dawn*. 7th Edition. Atlanta: Commission on Interracial Cooperation, 1942, 1943, 10.

Gilbert, Sandra M., and Susan Gubar, eds. *The Norton Anthology of Literature by Women: The Tradition in English*. New York: W. W. Norton, 1985. 1336.

Johnson, James Weldon, ed. *The Book of American Negro Poetry*. New York: Harcourt, Brace, 1922.

Kerlin, Robert, ed. *Negro Poets and Their Poems*. Washington, DC: Associated Publishers, 1923.

Masterpieces of Negro Eloquence. New York: The Bookery, 1914, 425–44; The Basic Afro-American Reprint Library, 1970; Johnson Reprints, 1970.

Shockley, 267–72.

Stetson, Erlene, ed. *Black Sister: Poetry by Black American Women, 1746–1980*. Bloomington: Indiana University Press, 1981. 65–67.

Writings about

"Alice Dunbar-Nelson" [Editorial]. *Negro History Bulletin* (Apr. 1968): 5–6.

Bardolph, Richard. *The Negro Vanguard*. New York: Random House, 1961. 202.

"Biography of Alice Dunbar-Nelson." *Negro History Bulletin* (Apr. 1968): 5.

Blair, Emily N. *The Woman's Committee, U.S. Council of National Defense*. Washington, DC: Government Printing Office, 1920. 106.

Brawley, *NBH*, 237.

Brawley, *NG*, 154, 193, 216–19.

Brawley, Benjamin. *Paul Laurence Dunbar, Poet of His People*. Chapel Hill: University of North Carolina Press, 1936.

Breen, William J. "Black Women and the Great War: Mobilization and Reform in the South." *Journal of Southern History* 44.3 (1978): 421–40.

Brown, Sterling. *Negro Poetry and Drama and the Negro in American Fiction*. New York: Arno Press, 1969. Republication of *Negro Poetry and Drama*. Washington, DC: The Associates in Negro Folk Education, 1937; and *The Negro in American Fiction*. Washington, DC: The Associates in Negro Folk Education, 1937.

Bullock, 90, 98, 137, 192.

Culp, 130.

Cunningham, Virginia. *Paul Laurence Dunbar and His Song*. New York: Dodd, Mead, 1947.

Dannett, 1: 299.

Du Bois, W.E.B. *The Gift of Black Folk. The Negroes in the Making of America*. Boston: Stratford, 1924. 68–69, 83, 87, 97, 100, 145, 155, 267, 268–89.

"The Dunbar Speaker and Entertainer" [Review]. *Crisis* 22 (1921): 218.

Dwight, Margaret L. *"Give Us Each Day: The Diary of Alice Dunbar-Nelson"* [Review]. *Journal of Southern History* (Feb. 1986): 128–30.

Gayle, Addison. *Black Expression*. New York: Weybright and Talley, 1969. 233.

Gloster, Hugh. *Negro Voices in American Fiction*. Chapel Hill: University of North Carolina Press, 1948.

"The Goodness of St. Rocque and Other Stories" [Review]. *Critic* (Feb. 1900): 183.

"The Goodness of St. Rocque and Other Stories" [Review]. *Nation* (Aug. 1900): 157.

"The Goodness of St. Rocque" [Review]. *Southern Workman* (March 1900): 187.

Huggins, Nathan Irvin. *Harlem Renaissance*. New York: Oxford University Press, 1971. 196, 261, 276.

Hull, Gloria T. "Alice Dunbar-Nelson: Delaware Writer and Woman of Affairs." *Delaware History* 17 (Fall–Winter 1976): 87–103.

————. "Black Women Poets from Wheatley to Walker." *Negro American Literature Forum* 9 (1975): 91–96.

————. *Color, Sex, and Poetry: Three Women Writers of the Harlem Renaissance*. Bloomington: Indiana University Press, 1987.

Jackson, Blyden. *The Waiting Years: Essays in American Negro Literature*. Baton Rouge: Louisiana State University Press, 1976.

Loggins, 317–18, 453.

"Masterpieces" [Review]. *Crisis* (March 1914): 254.

"Masterpieces of Negro Eloquence" [Review]. *Southern Workman* (Nov. 1914): 636.

McNeil, Barbara, and Miranda C. Herbert, eds. *Historical*

Biographical Dictionary Master Index. Detroit: Gale Research Co., 1980.

Mossell, 16, 93.

"Mrs. Paul Laurence Dunbar, Wife of the Colored Poet and Novelist." *Recorder* [Chicago] (4 Aug. 1902).

NAW, 2: 614–15.

"Personal: The Passing of Distinguished Persons, Alice Dunbar Nelson." *Journal of Negro History* (January 1936): 95–96.

Redding, J. Saunders. *They Came in Chains: Americans from Africa*. Philadelphia: J. B. Lippincott, 1950. 207–49.

[Review.] *Christian Advocate* [Pittsburgh] (21 Dec. 1899).

Richings, B. F. *Evidences of Progress among Colored People*. 3rd Edition. Philadelphia: George S. Ferguson Co., 1897. 419.

Robinson, William H., Jr., ed. *Early Black American Prose*. Dubuque, IA: William C. Brown Company Publishers, 1971. xv.

Rush, 253–54.

Shockley, 262–67.

Wagner, Jean. *Black Poets of the United States: From Paul Laurence Dunbar to Langston Hughes*. Kenneth Douglas, trans. Urbana: University of Illinois Press, 1973.

Wesley, 111.

Whiteman, Maxwell. *A Century of Fiction by American Negroes, 1853–1952*. Philadelphia: Jacobs, 1955.

Williams, Ora. "Works by and About Alice Ruth (Moore) Dunbar-Nelson: A Bibliography." *CLA Journal* (March 1976): 322–26.

Yenser, Thomas, ed. *Who's Who in Colored America: Dictionary of Notable Living Persons of African Descent in America, 1930–1932*. 3rd Edition. Brooklyn, NY: Thomas Yenser, 1933. 316–17.

Young, James. *Black Writers of the Thirties*. Baton Rouge: Louisiana State University Press, 1973. 135.

Young, Pauline A. "Paul Laurence Dunbar: An Intimate Glimpse." *Freedomways* (Fourth Quarter 1972): 319–29.

Papers in Collections

Metcalf, Eugene W., Jr. "The Letters of Paul and Alice Dunbar: A Private History." Diss., University of California, Irvine, 1973.

Williams, Ruby Ora. "An In-Depth Portrait of Alice Dunbar-Nelson." Diss., University of California, Irvine, 1974.

Sarah Jane Woodson Early (1814–1907)

Writings by

Life and Labors of Rev. Jordan W. Early, One of the Pioneers of African Methodism in the West and South. Nashville: Publishing House of the A.M.E. Sunday-school Union, 1894; Freeport, NY: Books for Libraries, 1971.

"The Great Part Taken by the Women of the West in the Development of the A.M.E. Church." Scruggs, 148–53.

Writings about

Lawson, Ellen N. "Sarah Woodson Early: 19th Century Black Nationalist 'Sister.' " *Umoja* 5.2 (1981): 15–26.

"*Life and Labors of Rev. Jordan W. Early*" [Review]. *Christian Recorder* (10 Jan. 1895): 2.

Majors, 101–2.

Mossell, 12.

Scruggs, 71–74.

Zilpha Elaw

Writings by

Memoirs of the Life, Religious Experience, Ministerial Travels and Labours, of Mrs. Zilpha Elaw, an American Female of Colour; Together with Some Account of the Great Religious Revivals in America. London: the Author, 1846.

Letters

Letter to John Tradgold. 9 Aug. 1840. MSS British Empire, Rhodes House, Oxford, England. *(BAP)*.

Anthologies

Andrews, William L., ed. *Sisters of the Spirit: Three Black Women's Autobiographies of the Nineteenth Century*. Bloomington: Indiana University Press, 1986. 49–160.

Shockley, 36.

Writings about

"A Colored Teacher." *National Anti-Slavery Standard* (7 Apr. 1842): 174.

Shockley, 33–35.

Louisa May Fields

Papers in Collections

Fields, Louisa May. *Twelve Years a Slave* [Play]. Indianapolis: n.p., 1897. Manuscript Play Collection, Library of Congress.

Gertrude Arguere Fisher

Writings by

Original Poems. Parsons, KS: Foley Railway Printing Co., [c.1910].

Julia Ann J. Foote (1823–?)

Writings by

A Brand Plucked from the Fire. An Autobiographical Sketch.
Cleveland: W. F. Schneider, 1879; New York: G. Hughes
& Co., 1879; Cleveland: Lauer & Yost, 1886.

Anthologies

Andrews, William L., ed. *Sisters of the Spirit: Three Black
Women's Autobiographies of the Nineteenth Century.* Bloom-
ington: Indiana University Press, 1986. 161–234.
A Brand Plucked from the Fire. An Autobiographical Sketch. In
Spiritual Narratives. Introduction by Sue E. Houchins.
New York: Oxford University Press, 1988.

Mary Weston Fordham (1862?–?)

Writings by

Magnolia Leaves; Poems. Charleston, SC: Walker, Evans &
Cogswell, 1897.

Anthologies

Magnolia Leaves; Poems. In *Collected Black Women's Poetry.*
Joan R. Sherman, ed. Vol. 2. New York: Oxford University Press, 1988.

Writings about

Braithwaite, W. S. "Book Reviews." *Colored American Mag-
azine* (Nov. 1901): 73–74.
Loggins, 335.
Sherman, 240–41.

Charlotte L. Forten [Mrs. Francis J. Grimké; Charlotte Forten Grimké] (1837–1914)

Writings by

A Free Negro in the Slave Era, The Journal of Charlotte L. Forten. Ray Allen Billington, ed. New York: Dryden Press, 1953; Collier Books, 1961.

The Journals of Charlotte Forten Grimké. Brenda Stevenson, ed. New York: Oxford University Press, 1988.

Erckmann, Emile, and Alexandre Chatrian. *Madame Thèrése; or, the Volunteers of '92*. Trans. from the 13th Edition by Charlotte Forten Grimké. New York: Scribner's, 1869.

"The Angels Visit." In *The Black Man, His Antecedents, His Genius, and His Achievements*. William Wells Brown. New York: Thomas Hamilton; Boston: R. F. Wallcut, 1863; New York: Johnson Reprints, 1968. 196–99.

"At the Home of Frederick Douglass." In *The Life and Writings of the Grimké Family*. Anna Julia Haywood Cooper, ed. N.p.: the Author, 1951. 2: 56–61.

"At Newport." *A.M.E. Church Review* 4 (1888): 258.

"The Centennial Exposition: Philadelphia, 1876." In *The Life and Writings of the Grimké Family*. Anna Julia Haywood Cooper, ed. N.p.: the Author, 1951. 2: 62–77.

"Charles Sumner. On Seeing Some Pictures of the Interior of His House." In *The Life and Writings of the Grimké Family*. Anna Julia Haywood Cooper, ed. N.p.: the Author, 1951. 2: 24. Mossell, 77–78.

"Charles Sumner. Written on Seeing Some Pictures of the Interior of His House" [Handwriten poem]. N.d. Grimké Papers, Moorland-Spingarn Research Center, Howard University. *(BAP)*.

"Charlotte Corday: Suggested by Two Pictures in the Corcoran Art Gallery." In *The Life and Writings of the Grimké*

Family. Anna Julia Haywood Cooper, ed. N.p.: the Author, 1951. 2: 22–23.

"In the Country." *National Anti-Slavery Standard* (1 Sept. 1860).

"Glimpses of New England." *National Anti-Slavery Standard* (19 June 1858).

"The Grand Army of the Republic" [Also titled "The Gathering of the Grand Army"]. In *The Life and Writings of the Grimké Family*. Anna Julia Haywood Cooper, ed. N.p.: the Author, 1951. 2: 25–26.

"In Florida." In *The Life and Writings of the Grimké Family*. Anna Julia Haywood Cooper, ed. N.p.: the Author, 1951. 2: 21–22.

"Life on the Sea Islands." *Atlantic Monthly* (May and June 1864): 587–96, 666–76. *(BAP)*.

"A Parting Hymn." In *The Black Man, His Antecedents, His Genius, and His Achievements*. William Wells Brown. New York: Thomas Hamilton; Boston: R. F. Wallcut, 1863; New York: Johnson Reprints, 1968. 191.

"Personal Recollections of Whittier." *New England Magazine* (June 1893). 468–76.

"Poem." *Liberator* (24 Aug. 1856).

"The Slave Girl's Prayer." *Liberator* (3 Feb. 1860).

"To W[illiam] L[loyd] G[arrison] on Reading His 'Chosen Queen.' " *Liberator* (16 March 1855).

"The Two Voices." *National Anti-Slavery Standard* (15 Jan. 1859).

"The Wind Among the Poplars." *Liberator* (27 May 1859).

"Wordsworth." In *The Life and Writings of the Grimké Family*. Anna Julia Haywood Cooper, ed. N.p.: the Author, 1951. 2: 23.

Letters

"Interesting Letter from Miss Charlotte L. Forten." *Liberator* (19 Dec. 1862). *(BAP)*.

Letter. 7 Oct. 1862. Grimké Papers, Moorland-Spingarn Research Center, Howard University. *(BAP)*.

Letter. *Woman's Era* (May 1896): 7.

Letter to Frederick Douglass. 21 June [?]. Frederick Douglass Papers, Library of Congress. *(BAP)*.

"Letters from St. Helena's Island." *Liberator* (12, 19 Dec. 1862): 119, 203.

Anthologies

Calverton, Victor Francis, ed. *An Anthology of American Negro Literature*. New York: Modern Library, 1929.

Davis, Arthur P., and J. Saunders Redding, eds. *Cavalcade: Negro American Writing from 1760 to the Present*. Boston: Houghton Mifflin, 1971.

Dunbar-Nelson, Alice, ed. *The Dunbar Speaker and Entertainer*. Naperville, IL: J. L. Nichols, 1920.

Kerlin, Robert, ed. *Negro Poets and Their Poems*. Washington, DC: Associated Publishers, 1923. 338.

Loewenberg, Bert J., and Ruth Bogin, eds. *Black Women in Nineteenth-Century American Life: Their Words, Their Thoughts, Their Feelings*. University Park: Pennsylvania State University Press, 1976. 283–95.

Meltzer, Milton, ed. *In Their Own Words; A History of the American Negro, 1619–1865*. New York: Thomas Y. Crowell, [c.1964].

"New Year's Day on the Islands of South Carolina." In *The Freedmen's Book*. Lydia Maria Child, ed. Boston: Ticknor and Fields, 1865. 251–56.

Shockley, 75–81.

Sterling, Dorothy, ed. *Speak Out in Thunder Tones: Letters and Other Writings by Black Northerners, 1787–1865.* Garden City, NY: Doubleday, 1973. 251, 311–13, 375–76.

Stetson, Erlene, ed. *Black Sister: Poetry by Black American Women, 1746–1980.* Bloomington: Indiana University Press, 1981. 22–24.

Trachtenberg, Alan, ed. *Democratic Vistas.* New York: Braziller, [c.1970]. 112–24.

Wish, Harvey, ed. *Slavery in the South: First-hand Accounts of the Antebellum American Southland from Northern and Southern White, Negroes and Foreign Observers.* New York: Farrar, Straus, [c. 1964]. 87–108.

Writings about

Billington, Ray Allen. "A Social Experiment: The Port Royal Journal of Charlotte L. Forten, 1862–1863." *Journal of Negro History* (July 1950): 233–64.

Brown, William Wells. *The Black Man, His Antecedents, His Genius, and His Achievements.* New York: Thomas Hamilton; Boston: R. F. Wallcut, 1863; New York: Johnson Reprints, 1968.

Butterfield, Stephen. *Black Autobiography in America.* Amherst: University of Massachusetts Press, 1975.

Cooper, Anna Julia Haywood, ed. *The Life and Writings of the Grimké Family.* 2 vols. N.p.: the Author, 1951.

DANB, 233–34.

Dannett, 1: 81, 86–93, 111.

Douty, Esther M. *Charlotte Forten: Free Black Teacher.* Champaign, IL: Garrard Publishing Co., 1971.

Fishel, Leslie H., and Benjamin Quarles. *The Black American: A Documentary History.* 3rd Edition. Glenview, IL: Scott, Foresman, [c.1976]. 199, 219.

"The Forten Family." *Negro History Bulletin* (Jan. 1947): 75–79, 95.

Frazier, Susan Elizabeth. "Some Afro-American Women of Mark." *A.M.E. Church Review* (Apr. 1892): 381–83.

Grimké, Angelina W. "To the Dunbar High School." *Crisis* 13 (1917): 222.

———. "To Keep the Memory of Charlotte Forten Grimké." *Crisis* 9 (1915): 134; 38 (1931): 380.

———. "To Keep the Memory of Charlotte Forten Grimké— A Poem." *Negro History Bulletin* (Jan. 1947): 79, 95.

Loggins, 334, 428, 455.

Longsworth, Polly. *I, Charlotte Forten, Black and Free.* New York: Thomas Y. Crowell, 1970.

Majors, 213–15.

Majors, Gerri, and Doris E. Saunders. *Black Society.* Chicago: Johnson Publishing Co., 1976.

McNeil, Barbara, and Miranda C. Herbert, eds. *Historical Biographical Dictionary Master Index.* Detroit: Gale Research Co., 1980.

Mossell, 77–78.

NAW, 2: 95–97.

Negro History Bulletin 4 (1941): 64–65; (Jan. 1947): 47.

New National Era (23 July 1873).

Oden, Gloria C. "The Journal of Charlotte L. Forten: The Salem–Philadelphia Years (1854–1862) Re-examined." *Essex Institute Historical Collections* 119.2 (1983): 119–36.

"Our Literary Women." *Lancet* (10 Oct. 1885): 1.

Quarles, Benjamin. *Black Abolitionists.* New York: Oxford University Press, 1969. 179, 180, 197, 208, 233.

Robinson, 86.

Rose, Willie Lee. *Rehearsal for Reconstruction: The Port Royal*

    Experiment. Indianapolis: Bobbs-Merrill; New York: Vintage Books, 1964.

Rush, 304–5.

Scruggs, 193–96.

Sherman, 88–96.

Shockley, 71–75.

Vaught, Bonny. "Trying to Make Things Real." In *Between Women: Biographers, Novelists, Critics, Teachers and Artists Write about Their Work on Women*. Carol Ascher, Louise DeSalvo, and Sara Ruddick, eds. Boston: Beacon Press, 1984.

Wesley, 5, 58, 79, 177.

Wilson, Edmund. "Charlotte Forten and Colonel Higginson." *New Yorker* (10 Apr. 1954): 132–47.

———. *Patriotic Gore: Studies in the Literature of the American Civil War*. New York: Oxford University Press, 1962. 239–57.

Letters

Dutch, J. C. Letter with Enclosure. 24 Apr. 1863. Penn School Papers, University of North Carolina. *(BAP)*.

Pickard John B., ed. *The Letters of John Greenleaf Whittier, 1861–1892*. Vol. 3. Cambridge, MA: Harvard University Press, The Belknap Press, 1975.

Papers in Collections

Cooper, Anna Julia. "Reminiscences." Francis J. Grimké Papers, Moorland-Spingarn Research Center, Howard University.

Garrison, Ellen Wright. Letter to Martha Coffin Wright. 13 Dec. 1858. Sophia Smith Collection, Smith College.

Grimké, Charlotte L. Forten. Letter to Ednah Dow Cheney. 1871. Sophia Smith Collection, Smith College.

Francis J. Grimké Papers, Manuscript Collection, Moorland-Spingarn Research Center, Howard University.

Angelina Weld Grimké (1880–1958)

Writings by

Rachel: A Play in Three Acts. Boston: Cornhill Company, 1920; College Park, MD: McGrath, 1969.

Selected Works of Angelina Weld Grimké. Carolivia Herron, ed. New York: Oxford University Press, 1991.

"Beware Lest He Awakes." *Pilot* (10 May 1902).

"A Biographical Sketch of Archibald H. Grimké." *Opportunity* (Feb. 1925): 44.

"The Black Finger." *Opportunity* (Nov. 1923): 343; (Apr. 1927): 110.

"Black Is As Black Does (A Dream)." *Colored American Magazine* (Aug. 1900): 160.

"The Closing Door." *Birth Control Review* (Sept. 1919): 10; (Oct. 1919).

"Death." *Opportunity* (March 1925): 68.

"Dusk." *Opportunity* (Apr. 1924): 99.

"El Beso." *Boston Transcript* (27 Oct. 1909).

"For the Candle-Light." *Opportunity* (Sept. 1925): 263.

"*Gertrude of Denmark* by Lillie Buffum Chace Wyman" [Review]. *Opportunity* (Dec. 1924): 378.

"Goldie." *Birth Control Review* (Nov.–Dec. 1920).

"The Grave in the Corner." *Norfolk County Gazette* (27 May 1893).

"I Weep." *Opportunity* (July 1924): 196.

"Little Grey Dreams." *Opportunity* (Jan. 1924).

"Longing." *Boston Transcript* (16 Apr. 1901).

"May." *Boston Transcript* (7 May 1901).

" 'Rachel': The Play of the Month: The Reason and Synopsis by the Author." *Competitor* (Jan. 1920): 51.

"Street Echoes." *Boston Sunday Globe* (22 July 1894).

"To the Dunbar High School." *Crisis* 13 (1917): 222.

"To Joseph Lee." *Boston Evening Transcript* (11 Nov. 1908).

"To Keep the Memory of Charlotte Forten Grimké." *Crisis* 9 (1915): 134; 38 (1931): 380. *Opportunity* (March 1925).

"To Keep the Memory of Charlotte Forten Grimké—A Poem." *Negro History Bulletin* (Jan. 1947): 79, 95.

"To Theodore D. Weld—On His 90th Birthday." *Norfolk County Gazette* (25 Nov. 1893).

"Where Phillis Sleeps." *Boston Transcript* (31 July 1901).

Anthologies

Adoff, Arnold, ed. *The Poetry of Black America: Anthology of the 20th Century*. New York: Harper & Row, 1973.

Ammons, Elizabeth, comp. *Short Fiction by Black Women, 1900–1920*. New York: Oxford University Press, 1991.

Barksdale, Richard, and Keneth Kinnamon. *Black Writers of America: A Comprehensive Anthology*. New York: Macmillan, 1972. 626–27.

Bernikow, Louise, ed. *The World Split Open: Four Centuries of Women Poets in England and America, 1552–1950*. New York: Vintage Books, 1974.

Brown, Sterling A., Arthur P. Davis, and Ulysses Lee, eds. *The Negro Caravan: Writings by American Negroes*. New York: Dryden Press, 1941; Arno Press, 1970; 341–43.

Byars, J. C., comp. *Black and White*. Washington, DC: Crane Press, 1927. 14–20.

Cullen, Countee, ed. *Caroling Dusk: An Anthology of Verse by Negro Poets*. New York: Harper & Brothers, 1927.

Hatch, James V. *Black Theater, U.S.A.: Forty-five Plays by*

Black Americans, 1847–1974. New York: Free Press, 1974.

Hughes, Langston, and Arna Bontemps, eds. *The Poetry of the Negro, 1747–1970*. Revised Edition. Garden City, NY: Doubleday, 1970.

Kerlin, Robert T., ed. *Negro Poets and Their Poems*. Washington, DC: Associated Publishers, 1923.

Shockley, 377–79.

Stetson, Erlene, ed. *Black Sister: Poetry by Black American Women, 1746–1980*. Bloomington: Indiana University Press, 1981. 60–63.

Writings about

Abramson, Doris E. "Angelina Weld Grimké, Mary T. Burrill, Georgia Douglas Johnson, and Marita O. Bonner: An Analysis of Their Plays." *Sage* 2.1 (1985): 9–13.

Ammons, Elizabeth. "Stowe's Dream of the Mother-Savior: *Uncle Tom's Cabin* and American Women Writers before 1920." In *New Essays on Uncle Tom's Cabin*. Eric J. Sundquist, ed. Cambridge: Cambridge University Press, 1986. 155–95.

Brawley, *NG*, 229.

Fauset, Jessie. *"Rachel: A Play in Three Acts"* [Review]. *Crisis* 21 (1920): 64.

Hull, Gloria T. *Color, Sex and Poetry: Three Women Writers of the Harlem Renaissance*. Bloomington: Indiana University Press, 1987.

———. " 'Under the Days': The Buried Life and Poetry of Angelina Weld Grimké." In *Home Girls: A Black Feminist Anthology*. Barbara Smith, ed. New York: Kitchen Table: Women of Color Press, 1983.

Locke, Alain LeRoy, ed. *The New Negro: An Interpretation*. New York: Albert and Charles Boni, 1925.

Locke, Alain LeRoy, and Montgomery Gregory, eds. *Plays of Negro Life: A Sourcebook of Native American Drama*. New York and London: Harper & Row, 1927.

Miller, Jeanne-Marie A. "Angelina Weld Grimké: Playwright and Poet." *CLA Journal* 21 (1978): 513–24.

Rush, 345.

Segrest, M. "Lines I Dare to Write: Lesbian Writing in the South." *Southern Exposure* 9.2 (1981): 53–55, 57–62.

Shockley, 373–77.

Stubbs, Carolyn Amonitti. "Angelina Weld Grimké: Washington Poet and Playwright." Diss., George Washington University. *Dissertation Abstracts International* 39 (1979): 4941A–42A.

Young, Patricia Alzatia. "Female Pioneers in Afro-American Drama: Angelina Weld Grimké, Georgia Douglas Johnson, Alice Dunbar-Nelson, and Mary Powell Burrill." *Dissertation Abstracts International* 47 (1978): 3043A.

Papers in Collections

Ellington, Mary Davis. "Plays by Negro Authors with Special Emphasis upon the Period from 1916 to 1934." Master's thesis, Fisk University, 1934.

Papers in Negro Collection, Fisk University Library.

Papers, 1887–1958. Manuscript Collection, Moorland-Spingarn Research Center, Howard University.

Frances Ellen Watkins Harper [Frances Ellen Watkins; pseud. Effie Afton] (1825–1911)

Writings by

[Afton, Effie.] *Eventide. A Series of Tales and Poems*. Boston: Ferridge & Co., 1854.

Atlanta Offering: Poems. Philadelphia: George S. Ferguson, 1895.

Atlanta Offering: Poems. Philadelphia: 1006 Bainbridge Street, 1895; Miami: Mnemosyne Publications, Inc., 1969.

Complete Poems of Frances E. W. Harper. Maryemma Graham, ed. New York: Oxford University Press, 1988.

Forest Leaves. Baltimore: the Author, 1855.

Enlightened Motherhood. An Address before the Brooklyn Literary Society, November 15, 1892. N.p., n.d.

Idylls of the Bible. Philadelphia: 1006 Bainbridge Street, 1901; New York: AMS Press, 1975.

Iola Leroy; or, Shadows Uplifted. Philadelphia: Garrigues Brothers, 1892, 1893; College Park, MD: McGrath, 1969; New York: AMS Press, 1971.

Iola Leroy; or, Shadows Uplifted. Boston: James H. Earle, 1892, 1895.

Iola Leroy; or, Shadows Uplifted. New York: Panther House, 1968.

Iola Leroy, or Shadows Uplifted. Hazel V. Carby, ed. Boston: Beacon Press, 1987.

Iola Leroy, or Shadows Uplifted. Introduction by Frances Smith Foster. New York: Oxford University Press, 1988.

Light Beyond the Darkness. Chicago: Donohue and Henneberry, n.d.

The Martyr of Alabama and Other Poems. N.p.: n.p., n.d. [1894?].

Moses: A Story of the Nile. 2nd Edition [No 1st Edition Known]. Philadelphia: Merrihew & Son, 1869. 3rd Edition, 1870.

Moses: A Story of the Nile. 2nd Edition. Philadelphia: 1006 Bainbridge Street, 1889.

Poems. Philadelphia: Merrihew & Son, 1871.

Poems. Providence RI: A. Crawford Greene & Sons, 1880.

Poems. Philadelphia: G. S. Ferguson, 1895, 1896, 1898, 1900; Freeport, NY: Books for Libraries, 1970.

Poems on Miscellaneous Subjects. Boston: J. B. Yerrinton & Son, 1854, 1855.

Poems on Miscellaneous Subjects. 2nd Series. Philadelphia, 1855.

Poems on Miscellaneous Subjects. Philadelphia: Merrihew & Thompson, 1857; Rhistoric Publications, 1969.

Poems on Miscellaneous Subjects. 20th Edition. Philadelphia: Merrihew & Son, 1871, 1874.

Poems on Miscellaneous Subjects. Switzerland: Kraus-Thompson, 1971.

Sketches of Southern Life. Philadelphia: Merrihew & Son, 1872, 1873, 1887, 1888.

Sketches of Southern Life. Philadelphia: Ferguson Bros:, 1888, 1891, 1893, 1896.

The Sparrow's Fall and Other Poems. N.p.: n.p., n.d.

"An Appeal to the American People." *Christian Recorder* (21 July 1866): 113.

"Be Active." *Frederick Douglass' Paper* (11 Jan. 1856).

"Be Active." *Weekly Anglo-African* (30 July 1859). *(BAP).*

"Behold the Lilies!" *A.M.E. Church Review* (Apr. 1900): 468.

"The Black Hero." *A.M.E. Church Review* 9 (1892–1893): 178–79.

"The Building." *Christian Recorder* (1 Aug. 1895): 1.

"The Burdens of All." *Colored American* (4 May 1901): 5.

"Burial of Sarah." *Christian Recorder* (15 March 1883): 1.

"Bury Me in a Free Land." *Anti-Slavery Bugle* (20 Nov. 1858). *(BAP).*

"Bury Me in a Free Land." *Weekly Anglo-African* (2 June 1860). *(BAP).*

"The Careless Word." *National Anti-Slavery Standard* (3 July 1858). *(BAP).*

"Centennial of the A.M.E. Church." *Christian Recorder* (10 Nov. 1887): 5.

"A Christmas Carol." *Christian Recorder* (28 Dec. 1872): 4.

"Christmas Carol." *Christian Recorder* (3 Jan. 1889): 1.

"Coloured Women of America." *Englishwoman's Review* (15 Jan. 1878): 10–15.

"The Death of Moses" [Excerpt from *Moses: A Story of the Nile*]. Mossell, 76–77.

"The Democratic Return to Power." *A.M.E. Church Review* 1 (1884): 222–25.

"A Dialogue." *Christian Recorder* (31 July 1873): 1.

"The Dismissal of Tyng." *National Anti-Slavery Standard* (29 Nov. 1856). *(BAP)*.

"Duty to Dependent Races." In National Council of Women of the United States. *Transactions of the National Council of Women of the United States, Assembled in Washington, D.C., February 22 to 25, 1891*. Rachel Foster, ed. Philadelphia: J. B. Lippincott, 1891.

"The Dying Bondman." *A.M.E. Church Review* (July 1884): 45.

"The Dying Child to its Blind Father." *Weekly Anglo-African* (24 March 1860): 1.

"The Dying Fugitive." *Anglo-African Magazine* (Aug. 1859). *(BAP)*.

"The Dying Fugitive." *Weekly Anglo-African* (20 Aug. 1859). *(BAP)*.

"The Dying Queen." *Christian Recorder* (10 Feb. 1872): 1.

"The Dying Wife." *Christian Recorder* (3 Dec. 1870): 1.

"Easter." *Christian Recorder* (30 March 1899): 1.

"Eliza Harris." *Frederick Douglass' Paper* (23 Dec. 1853): 4. *(BAP)*.

"Eva's Farewell." *Frederick Douglass' Paper* (31 March 1854). *(BAP)*.

"A Fairer Hope, A Brighter Morn." Majors, 361–63.

"Fancy Etchings" [Serial]. *Christian Recorder* (24 Apr. 1873): 1; (1 May 1873): 1; (22 May 1873): 1; (3 July 1873): 1; (15 Jan. 1874): 1.

"The Fatal Pledge." *Christian Recorder* (6 Sept. 1883): 1.

"Fifteenth Amendment." *New National Era* (12 May 1870): 2.

["Finished Now the Weary Throbbing."] *Anglo-African Magazine* (Apr. 1859). *(BAP)*.

"For the Twenty-Fifth Anniversary of the Home for Aged and Infirm Colored Persons." *Annual Report of the Home for the Aged and Infirm Colored People*. Philadelphia, 1889.

"The Free Labor Movement." *Frederick Douglass' Paper* (29 June 1855). *(BAP)*.

"Give My Love to the World." *Christian Recorder* (13 Jan. 1898).

"Go, Work." *Christian Recorder* (17 July 1873): 1.

"God's Judgment." *Weekly Anglo-African* (8 Feb. 1862): 4.

"Gone to God." *Anglo-African Magazine* 1 (1859): 123.

"Gone to God." Mossell, 94–96.

"He Stood Before His Finished World." *Christian Recorder* (9 March 1861): 33.

"His Name." *Christian Recorder* (31 March 1887): 1.

"How Are the Mighty Fallen?" *Christian Recorder* (21 Sept. 1899): 1.

"An Ideal Thanksgiving" [Incomplete Serial]. *Howard's American Magazine* (Nov. 1899): 47–51.

"I Thirst." *Christian Recorder* (16 March 1872): 1.

"In Commemoration of the Centennial of the A.M.E. Church." *A.M.E. Church Review* 7 (1891): 292. Reprinted in *The Centennial Budget, Containing an Account of the Celebration, November 1887*. . . . Benjamin W. Arnett, ed. Philadelphia: A.M.E. Book Concern, 1888. 549–50.

"Is Money the Answer?" *Anglo-African* (May 1859). Reprinted in *In Their Own Words; A History of the American Negro, 1619–1865.* Milton Meltzer, ed. New York: Thomas Y. Crowell, [c.1964]. 133–34.

"It Shall Not Come Nigh Thee." *Christian Recorder* (14 Nov. 1878): 1.

"The Lady's Dream." *McGirt's Magazine* (June 1904): 16–17.

"Lessons of the Street." *Liberator* (14 May 1858).

"Let the Light Enter." *Weekly Anglo-African* (14 July 1860): 1.

"Let the Light Enter Goethe." *Christian Recorder* (17 June 1875): 1.

"Let There Be Light." *Christian Recorder* (7 Oct. 1897): 1.

"Lines." *National Anti-Slavery Standard* (29 Nov. 1856). *(BAP).*

"Lines to M.A.H." *Christian Recorder* (13 Apr. 1872): 1.

"Lines to Hon. Thaddeus Stevens." *Christian Recorder* (14 July 1866): 109.

"The Lord is Risen." *Christian Recorder* (22 March 1883): 3.

"Mary at Christ's Feet." *Christian Recorder* (28 Jan. 1871): 1.

"Minnie's Sacrifice" [Serial]. *Christian Recorder* (20 March 1869): 37; (27 March 1869): 41; (17 Apr. 1869): 48; (24 Apr. 1869): 49; (1 May 1869): 53; (22 May 1869): 61; (12 June 1869): 1; (26 June 1869): 1; (3 July 1869): 1; (10 July 1869): 1; (17 July 1869): 1; (31 July 1869): 1; (14 Aug. 1869): 1; (28 Aug. 1869): 1; (4 Sept. 1869): 1; (11 Sept. 1869): 1; (25 Sept. 1869): 1.

"Miss Watkins and the Constitution." *National Anti-Slavery Standard* (9 Apr. 1859): 3. *(BAP).*

"Mrs. Frances E. Watkins Harper on the War and the

President's Colonization Scheme." *Christian Recorder* (27 Sept. 1862). *(BAP)*.

"The National Women's Christian Temperance Union." *A.M.E. Church Review* 5 (1889): 242–45.

"The Neglected Rich." International Council of Women. *Report*. Washington, DC: R. H. Darby, printer, 1888.

"New York Anti-Slavery Society Fourth Anniversary." *National Anti-Slavery Standard* (23 May 1857). *(BAP)*.

"The Night of Death." *Christian Recorder* (29 Nov. 1894): 1.

"Nothing and Something." *Christian Recorder* (15 March 1883): 3.

"Opening the Gates." *Christian Recorder* (28 Oct. 1871): 1.

"Others Shall Sing the Song." *Christian Recorder* (18 Sept. 1902): 1.

"Our Greatest Want." *Anglo-African Magazine* (May 1859): 160. *(BAP)*.

"Peace." *Christian Recorder* (26 June 1873): 1.

"The Present Age." *A.M.E. Church Review* 11 (1894–1895): 470–71.

"The Ragged Stocking." *Christian Recorder* (13 Aug. 1885): 1.

"A Rallying Cry." *Southland* (Apr. 1891): 160–61.

"The Rallying Cry." *Christian Recorder* (15 Jan. 1891): 1.

"Saved at Last." *Christian Recorder* (7 Aug. 1873): 1.

"School-Girl Notions." Shockley, 193.

"Signing the Pledge." *Christian Recorder* (7 June 1883): 1.

"Sketches." In *Men of Maryland*. George F. Bragg. Baltimore: Church Advocate Press, 1914.

"The Slave Auction." *Frederick Douglass' Paper* (22 Sept. 1854): 4. *(BAP)*.

"Something to Do." *Christian Recorder* (6 Apr. 1872): 1.

"The Soul." In *History of the A.M.E. Church*. Daniel A. Payne. Nashville: Publishing House of the A.M.E. Sunday-school Union, 1891. 302.

"Sowing and Reaping: A Temperance Story" [Serial]. *Christian Recorder* (10 Aug. 1876): 1; (24 Aug. 1876): 1; (7 Sept. 1876): 1; (28 Sept. 1876): 1; (5 Oct. 1876): 1; (12 Oct. 1876): 8; (19 Oct. 1876): 1; (26 Oct. 1876): 1; (23 Nov. 1876): 8; (30 Nov. 1876): 5; (7 Dec. 1876): 1; (14 Dec. 1876): 5; (21 Dec. 1876): 1; (4 Jan. 1877): 1; (11 Jan. 1877): 1; (1 Feb. 1877): 1; (8 Feb. 1877): 1.

"A Tale of Ancient Rome." *Christian Recorder* (11 Oct. 1883): 1.

"Thank God for Little Children." *Southern Workman* (5 Apr. 1872): 4.

"Thank God for Little Children." *Weekly Anglo-African* (28 Jan. 1860): 1.

"That Household Word." *Pine and Palm* (25 May 1861). *(BAP)*.

"Thine Eyes Shall See the King in His Beauty." *Christian Recorder* (27 Aug. 1891): 1.

"To Bishop Payne." *Journal of the 20th Session and 19th Quadrennial Session of the Central Conference of the African Methodist Episcopal Church. . . .* Philadelphia: Bethel Church, 2 May 1892. 61.

"To Charles Sumner." *Weekly Anglo-African* (30 June 1860): 1.

"To the Cleveland Union-Savers." *Anti-Slavery Bugle* (23 Feb. 1861). *(BAP)*.

"Today is a King in Disguise." *Christian Recorder* (23 June 1866): 97.

"To Mrs. Harriet Beecher Stowe." *Frederick Douglass' Paper* (3 Feb. 1854). *(BAP)*.

"To My Daughter." *Weekly Anglo-African* (15 Feb. 1862): 4.

"To the Union-Savers of Cleveland: An Appeal from One of the Fugitive's Own Race." *Liberator* (8 March 1861): 40. *(BAP)*.

"To the Union-Savers of Cleveland: An Appeal from One of the Fugitive's Own Race." In *The Underground Railroad*. William Still. Philadelphia: Porter & Coates, 1872. 764–65.

"To White Ribbons of Maine Who Gave Me Their Blessed Gifts." *Christian Recorder* (25 Dec. 1890): 1.

[Transcription of Speech given to the Twenty-Fifth Annual Meeting of the American Anti-Slavery Society.] *National Anti-Slavery Standard* (22 May 1858).

"Trial and Triumph" [Serial]. *Christian Recorder* (4 Oct. 1888): 6; (11 Oct. 1888): 5; (18 Oct. 1888): 5; (1 Nov. 1888): 5; (8 Nov. 1888): 5; (15 Nov. 1888): 5; (22 Nov. 1888): 5; (29 Nov. 1888): 5; (6 Dec. 1888): 5; (13 Dec. 1888): 5–6; (20 Dec. 1888): 5; (3 Jan. 1889): 5; (10 Jan. 1889): 5; (17 Jan. 1889): 5; (24 Jan. 1889): 5; (31 Jan. 1889): 5; (7 Feb. 1889): 5; (14 Feb. 1889): 5.

"The Triumph of Freedom—A Dream." *Anglo-African Magazine* (Jan. 1860): 21.

"True and False Politeness." *A.M.E. Church Review* 14 (1889): 339–45.

"Truth." *Anglo-African Magazine* (March 1860): 87–88.

"The Two Offers." *Anglo-African Magazine* (Sept.–Oct. 1859): 288–91, 311–13. *(BAP)*.

"Vashti." *New National Era* (22 Sept. 1870): 4.

"The Vision of the Czar of Russia." *A.M.E. Church Review* (July 1889): 140–41.

"The Wanderer's Return." *Christian Recorder* (26 Nov. 1885): 1.

"We Are Rising." *Christian Recorder* (9 Nov. 1876): 5.

"The Widow's Mites." *Christian Recorder* (27 Dec. 1877): 1.

"The Woman's Christian Temperance Union and the Colored Woman." *A.M.E. Church Review* 4 (1888).

"Woman's Political Future." In *World's Congress of Representative Women*. May Wright Sewall, ed. Chicago and New York: Rand, McNally & Company, 1894.

"Woman's Work." *Christian Recorder* (7 Feb. 1889): 1.

"A Word from Miss Watkins." *National Anti-Slavery Standard* (18 Feb. 1860). *(BAP)*.

"Words for the Hour." *Christian Recorder* (26 Jan. 1899): 4.

"Youth in Heaven." *Anglo-African Magazine* (Feb. 1860): 64.

Letters

"An Appeal for the Philadelphia Rescuers" [Letter to the Editor]. *Weekly Anglo-African* (23 June 1860). *(BAP)*.

"Breathing the Air of Freedom" [Letter to the Editor]. *National Anti-Slavery Standard* (4 Oct. 1856). *(BAP)*.

[Excerpts from a Letter to a Friend.] *Liberator* (23 Apr. 1858). *(BAP)*.

"Letter from Ellen Watkins" [Letter to the Editor]. *Anti-Slavery Bugle* (9 July 1959). *(BAP)*.

"Letter from Miss Watkins" [Letter to the Editor]. *Anti-Slavery Bugle* (23 Apr. 1859; 21 May 1859). *(BAP)*.

Letter on John Brown. In *Echoes of Harper's Ferry*. James Redpath. Boston, 1860.

Letter to John Brown. 25 Nov. 1859. In *The Mind of the Negro as Reflected in Letters Written During the Crisis, 1800–1860*. Carter Woodson, ed. Washington, DC: Association for the Study of Negro Life and History, 1926. 508–9. New York: Negro Universities Press, 1969.

Letter to the Editor. *National Anti-Slavery Standard* (6 March 1858): 3; (7 July 1860): 3.

Letter to Friend. *National Anti-Slavery Standard* (4 Oct. 1856): 3.

Letter to Colonel Hinton. *National Anti-Slavery Standard* (10 Aug. 1867): 2.

Letter to J. [Extract.] *National Anti-Slavery Standard* (9 Apr. 1859): 3.

Letter to Mrs. J. Elizabeth Jones. *Anti-Slavery Bugle* (7 July 1860; 29 Sept. 1860). *(BAP)*.

Letter to Marius R. Robinson. *Anti-Slavery Bugle* (13 Nov. 1858). *(BAP)*.

Letters to William Still, 1854–1872. In *Still's Underground Railroad Records*. William Still. Philadelphia: the Author, 1886. 755–80.

Letter to Charles Sumner. 26 June 1860. Sumner Papers, Harvard University. *(BAP)*.

Anthologies

Adams, William, Peter Conn, and Barry Slepian, eds. *Afro-American Literature: Drama, Fiction, Non-Fiction and Poetry*. Boston: Houghton Mifflin, 1970.

Barksdale, Richard, and Keneth Kinnamon. *Black Writers of America: A Comprehensive Anthology*. New York: Macmillan, 1972.

Bragg, George F., ed. *Golden Jubilee of Henry Laird Phillips*. N.p.: n.p., [c.1929].

Brawley, Benjamin Griffth. *Early Negro American Writers: Selections with Biographical and Critical Introductions*. Chapel Hill: University of North Carolina Press, 1935; Freeport, NY: Books for Libraries Press, 1968; New York: Dover Publications, 1970. 290–98.

Brown, Sterling A., Arthur P. Davis, and Ulysses Lee, eds. *The Negro Caravan: Writings by American Negroes*. New York: Dryden Press, 1941; Arno Press, 1970. 293–96.

Calverton, Victor Francis, ed. *An Anthology of American Negro Literature*. New York: Modern Library, 1929.

Chambers, Bradford, and Rebecca Moon, eds. *Right On! An Anthology of Black Literature*. New York: New American Library, 1970.

Child, Lydia Maria. *The Freedmen's Book*. Boston: Ticknor and Fields, 1865.

Davis, Arthur P., and J. Saunders Redding, eds. *Cavalcade: Negro American Writing from 1760 to the Present*. Boston: Houghton Mifflin, 1971. 53, 101.

Dunbar, Alice Moore, ed. *Masterpieces of Negro Eloquence*. New York: The Bookery, 1914; The Basic Afro-American Reprint Library, 1970; Johnson Reprints, 1970.

Dunbar-Nelson, Alice, ed. *The Dunbar Speaker and Entertainer*. Naperville, IL: J. L. Nichols & Co., 1920.

Eleazer, Robert B., comp. *Singers in the Dawn*. 7th Edition. Atlanta: Commission on Interracial Cooperation, 1942, 1943.

Gilbert, Sandra M., and Susan Gubar, eds. *The Norton Anthology of Literature by Women: The Tradition in English*. New York: W. W. Norton, 1985. 829–33.

Haley, James T., comp. *Afro-American Encyclopedia*. . . . Nashville: Haley & Florida, 1895. 550–51, 558.

———. *Sparkling Gems of Race Knowledge Worth Reading*. . . . Nashville: J. T. Haley and Co., 1897. 146.

Hayden, Robert Earl, ed. *Kaleidoscope: Poems by American Negro Poets*. New York: Harcourt, Brace & World, 1967.

Hughes, Langston, and Arna Bontemps, eds. *Poetry of the Negro: 1746–1970*. Revised Edition. Garden City, NY: Doubleday, 1970.

Kendricks, Ralph, and Claudette Levitt, eds. *Afro-American Voices, 1770's–1970's*. New York: Oxford University Press, 1970.

Kerlin, Robert, ed. *Negro Poets and Their Poems*. Washington, DC: Associated Publishers, 1923. 26–32.

Loewenberg, Bert J., and Ruth Bogin, eds. *Black Women in Nineteenth-Century American Life: Their Words, Their Thoughts, Their Feelings*. University Park: Pennsylvania State University Press, 1976. 243–51.

Lomax, Alan, and Raoul Abdul, eds. *3000 Years of Black Poetry*. New York: Dodd, Mead, 1970.

Long, Richard A., and Eugenia W. Collier, eds. *Afro-American Writing: An Anthology of Prose and Poetry*. New York: New York University Press, 1972. 2nd and Enlarged Edition. University Park: Pennsylvania State University Press, 1985.

Patterson, Lindsay. *An Introduction to Black Literature in America From 1746 to the Present*. New York: Publishers Co., 1968.

———. *A Rock Against the Wind: Black Love Poems*. New York: Dodd, Mead, 1973.

Randall, Dudley, ed. *The Black Poets*. New York: Bantam Books, 1971.

Robinson, William H., Jr., ed. *Early Black American Poets*. Dubuque, IA: William C. Brown Company Publishers, 1969. 26, 38, 230.

Shockley, 59–61, 201.

Sterling, Dorothy, ed. *Speak Out in Thunder Tones: Letters and Other Writings by Black Northerners, 1787–1865*. Garden City, NY: Doubleday, 1973. 129–31, 232, 377.

———. *The Trouble They Seen: Black People Tell the Story of Reconstruction*. Garden City, NY: Doubleday, 1976. 257–58.

Stetson, Erlene, ed. *Black Sister: Poetry by Black American Women, 1746–1980*. Bloomington: Indiana University Press, 1981. 26–34.

Walrond, Eric, and Rosey Pool, eds. *Black and Unknown Bards: A Collection of Negro Poetry*. Aldington, England: Hand & Flower Press, 1958.

Watkins, Mel, and Jay David, eds. *To Be a Black Woman: Portraits in Fact and Fiction*. New York: William Morrow, 1970.

Writings about

Adams, Russell L. *Great Negroes Past and Present*. Chicago: Afro-American Publishing Co., [c.1963]. 147.

Ammons, Elizabeth. "Legacy Profile: Frances Ellen Watkins Harper (1825–1911)." *Legacy* 2.2 (Fall 1985): 61–66.

———. "Stowe's Dream of the Mother-Savior: *Uncle Tom's Cabin* and American Women Writers before 1920." In *New Essays on Uncle Tom's Cabin*. Eric J. Sundquist, ed. Cambridge: Cambridge University Press, 1986. 155–95.

Baker, Houston, Jr. *Long Black Song: Essays in Black American Literature and Culture*. Charlottesville: University Press of Virginia, 1972.

Bardolph, Richard, ed. *The Negro Vanguard*. New York: Random House, 1961. 80.

Baskin, Wade, and Richard Runes. *Dictionary of Black Culture*. New York: Philosophical Library, 1973. 201–2.

Bell, Bernard W. "Literary Sources of the Early Afro-American Novel." *CLA Journal* (Sept. 1974): 29–43.

Bone, Robert. *The Negro Novel in America*. New Haven: Yale University Press, 1965.

Bontemps, Arna. *The Harlem Renaissance Remembered*. New York: Dodd, Mead, 1972. 63–64, 74, 80.

———. "The Negro Contribution to American Letters." In *The American Negro Reference Book*. John Preston Davis, ed. Englewood Cliffs, NJ: Prentice-Hall, 1966. 827.

Brawley, *NBH*, 234.

Brawley, *NG*, 116–20.

Brawley, *NLA*, 44–45, 138.

Brawley, Benjamin. "Three Negro Poets: Horton, Mrs. Harper, and Whiteman." *Journal of Negro History* 11 (1917): 384–92.

Brown, 97–103.

Brown, Martha Hursey. "Literary Portrayals of Black Women as Moral Reformers: Novels by Harper, Henry and Hopkins." In *Transactions of the Conference Group for Social and Administrative History*. Vol. 6. Oshkosh, WI: State Historical Society, 1976.

Brown, Sterling. *Negro Poetry and Drama and the Negro in American Fiction*. New York: Arno Press, 1969. Republication of *Negro Poetry and Drama*. Washington, DC: The Associates in Negro Folk Education, 1937; and *The Negro in American Fiction*. Washington, DC: The Associates in Negro Folk Education, 1937.

Brown, William Wells. *The Black Man, His Antecedents, His Genius, and His Achievements*. New York: Thomas Hamilton; Boston: R. F. Wallcut, 1863; New York: Johnson Reprints, 1968.

————. *The Rising Son; or, the Antecedents and Advancement of the Colored Race.* Boston: A. G. Brown and Co., 1874.

Bryant, Joseph G. "Negro Poetry." *Colored American Magazine* (May 1905): 254–57.

Bullock, 47, 61, 66, 79, 84, 96, 98, 102, 155.

Burks, Mary Fair. "The First Black Literary Magazine in American Letters." *CLA Journal* (March 1976): 318–21.

Christian, Barbara. *Black Feminist Criticism.* New York: Pergamon Press, 1985. 3, 71, 73, 120–21, 165–70, 172–73.

————. *Black Women Novelists: The Development of a Tradition, 1892–1976.* Westport, CT: Greenwood Press, 1980. 3–34.

Christian Recorder (21 Dec. 1872): 8.

Clark, Alice. "Frances Ellen Watkins Harper." *Negro History Bulletin* (Jan. 1942): 83.

DANB, 289–90.

Dann, 67.

Dannett, 1: 102–9.

Davis, 231–32.

Davis, John Preston. *The American Negro Reference Book.* Englewood Cliffs, NJ: Prentice-Hall, 1966. 35, 854–56.

Du Bois, W.E.B. *The Gift of Black Folk, The Negroes in the Making of America.* Boston: Stratford, 1924. 300–304.

————. "Writers" [Editorial]. *Crisis* (Apr. 1911): 20–21.

Dunnigan, Alice E. "Early History of Negro Women in Journalism." *Negro History Bulletin* 28 (Summer 1965): 178.

Frazier, Susan Elizabeth. "Some Afro-American Women of Mark." *A.M.E. Church Review* (Apr. 1892): 378–86.

Fryar, Lillie B. "The Aesthetics of Language: Harper, Hurston and Morrison." *Dissertation Abstracts International* 47 (Aug. 1986): 529A.

Gayle, Addison, ed. *Black Expression*. New York: Weybright and Talley, 1969. 73–207.

Giddings, Paula. *When and Where I Enter: The Impact of Black Women on Race and Sex in America*. New York: William Morrow, 1984. 29, 58, 63, 66, 68, 71–73, 91, 93, 96, 122, 124–25, 130.

Gloster, Hugh M. *Negro Voices in American Fiction*. Chapel Hill: University of North Carolina Press, 1948; New York: Russell & Russell, 1965.

Goldstein, Rhoda L. *Black Life and Culture in the United States*. New York: Thomas Y. Crowell, 1971. 186.

Haley, James T., comp. *Afro-American Encyclopedia*. . . . Nashville: Haley & Florida, 1895. 550–51, 558, 592–93.

Hannaford, Phebe. *Daughters of America*. Augusta, ME: True and Co., 1882. 326.

Hill, Patricia Liggins. "Frances W. Harper's Aunt Chloe Poems from *Sketches of Southern Life:* Antithesis to the Plantation Literary Tradition." *Mississippi Quarterly* 34.4 (1981): 403–13.

———. "Let Me Make the Songs for the People: A Study of Frances Watkins Harper's Poetry." *Black American Literature Forum* (Summer 1981): 60–65, 91–96.

"Iola Leroy" [Review]. *A.M.E. Church Review* 9 (1893): 416–17.

"Iola Leroy" [Review]. *Independent* (5 Jan. 1893): 21; (29 Oct. 1896): 1463.

"Iola Leroy" [Review]. *Nation* (23 Feb. 1893): 146–47.

"Iola Leroy" [Review]. *Southern Workman* (Sept. 1899): 359.

"Iola Leroy, or Shadows Uplifted" [Review]. *Christian Recorder* (12 Jan. 1893): 3.

Jackson, Blyden. *The Waiting Years: Essays in American Negro Literature*. Baton Rouge: Louisiana State University Press, 1976.

Jahn, Janheinz. *Neo-African Literature: A History of Black Writing*. New York: Grove Press, 1968. 131, 138, 140.

Jet (23 Feb. 1961): 9; (24 Feb. 1966): 11.

Johnson, Lonnell Edward. "Portrait of the Bondslave in the Bible: Slavery and Freedom in the Works of Four Afro-American Poets." *Dissertation Abstracts International* 47 (Feb. 1987): 3038A–39A.

Journal of Negro History 2 (1917): 386–87.

"Lecture on the Mission of the War." *Christian Recorder* (21 May 1864). *(BAP)*.

Lewis, Vashti. "The Near-White Female in Frances Ellen Harper's *Iola Leroy*." *Phylon* 45.4 (1984): 319–22.

Loggins, 211, 245–49, 324–26.

Majors, 23–27, 361–63.

Mays, Benjamin. *The Negro's God: As Reflected in His Literature*. Boston: Chapman and Grimes, 1938. 118, 120.

McClellan, G. M. "The Negro as a Writer." Culp, 275.

McDowell, Deborah E. "The Changing Same: Generational Connections and Black Women Novelists." *New Literary History* (Winter 1987): 281–302.

McNeil, Barbara, and Miranda C. Herbert, eds. *Historical Biographical Dictionary Master Index*. Detroit: Gale Research Co., 1980.

Miller, Ruth, and Peter J. Katopes. "Modern Beginnings: William Wells Brown, Charles Waddell Chesnutt, Martin R. Delany, Paul Laurence Dunbar, Sutton E. Griggs, Frances Ellen Watkins Harper, and Frank J. Webb." In *Black American Writers: Bibliographical Essays, I: The Beginnings Through the Harlem Renaissance and Langston Hughes*. Thomas M. Inge, Maurice Duke, and Jackson

R. Bryer, eds. New York: St. Martin's Press, 1978. 133–60.

"Miss Watkins and the Constitution" [Reprinted Letter]. *National Anti-Slavery Standard* (9 Apr. 1859). *(BAP)*.

Montgomery, Janey Weinhold. *A Comparative Analysis of the Rhetoric of Two Negro Women Orators: Sojourner Truth and Frances E. Watkins Harper.* Hays: Fort Hays Kansas State College, 1968.

Mossell, 13–14, 60–61, 75–77.

"Mrs. F.E.W. Harper." *Christian Recorder* (30 Oct. 1873): 5.

"Mrs. F.E.W. Harper" [Review]. *Christian Recorder* (7 Aug. 1890): 4.

"Mrs. F.E.W. Harper." *New National Era* (13 July 1871): 3.

"Mrs. Frances E. W. Harper on Reconstruction." *Liberator* (3 March 1865). *(BAP)*.

"Mrs. Harper's Book." *Christian Recorder* (12 Dec. 1895): 2.

NAW, 137–38.

Negroes of Achievement: 1865–1915 [Study Prints]. Chicago: Afro-American, 1968.

Negro History Bulletin (Jan. 1942): 83, 96.

"Negro Novelists Blazing the Way in Fiction." *Negro History Bulletin* (Dec. 1938): 17.

"Notes and Muse." *Woman's Journal* (18 Oct. 1890).

O'Connor, Lillian. *Pioneer Women Orators.* New York: Columbia University Press, 1954.

"Our Literary Women." *Lancet* (10 Oct. 1885): 1.

Oxley, Thomas L. G. "Survey of Negro Literature, 1760–1926." *Messenger* (Feb. 1927): 37–39.

Penn, 420.

Ploski, Harry A., and Earnest Kaiser. *The Negro Almanac.* New York: Bellwether, 1971. 678–79.

"*Poems*" [Review]. *Voice of the Negro* (Oct. 1905): 720.

"*Poems on Miscellaneous Subjects*" [Review]. *Christian Recorder* (16 Sept. 1854): 79.

Pollard, Leslie J. "Frances Harper and the Old People: Two Recently Discovered Poems." *Griot* (Winter–Summer 1985): 52–56.

Quarles, Benjamin. *Black Abolitionists*. New York: Oxford University Press, 1969. 75, 76, 83, 179, 214, 233, 241, 244, 247.

Redding, J. Saunders. *They Came in Chains; Americans from Africa*. Philadelphia: J. B. Lippincott, 1950. 103, 210.

———. *To Make a Poet Black*. Chapel Hill: University of North Carolina Press, 1939.

[Review of Speech.] *Liberator* (24 March 1865). *(BAP)*.

Richings, G. F. *Evidences of Progress among Colored People*. Philadelphia: George S. Ferguson, 1901.

Riggins, Linda. "The Works of Frances E. W. Harper." *Black World* (Dec. 1972): 30–36.

Robinson, 88.

Robinson, William H., Jr., ed. *Early Black American Prose*. Dubuque, IA: William C. Brown Company Publishers, 1971. xiv, xvii.

Rollins, Charlemae Hill. *Famous American Negro Poets*. New York: Dodd, Mead, 1965. 22–27.

———. *They Showed the Way: Forty American Negro Leaders*. New York: Thomas Y. Crowell, 1964. 80–82.

Rubin, Louis D. "The Search for a Language, 1746–1923." In *Black Poetry in America: Two Essays in Historical Interpretation*. Blyden Jackson and Louis D. Rubin, Jr. Baton Rouge: Louisiana State University Press, 1974. 1–35.

Rush, 361–62.

Rushing, Andrea Benton. "Images of Black Women in Afro-American Poetry." *Black World* (Sept. 1975): 18–30.

Scruggs, 6–13.

Sherman, xvii, xviii, xxiii, xxiv, xxv, xxvii, 14, 62–74, 140, 190.

Shockley, 56–58, 190–93.

Sillen, Samuel. *Women Against Slavery*. New York: Masses & Mainstream, 1955.

"Speech given to the Twenty-Fifth Annual Meeting of the American Anti-Slavery Society" [Transcription]. *National Anti-Slavery Standard* (22 May 1858). *(BAP)*.

"Speech of Mrs. Frances E. W. Harper." *Liberator* (11 Aug. 1865). *(BAP)*.

Stanton, Elizabeth Cady, et al., eds. *History of Woman Suffrage*. New York: Fowler and Wells, 1881. 2: 171, 391–92; 6: 425.

Still, William. *Still's Underground Rail Road Records*. Philadelphia: the Author, 1886.

———. *The Underground Railroad. . . .* Philadelphia: Porter & Coates, 1872.

Tischler, Nancy Marie. *Black Masks; Negro Characters in Modern Southern Fiction*. University Park: Pennsylvania State University Press, 1969. 150.

Toppin, Edgar A. *A Biographical History of Blacks in America Since 1528*. New York: David McKay, 1971.

" 'Trial and Triumph,' the story now running. . . ." *Christian Recorder* (15 Nov. 1888): 4.

Wagner, Jean. *Black Poets of the United States from Paul Laurence Dunbar to Langston Hughes*. Urbana: University of Illinois Press, 1973. 22–23.

Watson, Carole McAlpine. *Prologue: The Novels of Black American Women, 1891–1965*. Westport, CT: Greenwood Press, 1985.

Wesley, 4, 9, 13, 35–36, 38, 43, 45–46, 63, 70, 218.

White, Charles F. *Who's Who in Philadelphia*. Philadelphia: A.M.E. Book Concern, 1912.

Williams, Kenny J. *They Also Spoke: An Essay on Negro Literature in America, 1787–1930*. Nashville: Townsend, 1970. 120–36, 143, 217, 223, 243, 269.

Woman's Journal (30 Jan. 1892; 3 March 1894; 7 Oct. 1899; 1 Nov. 1902).

Woodson, Carter G., and Charles H. Wesley. *The Negro in Our History*. Washington, DC: Associated Publishing Co., 1922. 469.

"A Word from Miss Watkins." *National Anti-Slavery Standard* (18 Feb. 1860). *(BAP)*.

Papers in Collections

Daniel, Theodora Williams. "The Poems of Frances E. W. Harper, Edited with a Biographical and Critical Introduction, and Bibliography." Master's thesis, Howard University, 1937.

Fryar, Lillie B. "The Aesthetics of Language: Harper, Hurston and Morrison." Diss., State University of New York, 1986.

Graham, Maryemma. "The Threefold Cord: Blackness, Womanness and Art, A Study of the Life and Work of Frances Ellen Watkins Harper." Master's thesis, Cornell University, 1973.

Harper, Frances Ellen Watkins. *Iola Leroy; or, Shadows Uplifted*. Boston: J. H. Earle, [c. 1892]. Presentation inscription to A. G. Wills, 1904. Beinecke Library, Yale University.

———. *Poems*. Philadelphia: Merrihew & Son, 1871. 1876 cover (Providence, RI: Crawford & Greene) and 1871 title page, Library of Congress.

———. *Poems*. 1880 cover (Crawford & Greene) and 1871 title page, Moorland-Spingarn Collection, Howard University.

Photograph, Sophia Smith Collection, Smith College.

Josephine Delphine Henderson Heard
(1861–1921)

Writings by

Morning Glories. Philadelphia: n.p., 1890.

Morning Glories. 2nd Edition. Atlanta: Franklin Printing and Publishing Co., 1901.

"And It Shall Come to Pass." *Christian Recorder* (30 Aug. 1894): 1.

"The Birth of Time." *Christian Recorder* (10 Oct. 1889): 1.

"The Debt of Love." *Christian Recorder* (24 Sept. 1896): 1.

"Deception." *Christian Recorder* (6 March 1890): 1.

"Decoration Day." *Christian Recorder* (13 June 1889): 1.

"The Deserted Church; or, the Day After the Conference." *Christian Recorder* (21 June 1888): 1.

"Easter Morn, 1890." *Christian Recorder* (17 Apr. 1890): 1.

"An Epitaph." Mossell, 86.

"He That Cometh to Me, I Will in No Wise Cast Out." *Christian Recorder* (16 Apr. 1891): 1.

"Hope." *Christian Recorder* (19 Sept. 1889): 1.

"I Will Look Up." *Christian Recorder* (1 Aug. 1889): 1.

"In Memory of Rev. James M. Bathel." *Christian Recorder* (20 Feb. 1890): 1.

"Lend a Hand." *Christian Recorder* (11 Nov. 1897): 1.

"Life's Journey." *Christian Recorder* (13 Nov. 1890): 1.

"Morning Prayer." *Christian Recorder* (16 Aug. 1894): 1.

"Night." *A.M.E. Church Review* 3 (1886–1887): 363.

"Out in the Desert." *Christian Recorder* (1 May 1890): 5.

"Resting." *Christian Recorder* (22 Aug. 1889): 1.

"Retrospect." *Christian Recorder* (10 Jan. 1889): 1.

"Sabbath Bells." *Christian Recorder* (27 Sept. 1888): 1.

"Solace." *Christian Recorder* (27 March 1890): 1.

"Spectre Fancies." *Christian Recorder* (14 Aug. 1890): 1.

"They Are Coming." *A.M.E. Zion Quarterly Review* (Jan. 1894): 176–77.

"Thou Leadest Me." *Christian Recorder* (2 Jan. 1890): 1.

"Time and Things Have Changed." *Christian Recorder* (7 March 1895): 1.

"To Clement's Ferry." *Christian Recorder* (20 Sept. 1888): 1.

"To Whittier." *Christian Recorder* (6 March 1890): 1.

"To Youth." *Christian Recorder* (5 Sept. 1889): 1.

"Unuttered Prayer." *Christian Recorder* (4 Apr. 1889): 1.

"Vesper Hymn." *Christian Recorder* (16 July 1891): 6.

"When I Would Die." *Christian Recorder* (29 Aug. 1889): 1.

"Who Is My Neighbor?" *Christian Recorder* (13 Sept. 1888): 1.

"Whoever Gives Freely Shall Freely Receive." *Christian Recorder* (18 Oct. 1888): 1.

"Wilberforce." *A.M.E. Church Review* (Oct. 1888): 113–14.

"Wilberforce." *Christian Recorder* (25 Oct. 1888): 1.

Anthologies

Morning Glories. In *Collected Black Women's Poetry*. Joan R. Sherman, ed. Vol. 4. New York: Oxford University Press, 1988.

Robinson, William H., Jr., ed. *Early Black American Poets*. Dubuque, IA: William C. Brown Company Publishers, 1969. 261–63.

Shockley, 173–74.

Writings about

Heard, William Henry. *From Slavery to the Bishopric in the A.M.E. Church: An Autobiography.* Philadelphia: A.M.E. Book Concern, 1924.

Majors, 261–68.

"Morning Glories" [Review]. *Christian Recorder* (19 June 1890): 4.

Mossell, 14, 85–86.

Rush, 372.

Sherman, 209, 241.

Shockley, 171–73.

Simson, Renate Maria. "Whoever Heard of Josephine Heard?" *College Language Association Journal* (Dec. 1982): 256–61.

Pauline Elizabeth Hopkins
[pseud. Sarah A. Allen] (1859–1930)

Writings by

Contending Forces: A Romance Illustrative of Negro Life North and South. Boston: The Colored Co-operative Publishing Co., 1900; Miami: Mnemosyne Publishing Co., 1969.

Contending Forces: A Romance Illustrative of Negro Life North and South. Afterword by Gwendolyn Brooks. Carbondale: Southern Illinois University Press, 1978.

Contending Forces: A Romance Illustrative of Negro Life North and South. Introduction by Richard Yarborough. New York: Oxford University Press, 1988.

The Magazine Novels of Pauline Hopkins. Introduction by Hazel V. Carby. New York: Oxford University Press, 1988.

One Scene from the Drama of Early Days. N.p.: n.p., n.d.

A Primer of Facts Pertaining to the Early Greatness of the African Race and the Possibility of Restoration by Its Descendants. Cambridge, MA: P. E. Hopkins & Co., 1905.

Slaves' Escape: or The Underground Railroad, 1879; later titled *Peculiar Sam, or The Underground Railroad.* A Musical Drama in 4 Acts. Boston: N.p., 1879.

[Allen, Sarah A.] "Hagar's Daughter. A Story of Southern Caste Prejudice" [Serial]. *Colored American Magazine* (March 1901): 337–52; (Apr. 1901): 431–45; (May 1901): 24–34; (June 1901): 117–28; (July 1901): 185–95; (Aug. 1901): 262–72; (Sept. 1901): 343–53; (Oct. 1901): 425–35; (Nov. 1901): 23–33; (Dec. 1901): 113–24; (Jan.–Feb. 1902): 188–200, 281–91.

[———.] "Latest Phases of the Race Problem in America." *Colored American Magazine* (Feb. 1903): 244–51.

[———.] "Mr. M. Hamilton Hodges." *Colored American Magazine* (March 1904): 167–69.

[———.] "A New Professional." *Colored American Magazine* (Sept. 1903): 661–63.

[———.] "The Test of Manhood." *Colored American Magazine* (Dec. 1902): 114–19.

"Artists." *Colored American Magazine* (Sept. 1902): 362–67.

"As the Lord Lives, He Is One of Our Mother's Children." *Colored American Magazine* (Nov. 1903): 795–801.

"Booker T. Washington." *Colored American Magazine* (Oct. 1901): 436–41.

"Bro'r Abr'm Jimson's Wedding, A Christmas Story." *Colored American Magazine* (Dec. 1901): 103–12.

"Club Life among Colored Women." *Colored American Magazine* (Aug. 1902): 273–77.

"Dark Races of the Twentieth Century" [Series]. *Voice of the Negro* (Feb. 1905): 108; (March 1905): 187; (May 1905): 330; (June 1905): 415; (July 1905): 459.

"A Dash for Liberty." *Colored American Magazine* (Aug. 1901): 243–47.

"Echoes from the Annual Convention of Northeastern Federation of Colored Women's Clubs." *Colored American Magazine* (Oct. 1903): 709–13.

"Famous Men of the Negro Race. Charles Lenox Remond." *Colored American Magazine* (May 1901): 34–39.

"Famous Women of the Negro Race" [Series]. *Colored American Magazine* "I: Phenomenal Vocalists" (Nov. 1901): 45–53; "II: Sojourner Truth" (Dec. 1901): 124–32; "III: Harriet Tubman ('Moses')" (Jan.–Feb. 1902): 210–23; "IV: Some Literary Workers" (March 1902): 277–80; "V: Literary Workers" (Apr. 1902): 366–71; "VI: Educators" (May 1902): 41–46; "VII: Educators" (June 1902): 125–30; "VIII: Educators" (July 1902): 206–13.

"The First Pan-African Conference of the World." *Colored American Magazine* (Sept. 1900): 223–31.

"General Washington, A Christmas Story." *Colored American Magazine* (Dec. 1900): 95–104.

"Heroes and Heroines in Black." *Colored American Magazine* (Jan. 1903): 206–11.

"Higher Education of Colored Women in White." *Colored American Magazine* (Oct. 1902): 445–50.

"Hon. Frederick Douglass." *Colored American Magazine* (Dec. 1900): 121.

"How a New York Newspaper Man Entertained a Number of Colored Ladies and Gentlemen at Dinner in the Revere House, Boston, and How the Colored American League

Was Started." *Colored American Magazine* (Jan. 1904): 151–60.

"In the Editor's Sanctum." *Colored American Magazine* (Apr. 1904): 297.

"Josephine St. Pierre Ruffin at Milwaukee, 1900." *Colored American Magazine* (July 1902): 210–13.

"Monroe Rodgers." *Colored American Magazine* (Nov. 1902): 20–26.

"The Mystery Within Us." *Colored American Magazine* (May 1900): 14–18.

"The New York Subway." *Voice of the Negro* (Dec. 1904): 605, 608–12.

"Of One Blood. Or, the Hidden Self" [Serial]. *Colored American Magazine* (Nov. 1902): 29–40; (Dec. 1902): 102–13; (Jan. 1903): 191–200; (Feb. 1903): 264–72; (March 1903): 339–48; (May–June 1903): 423–32; (July 1903): 492–501; (Aug. 1903): 580–86; (Sept. 1903): 643–47; (Oct. 1903): 726–31; (Nov. 1903): 802–7.

"Reminiscences of the Life and Times of Lydia Maria Child." *Colored American Magazine* (Feb. 1903): 271; (March 1903): 353; (May–June 1903): 460.

"A Retrospect of the Past" [Excerpt from *Contending Forces*]. *Colored American Magazine* (Nov. 1900): 64–72.

"Some Famous Women." *Colored American Magazine* (Aug. 1902): 273–77.

"Talma Gordon." *Colored American Magazine* (Oct. 1900): 271–90.

"Venus and Apollo Modelled from Ethiopians." *Colored American Magazine* (May–June 1903): 465.

"William Wells Brown." *Colored American Magazine* (Jan. 1901): 232.

"Winona. A Tale of Negro Life in the South and Southwest"
[Serial]. *Colored American Magazine* (May 1902): 29–
41; (June 1902): 97–110; (July 1902): 177–87; (Aug.
1902): 257–68; (Sept. 1902): 348–58; (Oct. 1902):
422–31.

Anthologies

Ammons, Elizabeth, comp. *Short Fiction by Black Women,
1900–1920*. New York: Oxford University Press, 1991.
Shockley, 295–303.

Writings about

Bell, Bernard W. "Literary Sources of the Early Afro-
American Novel." *CLA Journal* (Sept. 1974): 29–43.
Bone, Robert A. *The Negro Novel in America*. New Haven:
Yale University Press, 1958. 14, 19, 26.
Braithwaite, William Stanley. "Negro America's First Mag-
azine." *Negro Digest* (Dec. 1947).
Brown, Martha Hursey. "Literary Portrayals of Black Women
as Moral Reformers: Novels by Harper, Henry and
Hopkins." In *Transactions of the Conference Group for
Social and Administrative History*. Vol. 6. Oshkosh, WI:
State Historical Society, 1976.
Bullock, 65, 67, 83, 107–10, 112, 115, 125.
Campbell, Jane. "Pauline Elizabeth Hopkins." In *Afro-
American Writers before the Harlem Renaissance*. Vol. 50
of *Dictionary of Literary Biography*. Trudier Harris and
Thadious M. Davis, eds. Detroit: Bruccoli-Clark, 1986.
DANB, 325–26.
Dannett, 1: 215.
"Editorial and Publisher's Announcements." *Colored Ameri-
can Magazine* (Oct. 1901): 478.
Gloster, Hugh M. *Negro Voices in American Fiction*. Chapel

Hill: University of North Carolina Press, 1948; New York: Russell & Russell, 1965. 33–34, 56.

"Pauline E. Hopkins." *Colored American Magazine* (Jan. 1901): 218–19; (May 1901): 47.

Lamping, Marilyn. "Pauline Elizabeth Hopkins." In *American Women Writers: A Critical Reference Guide from Colonial Times to the Present*. Lina Mainiero, ed. Vol. 2. New York: Frederick Ungar, 1980. 325–27.

Loggins, 326, 405, 453.

[Notice regarding *Contending Forces*.] *Woman's Journal* (25 Nov. 1899).

[Photograph.] *Colored American Magazine* (Jan. 1901): 201; (May 1901): 52.

"Prospectus of *Contending Forces*. . . ." *Colored American Magazine* (Sept. 1900): 195, 262.

"Publisher's Announcements." *Colored American Magazine* (Nov. 1904): 700.

"Reply to Letter to the Editor." *Colored American Magazine* (March 1903): 399.

[Review of *Contending Forces*.] *Colored American Magazine* (Sept. 1900): 1.

Robinson, William, H., Jr., ed. *Early Black American Prose*. Dubuque, IA: William C. Brown Company Publishers, 1971. xviii.

Rush, 389–90.

Shockley, 289–95.

Shockley, Ann Allen. "Pauline Elizabeth Hopkins: A Biographical Excursion into Obscurity." *Phylon* (Spring 1972): 22–26.

Smith, Albreta Moore. "Comment." *Colored American Magazine* (Oct. 1901): 479.

Tate, Claudia. "Pauline Hopkins: Our Literary Foremother." In *Conjuring: Black Women, Fiction, and Liter-*

ary Tradition. Marjorie Pryse and Hortense J. Spillers, eds. Bloomington: Indiana University Press, 1985.

Toppin, Edgar A. *A Biographical History of Blacks in America Since 1528*. New York: David McKay, 1971.

"The Voice of the Negro for March." *Voice of the Negro* (Feb. 1905).

"The Voice of the Negro for 1905." *Voice of the Negro* (Dec. 1904).

Watson, Carole McAlpine. *Prologue: The Novels of Black American Women, 1891–1965*. Westport, CT: Greenwood Press, 1985.

Papers in Collections

Burks, Mary Fair. "A Survey of Black Literary Magazines in the United States: 1859–1940." Diss., Columbia University, 1975.

Pauline E. Hopkins Papers, Negro Collection, Fisk University Library.

Lucy E. Hubert

Writings by

Hints on the Care of Children. Philadelphia: George S. Ferguson Co., 1898.

Writings about

Ethridge, Willie Snow. *An Aristocracy of Achievement*. Savannah, GA: Presses of Review Printing Co., [1929?].

Addie D. Waites Hunton (1875–1943)

Writings by

Two Colored Women with the American Expeditionary Forces. With Kathryn M. Johnson. Brooklyn, NY: Eagle Press, 1920.

William Alphaeus Hunton: A Pioneer Prophet of Young Men. New York: Association Press, 1938.

"The American Carlsbad." *Voice of the Negro* (May 1906): 329.

"The Cosmopolitan Society of Greater New York." *Voice of the Negro* (May 1907): 185.

"A Deeper Reverence for Home Ties." *Colored American Magazine* (Jan. 1907): 58–59.

"The Detroit Convention of the National Association of Colored Women." *Voice of the Negro* (Aug. 1906): 589–93.

"The National Association of Colored Women: Its Real Significance." *Colored American Magazine* (July 1908): 416–24.

"Negro Womanhood Defended." *Voice of the Negro* (July 1904): 280–82.

"The Southern Federation of Colored Women." *Voice of the Negro* (Dec. 1905): 850–54.

[Hunton, Addie, et al.] "Woman's Part in the Uplift of the Negro Race." *Colored American Magazine* (Jan. 1907): 53–61.

Writings about

Balch, Emily Greene, ed. *Occupied Haiti* [Committee Report]. New York: The Writers Publishing Co., 1927; Garland, 1972.

Brawley, Benjamin. *"William Alphaeus Hunton: A Pioneer Prophet of Young Men"* [Review]. *Opportunity* (Aug. 1938): 150.

DANB, 337–38.

Dannett, 2: 199–206.

Davis, 64.

NAW, 2: 240–41.

[Notice.] *Woman's Era* (Aug. 1896): 8.

Rice, Anna V. *History of the World's YWCA*. New York: Woman's Press, 1947.

Wesley, 38, 67, 88, 99, 112, 202, 209, 292.

Wilson, Elizabeth. *Fifty Years of Associated Work among Young Women, 1806–1916*. New York: National Board of the Young Women's Christian Associations of the United States of America, 1916.

Yenser, Thomas, ed. *Who's Who in Colored America: Dictionary of Notable Living Persons of African Descent in America, 1938–39–40*. 5th Edition. Brooklyn, NY: Thomas Yenser, 1940. 271.

Harriet Ann Jacobs [pseud. Linda Brent] (1813–1897)

Writings by

The Deeper Wrong; or, Incidents in the Life of a Slave Girl. London: W. Tweedie, 1862.

Incidents in the Life of a Slave Girl, Written by Herself. Lydia Maria Child, ed. Boston: Published for the Author, 1861; Miami: Mnemosyne Publishing Co., 1969.

Incidents in the Life of a Slave Girl, Written by Herself. Lydia Maria Child, ed. New introduction and notes by Walter Teller. New York: Harcourt Brace Jovanovich, 1973.

Incidents in the Life of a Slave Girl, Written by Herself. Jean Fagan Yellin, ed. Cambridge, MA, and London: Harvard University Press, 1987.

Incidents in the Life of a Slave Girl. Introduction by Valerie Smith. New York: Oxford University Press, 1988.

Letters

A Fugitive [Harriet Jacobs]. "Cruelty to Slaves." Letter to New York *Tribune* (25 July 1853): 3.

A Fugitive Slave [Harriet Jacobs]. "Letter from a Fugitive Slave: Slaves Sold Under Peculiar Circumstances." New York *Tribune* (21 July 1853): 6.

[Jacobs, H. B., and L. Jacobs.] "Letter from Teachers of the Freedmen" [Letter to Lydia M. Child]. *National Anti-Slavery Standard* (16 Apr. 1864): 2. *(BAP)*.

"Letter from Mrs. Jacobs" [Letter to the Editor of *Liberator*]. *National Anti-Slavery Standard* (16 Apr. 1864). *(BAP)*.

Letter to Lydia Maria Child. *National Anti-Slavery Standard* (18 Apr. 1863): 4.

Letter to J. Sella Martin, 13 April 1863, Alexandria, VA. *Freeman's Aid Society*, 7. Presscopy, MSS British Empire, Rhodes House. *(BAP)*.

Letter to N. N. *Liberator* (10 Apr. 1863): 61.

Letter to Amy Post. [185?], [n.p.]; 11 Jan. [185?], [Cornwall?]; [12 Feb.? 185(?)], New York; 14 Feb. [?], [n.p.]; 3 March [185?]; March [?], Idlewild; 7 Apr. [185?]; 3 May [18??], [n.d. #87], [Cambridge?]; 1 March [186?], New York; 18 May [186?], [n.p.]; 23 May [18??], [n.d. #89], [Idlewild?]; 18 June [186?], New York; 21 June [n.d. #90], [n.p.]; 25 June [186?], [Cornwall?]; 27 July [?], Idlewild; 31 July [18??], [n.d. #88], [Cornwall?]; 7 Aug [?], Idlewild; 9 Aug. [186?], New Bedford, MA; 19 Aug. [18??], [n.d. #91]; [n.d. #92], [n.p.]; 8 Oct. [186?]; 9 Oct. [?], [n.p.]; [8 Nov. 1861?]; 8 Dec. [186?], Idlewild; 20 Dec. [?], [Cornwall?]; 27 Dec. [?], Idlewild; [n.d.], [Cornwall?]; [n.d.], [n.p.], [n.d.], [n.p.]. Post Papers, University of Rochester. *(BAP)*.

Letter to Anne Warren Weston. June 28, [1861?]. Boston Public Library, Anti-Slavery Collections. *(BAP)*.

Anthologies

Child, Lydia Maria, ed. *The Freedmen's Book*. Boston: Ticknor and Fields, 1865. 206–18.

Gilbert, Sandra M., and Susan Gubar, eds. *The Norton Anthology of Literature by Women*. New York: W. W. Norton, 1985. 752–57.

Incidents in the Life of a Slave Girl. In *The Classic Slave Narratives*. Henry Louis Gates, Jr., ed. New York: Mentor, 1987. 333–513.

Shockley, 99–105.

Sterling, Dorothy, ed. *We Are Your Sisters: Black Women in the Nineteenth Century*. New York: W. W. Norton, 1984. 20–24, 73–84, 245–48, 255, 257, 398n, 401–3.

Writings about

Blassingame, John. "Critical Essay on Sources." *The Slave Community: Plantation Life in the Antebellum South*. 2nd Edition. New York: Oxford University Press, 1979.

Braxton, Joanne M. "Harriet Jacobs' *Incidents in the Life of a Slave Girl:* The Re-definition of the Slave Narrative Genre." *Massachusetts Review* (Summer 1986): 379–87.

Deck, Alice A. "Whose Book Is This? Authorial Versus Editorial Control of Harriet Brent Jacobs' *Incidents in the Life of a Slave Girl: Written by Herself.*" *Women's Studies International Forum* 10.1 (1987): 33–40.

Diedrich, Maria. " 'My Love Is Black as Yours Is Fair': Premarital Love and Sexuality in the Antebellum Slave Narrative." *Phylon* 47.3 (1986): 238–47.

Doherty, Thomas. "Harriet Jacobs' Narrative Strategies: *Incidents in the Life of a Slave Girl.*" *Southern Literary Journal* 19.1 (1986): 79–91.

Franklin, H. Bruce. " 'A' is for Afro-American: A Primer

on the Study of American Literature." *Minnesota Review,* n.s., 5 (1975): 53–64.

———. *The Victim as Criminal and Artist: Literature from the American Prison.* New York: Oxford University Press, 1978. 22–34, 50, 61, 108, 249.

Gates, Henry Louis,.Jr. "To Be Raped, Bred or Abused" [Review]. *New York Times Book Review* (12 Nov. 1987): 12.

Gwin, Minrose C. *Black and White Women of the Old South: The Peculiar Sisterhood in American Literature.* Knoxville: University of Tennessee Press, 1985. 7, 50–56, 59–65, 68, 132, 146, 154, 158, 160, 172–73.

———. "Green-eyed Monsters of the Slavocracy: Jealous Mistresses in Two Slave Narratives." In *Conjuring: Black Women, Fiction, and Literary Tradition.* Marjorie Pryse and Hortense J. Spillers, eds. Bloomington: Indiana University Press, 1985. 39–52.

Hewitt, Nancy A. *Women's Activism and Social Change: Rochester, New York, 1822–72.* Ithaca, NY: Cornell University Press, 1984. 42, 193, 214.

Hooks, Bell. *Ain't I a Woman: Black Women and Feminism.* Boston: South End Press, 1981.

"Linda." *Christian Recorder* (11 Jan. 1862): 6.

Loggins, 288, 434.

New England Anti-Slavery Convention. *Liberator* (5 June 1863). *(BAP).*

Niemtzow, Annette. "The Problematic of Self in Autobiography: The Example of the Slave Narrative." *The Art of the Slave Narrative: Original Essays in Criticism and Theory.* Macomb: Western Illinois University, 1982.

Porter, Dorothy B. "Women Activists, Wives, Intellectuals, Mothers, and Artists." *Candidates for Rediscovery: The*

Boston Version. Proceedings of a Symposium at the Afro-American Studies Center, Boston University, 12 April 1975. 76–84. Boston: Afro-American Studies Center, Boston University, 1975.

Shockley, 96–99.

White, Deborah Gray. *Ar'n't I a Woman? Female Slaves in the Plantation South*. New York: W. W. Norton, 1985. 41, 42–43, 71, 74, 93–94, 95, 96, 117, 146, 155.

Yellin, Jean Fagan. "Text and Contexts of Harriet Jacobs' *Incidents in the Life of a Slave Girl: Written by Herself*." In *The Slave's Narrative*. Charles T. Davis and Henry Louis Gates, Jr., eds. New York: Oxford University Press, 1985. 262–82.

———. *Women and Sisters: The Antislavery Feminists in American Culture*. New Haven: Yale University Press, 1990. Chapter 4.

———. "Written by Herself: Harriet Jacobs' Slave Narrative." *American Literature* 53.3 (1981): 479–86.

Papers in Collections

Incidents in the Life of a Slave Girl. Boston: published for the Author, 1861. Author's presentation copy to R. Smith. Library Company of Philadelphia.

Jacobs, Harriet. Letter to Ednah Dow Cheney. Sophia Smith Collection, Smith College.

———. Letter to R. Smith. Library Company of Philadelphia.

Amelia Etta Hall Johnson (1858–1922)

Writings by

Clarence and Corinne; or, God's Way. Philadelphia: American Baptist Publication Society, 1890.

Clarence and Corinne; or, God's Way. Introduction by Hortense J. Spillers. New York: Oxford University Press, 1988.

The Hazeley Family. Philadelphia: American Baptist Publication Society, 1894.

The Hazeley Family. Introduction by Barbara Christian. New York: Oxford University Press, 1988.

Martina Meriden; or, What Is My Motive? Philadelphia: American Baptist Publication Society, 1901.

Anthologies

Shockley, 165–70.

Writings about

Dann, 67.

Majors, 210, 216.

Pegues, A. W. *Our Baptist Ministers and Schools*. Springfield, MA: Wiley & Co., 1892.

Penn, 422–25.

Robinson, William H., Jr., ed. *Early Black American Prose*. Dubuque, IA: William C. Brown Company Publishers, 1971. xvii.

Rush, 422–23.

Scruggs, 116–19.

Schockley, 162–65.

Watson, Carole McAlpine. *Prologue: The Novels of Black American Women, 1891–1965*. Westport, CT: Greenwood Press, 1985.

Maggie Pogue Johnson

Writings by

Thoughts for Idle Hours. Roanoke, VA: The Stone Printing and Manufacturing Co., [c.1915].

Virginia Dreams: Lyrics for the Idle Hour. Tales of the Time Told in Rhyme. N.p.: John M. Leonard, 1910.

Anthologies

Virginia Dreams: Lyrics for the Idle Hour. Tales of the Time Told in Rhyme. In *Collected Black Women's Poetry.* Joan R. Sherman, ed. Vol. 4. New York: Oxford University Press, 1988.

Elizabeth Keckley (c.1818?1824?–1907)

Writings by

Behind the Scenes. Or, Thirty Years a Slave, and Four Years in the White House. New York: G. W. Carleton & Co., 1868; Arno Press, [c.1968].

Behind the Scenes. Or, Thirty Years a Slave, and Four Years in the White House. Buffalo, NY: Stansil and Lee, 1931.

Behind the Scenes. Or, Thirty Years a Slave, and Four Years in the White House. Introduction by James Olney. New York: Oxford University Press, 1988.

Anthologies

Barksdale, Richard, and Keneth Kinnamon. *Black Writers of America: A Comprehensive Anthology.* New York: Macmillan, 1972. 305–11.

Brown, Sterling A., Arthur P. Davis, and Ulysses Lee, eds. *The Negro Caravan: Writings by American Negroes.* New York: Dryden Press, 1941; Arno Press, 1970.

Davis, Arthur P., and Redding, J. Saunders, eds. *Cavalcade: Negro American Writing from 1760 to the Present.* Boston: Houghton Mifflin, 1971.

Katz, William L. *Eyewitness: The Negro in American History.* New York, Toronto, and London: Pitman, 1967. 215.

Loewenberg, Bert J., and Ruth Bogin, eds. *Black Women in Nineteenth-Century American Life: Their Words, Their Thoughts, Their Feelings*. University Park: Pennsylvania State University Press, 1976. 70–77.

Shockley, 139–43.

Writings about

Barksdale, Richard. "White Triangles, Black Circles." *CLA Journal* (June 1975): 465–76.

Brawley, *NG*, 121.

Brown, 147–49.

Cowden, Gerald Steffens. " 'My Dear Mr. W.': Mary Lincoln Writes to Alexander Williamson." *Journal of the Illinois State Historical Society* 76.1 (1983): 71–74.

DANB, 375–76.

Dannett, 1: 174–75.

Ebony (March 1970): 99.

First Annual Report of the Contraband Relief Association of the District of Columbia. 1863.

Fry, Smith D. "Lincoln Liked Her." *Minneapolis Register* (6 July 1901).

Gwin, Minrose C. *Black and White Women of the Old South: The Peculiar Sisterhood in American Literature*. Knoxville: University of Tennessee Press, 1985. 59–61, 65–68, 146, 160, 173.

———. "Green-eyed Monsters of the Slavocracy: Jealous Mistresses in Two Slave Narratives." In *Conjuring: Black Women, Fiction, and Literary Tradition*. Marjorie Pryse and Hortense J. Spillers, eds. Bloomington: Indiana University Press, 1985. 39–52.

Kickley, Bettsey [pseud.]. *Behind the Seams; by a Nigger Woman Who Took in Work from Mrs. Lincoln and Mrs. Davis. . .* [Parody]. New York, 1868.

Loggins, 259–61, 440.

Majors, 259–61.

Miers, Earl S., et al., eds. *Lincoln Day by Day: A Chronology, 1809–1865*. Washington, DC: Lincoln Sesquicentennial Commission, 1960.

Murray, Daniel. "Bibliographia Africania." *Voice of the Negro* (May 1904): 190

NAW, 2: 310–11.

Ostendorf, Lloyd. "Elizabeth Keckley's Lost Lincoln Relics." *Lincoln Herald* 71.1 (1969): 14–18.

Randall, Ruth Painter. *Mary Lincoln: Biography of a Marriage*. Boston: Little, Brown, 1953.

Rush, 452.

Shockley, 134–38.

Washington, John E. *They Knew Lincoln*. New York: E. P. Dutton, 1942.

Emma Dunham Kelley-Hawkins
[Emma Dunham Kelley; pseud. Forget-me-not]

Writings by

[Forget-me-not.] *Megda*. Boston: James H. Earle, 1891, 1892.

[———.] *Megda*. Introduction by Molly Hite. New York: Oxford University Press, 1988.

Four Girls at Cottage City. Boston: James H. Earle, 1898.

Four Girls at Cottage City. Introduction by Deborah E. McDowell. New York: Oxford University Press, 1988.

Anthologies

Shockley, 178–80.

Writings about

Robinson, William H., Jr., ed. *Early Black American Prose.*
Dubuque, IA: William C. Brown Company Publishers,
1971. xvii.

Shockley, 176–78.

Watson, Carole McAlpine. *Prologue: The Novels of Black
American Women, 1891–1965.* Westport, CT: Greenwood Press, 1985.

Jarena Lee (1783–?)

Writings by

*Life and Religious Experience of Jarena Lee, A Coloured Lady,
Giving an Account of Her Call to Preach.* Philadelphia:
printed and published for the Author, 1836.

*Religious Experience and Journal of Mrs. Jarena Lee, Giving
an Account of Her Call to Preach the Gospel.* Philadelphia:
printed for the Author, 1849.

Anthologies

Andrews, William L., ed. *Sisters of the Spirit: Three Black
Women's Autobiographies of the Nineteenth Century.* Bloomington: Indiana University Press, 1986.

Loewenberg, Bert J., and Ruth Bogin, eds. *Black Women in
Nineteenth-Century American Life: Their Words, Their
Thoughts, Their Feelings.* University Park: Pennsylvania
State University Press, 1976. 135–41.

Mason, Mary Grimley, and Carol Hurd Green, eds. *Jour-
neys: Autobiographical Writings by Women.* Boston: G. K.
Hall, [c.1979].

Porter, Dorothy, ed. *Early Negro Writing*. Boston: Beacon
    Press, 1971. 494–514.
*Religious Experience and Journal of Mrs. Jarena Lee, Giving
    an Account of Her Call to Preach the Gospel*. In *Spiritual
    Narratives*. Introduction by Sue E. Houchins. New York:
    Oxford University Press, 1988.
Shockley, 44.

Writings about

Foster, Frances Smith. "Adding Color and Contour to Early
    American Self-Portraitures: Autobiographical Writings
    of Afro-American Women." In *Conjuring: Black Women,
    Fiction, and Literary Tradition*. Marjorie Pryse and Hor-
    tense J. Spillers, eds. Bloomington: Indiana University
    Press, 1985. 25–38.
———. "Neither Auction Block nor Pedestal: The Life and
    Religious Experience of Jarena Lee, a Coloured Lady."
    New York Literary Forum 12–13 (1984): 143–69.
Loggins, 229, 437.
McMahon, Jean, ed. *Gifts of Power: The Writings of Rebecca
    Jackson, Black Visionary, Shaker Eldress*. Amherst: Uni-
    versity of Massachusetts Press, 1981.
Payne, Daniel Alexander. *History of the African Methodist
    Episcopal Church*. C. S. Smith, ed. Nashville: Publishing
    House of the A.M.E. Sunday-school Union, 1891.
Shockley, 41–43.

Charlotte E. Linden [Mrs. Henry Linden] (1859–?)

Writings by

Autobiography and Poems. 3rd Edition. Springfield, OH:
    n.p., n.d.

Scraps of Time; Poems by Mrs. Henry Linden. Springfield, OH: n.p., n.d.

Anthologies

Autobiography and Poems. In *Collected Black Women's Poetry*. Joan R. Sherman, ed. Vol. 4. New York: Oxford University Press, 1988.

Adella Hunt Logan

Writings by

Methods of Restraining Pre-Natal and Hereditary Influences [Pamphlet]. Atlanta: Atlanta University, 1897.

"What Are the Causes of the Great Mortality among the Negroes in the Cities of the South, and How Is That Mortality to Be Lessened?" Culp, 199–202.

"Woman Suffrage." *Colored American Magazine* (Sept. 1905): 487–89.

Writings about

Alexander, Adele Logan. "Adella and Ruth: A Granddaughter's Story." *Sage: A Scholarly Journal on Black Women* 1.2 (1984): 32–33.

———. "School Days, School Days: Discovering My Grandmother, Adella Hunt Logan." *Journal of the Afro-American Historical and Genealogical Society* 6.2 (1985): 65–73.

Culp, 199.

Dannett, 1: 283.

"Methods of Restraining Pre-Natal and Hereditary Influences" [Review]. *Southern Workman* (Oct. 1897): 206–7.

Woman's Journal (4 July 1903).

Helena Arkansas Mason

Writings by

The Lord's Prayer in Poetry. Hannibal, MO: n.p., 1910.

Victoria Earle Matthews [Victoria Earle] (1861–1907)

Writings by

Aunt Lindy: A Story Founded on Real Life. New York: J. J. Little & Co., 1893.

The Awakening of the Afro-American Woman; An Address Delivered at the Annual Convention of the Society of Christian Endeavor, San Francisco, July 11th, 1897. Brooklyn, NY: n.p., [1897?].

Black-belt Diamonds: Gems from the Speeches, Addresses and Talks to Students of Booker T. Washington. Victoria E. Matthews, ed. New York: Fortune & Scott, 1898; Negro Universities Press, 1969.

"Cedar Hill and Its Master." *Woman's Era* (Nov. 1894): 2–4.

"Dangers Encountered by Southern Girls in Northern Cities." *Hampton Negro Conference. Number II* (July 1898). Hampton, VA: Hampton Institute Press, 1898–1903. 62–69.

"An Explanation." *Woman's Era* (May 1896): 7–8.

"Greeting." *Woman's Era* (Nov. 1894): 2.

"Harriet Tubman." *Woman's Era* (June 1896): 8.

"Harriet Tubman. *Woman's Era* Eminent Women Series." *Woman's Era* (July 1896): 3.

Letter. *Woman's Era* (1 May 1894): 4.

"Memoranda of 'the Conference Committee' of the National Federation, the National League, and the Atlanta Congress." *Woman's Era* (Feb. 1896): 3–4.

"New York." *Woman's Era* (May 1895): 1–2; (June 1895): 2–3; (July 1895): 2–3.

"Note on the Atlanta 'Lynch Law Resolution.' " *Woman's Era* (Feb. 1896): 9.

"An Open Appeal to Our Women for Organization." *Woman's Era* (Jan. 1897): 2–3.

"Open Letter from Chairman of Ex. Com. of N.F.A.-A.W." *Woman's Era* (June 1896): 7.

"Suggestions of Committee on Domestic Science." *Hampton Negro Conference. Number II* (July 1898). Hampton, VA: Hampton Institute Press, 1898–1903.

"Thomas Clarkson's Seal." *Woman's Era* (Aug. 1896): 4.

"The Value of Race Literature: An Address Delivered at the First Congress of Colored Women, Boston, Massachusetts, 1895." Afterword by Fred Miller Robinson. *Massachusetts Review* 27.2 (Summer 1986): 169–91.

"The Value of Race Literature: An Address Delivered at the First Congress of Colored Women of the United States, at Boston, Massachusetts, July 30th, 1895." [Boston? 1895?]

"Zelika: A Story." *A.M.E. Church Review* 9 (1892–1893): 72–78.

Anthologies

Robinson, William H., Jr., ed. *Early Black American Prose.* Dubuque, IA: William C. Brown Company Publishers, 1971. 159–64.

Shockley, 184–89.

Writings about

Brown, 208–16.
Bullock, 98, 192, 310.
DANB, 428–29.
Dann, 63–64.

Dannett, 1: 289.

Davis, 21–23, 232–33.

Dunnigan, Alice E. "Early History of Negro Women in Journalism." *Negro History Bulletin* 28 (Summer 1965): 178.

Frazier, Susan Elizabeth. "Mrs. William E. Matthews." *Woman's Era* (1 May 1894): 1.

Gould, Medora M. "Literature Department." *Woman's Era* (Aug. 1894): 14.

Majors, 211–13.

Mossell, 15–16, 61–63.

NAW, 510–11.

Osofsky, Gilbert. *Harlem: The Making of a Ghetto: Negro New York, 1890–1930*. New York: Harper & Row, 1966.

———. "Progressivism and the Negro: New York, 1900–1915." *American Quarterly* 16.2 (1964): Part 1, 153–68.

Penn, 375–77.

Scruggs, 30.

Shockley, 181–83.

Wesley, 9, 18–19, 26, 32, 35–38, 43, 88, 208.

"Working Girl's Home." *Christian Recorder* (10 Apr. 1902): 3.

Papers in Collections

Aunt Lindy; A Story Founded on Real Life. Author's presentation copy to Hon. John M. Langston, 1893. New York: J. J. Little & Co., 1893. Fisk University.

Adah Isaacs Menken (1835–1868)

Writings by

Infelicia. Philadelphia: J. B. Lippincott, 1868, 1870, 1873; London: Chatto & Windus, Piccadilly, 1888.

Anthologies

Infelicia. In *Collected Black Women's Poetry*. Joan R. Sherman, ed. Vol. 1. New York: Oxford University Press, 1988.

Writings about

Barclay, George Lippard. *The Life and Remarkable Career of Adah Isaacs Menken, the Celebrated Actress*. Philadelphia: Barclay & Co., 1868.

Bontemps, Arna Wendell. *They Seek a City*. Garden City, NY: Doubleday, Doran and Co., 1945.

Deltwyn, Agnes Proctor. *Echoes from Shadow-land*. New York: Alliance, 1900. Republished as *Believest Thou This*. Chicago: M. A. Donahue, 1913.

Falk, Bernard. *The Naked Lady; or, Storm over Adah*. London: Hutchinson & Co., 1934.

Jenkins, William D. "We Were Both in the Photographs: I. Adler and Adah I." *The Baker Street Journal: An Irregular Quarterly of Sherlockiana* (March 1986): 6–16.

Kendall, John S. "The World's Delight: The Story of Adah Isaacs Menken." *Louisiana Historical Quarterly* (Jan.–Oct. 1938).

Krich, John F. "The Amiable Lady Charms the Iron City: Adah Isaacs Menken Charms Pittsburgh." *Western Pennsylvania Historical Magazine* 51.3 (1968): 259–78.

Lesser, Allen. *Enchanting Rebel (The Secret of Adah Isaacs Menken)*. New York: Jewish Book Guild, 1947; Beechhurst Press, [c.1947].

Lewis, Paul. *Queen of the Plaza; a Biography of Adah Isaacs Menken*. New York: Funk & Wagnalls, [c.1964].

Mankowitz, Wolf. *Mazeppa: The Lives, Loves and Legends of Adah Isaccs Menken*. New York: Stein and Day, 1982.

Marberry, M. M. " 'The Naked Lady,' or Don't Take Your Sister to Astley's." *Horizon* 6.1 (1964): 112–18.

Miller, Joaquin. *Adah Isaacs Menken*. Ysleta, TX: E. B. Hill, 1934.

NAW, 2: 526–29.

Palmer, Pamela Lynn. "Adah Isaacs Menken: From Texas to Paris." In *Legendary Ladies of Texas*. Francis Edward Abernethy, ed. Dallas: E-Heart, 1981.

Pegnato, Lisa. "Produced in Magnificent Style." *Civil War Times Illustrated* 24.10 (1986): 36–43, 49.

Swinburne, Algernon Charles. *Adah Isaacs Menken, a Fragment of Autobiography*. London: printed for private circulation only, 1917. [Beinecke Library, Yale University.]

———. *In the Album of Adah Menken*. London: R. H. Shepherd, 1883.

Sarah A. Mix [Mrs. Edward Mix]

Writings by

In Memory of Departed Worth: The Life of Mrs. Edward Mix, Written by Herself in 1880. Torrington, CT: Press of Register Printing Co., 1884.

Lizelia Augusta Jenkins Moorer

Writings by

Prejudice Unveiled and Other Poems. Boston: Roxburgh Publishing Co., 1907.

"Refining Fire." *Voice of the Negro* (Feb. 1904): 74.

Anthologies

Prejudice Unveiled and Other Poems. In *Collected Black Women's Poetry.* Joan R. Sherman, ed. Vol. 3. New York: Oxford University Press, 1988.

Writings about

Wesley, 328, 331.

Gertrude E. H. Bustill Mossell [Mrs. Nathan F. Mossell; E. H. Bustill] (1855–1948)

Writings by

Little Dansie's One Day at Sabbath School. Germantown, PA: Philander V. Baugh, [19?].

The Work of the Afro-American Woman. Philadelphia: George S. Ferguson Company, 1894, 1898, 1908; Freeport, NY: Books for Libraries Press, 1971.

The Work of the Afro-American Woman. Introduction by Joanne Braxton. New York: Oxford University Press, 1988.

"Baby Bertha's Temperance Lesson." *Christian Recorder* (8 Jan. 1885): 1.

"Beautiful Things." *Christian Recorder* (12 Sept. 1878): 1.

"The Colored Woman in Verse." *A.M.E. Church Review* 2 (1885): 60–67.

"Earth's Sorrows." *Christian Recorder* (12 Feb. 1885): 1.

"Mizeriah Johnson: Her Arisings and Shinings." *Colored American Magazine* (Jan.–Feb. 1902): 229–33.

"The National Afro-American Council." *Colored American Magazine* (Aug. 1901): 291–305.

"Only." *Christian Recorder* (19 Sept. 1878).

"The Open Court." *Woman's Era* (May 1895): 19–20; (June 1895): 13; (Aug. 1895): 25.

"Opinion of Mrs. N. F. Mossell." Penn, 487–91.

"The Power of the Press." In *Afro-American Encyclopedia.* . . . James T. Haley, comp. Nashville: Haley & Florida, 1895. 167–69.

"The Story of a Life." *Christian Recorder* (10 Nov. 1881): 1.

"Tell the North That We Are Rising." *Christian Recorder* (15 Aug. 1889): 1.

"That Reminds Me." *Christian Recorder* (15 Dec. 1881): 1.

"Three Glimpses of Mission Work." *Christian Recorder* (27 Jan. 1881): 1.

"Words." *Christian Recorder* (5 Dec. 1878): 1.

Anthologies

Ammons, Elizabeth, comp. *Short Fiction by Black Women, 1900–1920.* New York: Oxford University Press, 1991.

Writings about

Bullock, 98, 155, 192.

DANB, 457.

Dann, 61–62, 364–65.

Dannett, 1: 295.

Dunnigan, Alice E. "Early History of Negro Women in Journalism." *Negro History Bulletin* (Summer 1965): 178.

Giddings, Paula. *When and Where I Enter: The Impact of Black Women on Race and Sex in America.* New York: William Morrow, 1984.

Lee, Mary E. "To Mrs. N. F. Mossell on Her Book, *The Work of the Afro-American Woman*." *Christian Recorder* (10 Jan. 1895): 1.

Majors, 129.

Penn, 405–7.
Scruggs, 23–25.
Sherman, 242.
Wesley, 9–10, 59.
"The Work of the Afro-American Woman" [Review]. *Christian Recorder* (10 Jan. 1895): 2.

Susan Paul (1809–1841)

Writings by

Memoir of James Jackson, an Attentive and Obedient Student. Boston: James Loring, 1835. [First published *Liberator* (1 Aug. 1835): 22; republished (4 March 1837): 48].

[Paul, Susan, et al. (Massachusetts Anti-Slavery Women).] "Regarding the Massachusetts Anti-Slavery Fair." *National Anti-Slavery Standard* (6 May 1841). *(BAP)*.

———. "To the Friends of the Anti-Slavery Cause in Massachusetts." *Liberator* (13 March 1840). *(BAP)*.

"Temptation Resisted. Communicated by Miss Susan Paul of Boston." *American Anti-Slavery Almanac for 1837.* Vol. 2. Boston: N. Southard and D. K. Hitchcock, 1837. 42. [Illustrated.]

Letters

Letter to the Editor [William Lloyd Garrison]. *Liberator* (5 Apr. 1834): 55.

Letter to William Lloyd Garrison. 1 Apr. 1834. Anti-Slavery Collections, Boston Public Library. *(BAP)*.

Letter to A. Morrill. *Liberator* (13 Aug. 1836). *(BAP)*.

"Reply to the Children of the Union Evangelical Sabbath School of Amesbury and Salisbury" [Letter]. *Liberator* (13 Aug. 1836): 130. *(BAP)*.

[With Anne C. Smith, Mary Stockbridge, and Mary Williams.] Letter to Ladies' Negro's Friend Society, for Birmingham, West Bromwich, Wednesburg, Walsall, and Their Respective Neighborhoods, Established 1825. Boston. 2 Apr. 1833. *Monthly Report*. Birmingham: B. Hudson, 1834. 32–35.

Writings about

Bracey, John H., comp. *Blacks in the Abolitionist Movement*. Belmont, CA: Wadsworth Publishing Co., 1971.

Juvenile Concert (Program), ["S. Paul, Director"]. Cornell University, Anti-Slavery Pamphlets. *(BAP)*.

Loggins, 97.

Nell, William C. *Colored Patriots of the American Revolution*. Boston: Robert F. Wallcut, 1855; New York: Arno Press, 1968. 346–47, 351.

[Obituary.] *National Anti-Slavery Standard* (29 Apr. 1841): 187.

Porter, Dorothy B. "Women Activists, Wives, Intellectuals, Mothers, and Artists." In *Candidates for Rediscovery: The Boston Version*. Proceedings of a Symposium at the Afro-American Studies Center, Boston University, 12 Apr. 1975. 76–84. Boston: Afro-American Studies Center, Boston University, 1975.

Quarles, Benjamin. *Black Abolitionists*. New York: Oxford University Press, 1969. 27, 30, 31, 49, 94, 136.

"Report from the Treasurer of The New England Anti-Slavery Society." *Abolitionist* (Nov. 1833): 176.

Wesley, 4.

Letters

[Letter from N. N. to Joshua Levit regarding Susan Paul's *Juvenile Concert*.] *New York Evangelist* (25 Feb. 1837). *(BAP)*.

Morrill, A., et al. [Letter to Susan Paul.] *Liberator* (13 Aug. 1836). *(BAP)*.

Ann Plato (1820–?)

Writings by

Essays; Including Biographies and Miscellaneous Pieces, in Prose and Poetry. Hartford, CT.: printed for the Author, 1841.

Essays; Including Biographies and Miscellaneous Pieces, in Prose and Poetry. Introduction by Kenny J. Williams. New York: Oxford University Press, 1988.

"Lines on Visiting the Grave of a Venerated Friend." *Colored American* (5 Sept. 1840): 4.

Anthologies

Loewenberg, Bert J., and Ruth Bogin, eds. *Black Women in Nineteenth-Century American Life: Their Words, Their Thoughts, Their Feelings.* University Park: Pennsylvania State University Press, 1976. 174–80.

Robinson, William H., Jr., ed. *Early Black American Poets.* Dubuque, IA: William C. Brown Company Publishers, 1969. 113–20.

Shockley, 28–31.

Stetson, Erlene, ed. *Black Sister: Poetry by Black American Women, 1746–1980.* Bloomington: Indiana University Press, 1981. 43–46.

White, Newman Ivey, and Walter Clinton Jackson, eds. *An Anthology of Verse by American Negroes.* Durham, NC: Trinity College Press, 1924.

Writings about

Baker, Houston, Jr. *Long Black Song: Essays in Black American Literature and Culture.* Charlottesville: University Press of Virginia, 1972.

Loggins, 248–49, 397, 439.

Rush, 595–96.

Sherman, 33–34.

Shockley, 26–28.

White, David O. "Hartford's African Schools, 1830–1868." *Connecticut Historical Society Bulletin* (Apr. 1974): 47–53.

Eliza Potter

Writings by

A Hairdresser's Experience in High Life. Cincinnati: published for the Author, 1859.

A Hairdresser's Experience in High Life. Introduction by Sharon G. Dean. New York: Oxford University Press, 1991.

Writings about

Blassingame, John W. *Black New Orleans, 1860–1880*. Chicago: University of Chicago Press, 1973. 17, 20, 21.

Census Population Schedule, Ohio. City of Cincinnati, Hamilton County, Ward 14, 1860. 373.

Dabney, Wendell Phillips. *Cincinnati's Colored Citizens: Historical, Sociological, and Biographical*. Cincinnati: the Author, 1926.

Harlow, Alvin Fay. *The Serene Cincinnatians*. New York: E. P. Dutton, 1950. 172.

Nancy Gardner Prince (1799–?)

Writings by

A Narrative of the Life and Travels of Mrs. Nancy Prince. Boston: the Author, 1850. 2nd Edition. Boston: the

Author [Wm. A. Hall, Printer], 1853. 3rd Edition. Boston: the Author, 1856.

The West Indies: Being a Description of the Islands, Progress of Christianity, Education, and Liberty among the Colored Population Generally. Boston: Dow & Jackson Printers, 1841.

Letters

Letter to William Lloyd Garrison. *Liberator* (17 Sept. 1841). *(BAP).*

Letter to n. n. *National Anti-Slavery Standard* (25 May 1843): 202.

Anthologies

Loewenberg, Bert J., and Ruth Bogin, eds. *Black Women in Nineteenth-Century American Life: Their Words, Their Thoughts, Their Feelings.* University Park: Pennsylvania State University Press, 1976. 201–18.

A Narrative of the Life and Travels of Mrs. Nancy Prince. In *Collected Black Women's Narratives.* Introduction by Anthony G. Barthelemy. New York: Oxford University Press, 1988.

Shockley, 52.

Writings about

Foster, Frances Smith. "Adding Color and Contour to Early American Self-Portraitures: Autobiographical Writings of Afro-American Women." In *Conjuring: Black Women, Fiction, and Literary Tradition.* Marjorie Pryse and Hortense J. Spillers, eds. Bloomington: Indiana University Press, 1985. 25–38.

Hilton, Thomas B. *Woman's Era* (Aug. 1894).

Liberator (8 March 1839).

Loggins, 229, 429, 437.

Shockley, 48–51.

Stanton, Elizabeth Cady, et al., eds. *History of Woman Suffrage*. New York: Fowler and Wells, 1881. 1: 384.

Wesley, Charles. *Prince Hall: Life and Legacy*. Washington, DC: United Supreme Council, Southern Jurisdiction, Prince Hall Affiliation, 1977.

Charlotte E. Ray (1850–1911)

Writings by

Sketch of the Life of Rev. Charles B. Ray. With Florence T. Ray and Henrietta C. Ray. New York: J. J. Little & Co., 1887.

Writings about

Alexander, Sadie T. M. "Women as Practitioners of Law in the United States." *National Bar Journal* (July 1941): 56–64.

Chicago Legal News (23 Oct. 1897): 80.

Hannaford, Phebe. *Daughters of America*. Augusta, ME: True and Co., 1882.

Howard University *Annual Report*. Washington, DC: Howard University, 1870.

Howard University *Catalogue*. Washington, DC: Howard University, 1869–1872.

Hughes, Joyce Anne. "The Black Portia." *Crisis* 82.5 (1975): 167–72.

Majors, 183–84.

NAW, 3: 121–22.

New National Era (20 Feb. 1872).

Stanton, Elizabeth Cady, et al., eds. *History of Woman Suffrage*. New York: Fowler and Wells, 1881. 3: 19.

Thomas, Dorothy. *Women Lawyers in the United States.* New
   York: Scarecrow Press, 1957.
Wesley, 8–9.
Woman's Journal (25 May 1872): 161.

Florence T. Ray (c.1849–1916)

Writings by

Sketch of the Life of Rev. Charles B. Ray. With Charlotte E.
   Ray and Henrietta C. Ray. New York: J. J. Little &
   Co., 1887.

Writings about

Majors, 179–80.
Mossell, 81.
Wesley, 66.

Henrietta Cordelia Ray (c.1850–1916)

Writings by

*Commemoration Ode on Lincoln: Written for the Occasion of the
   Unveiling of the Freed-Man's Monument in Memory of
   Abraham Lincoln, April 14, 1876.* New York: J. J. Little
   & Co., 1893.
Poems. New York: Grafton, 1910.
Sketch of the Life of Rev. Charles B. Ray. With Charlotte E.
   Ray and Florence T. Ray. New York: J. J. Little & Co.,
   1887.
Sonnets. New York: J. J. Little & Co., 1893.
"Charles Lamb." *A.M.E. Church Review* (July 1891): 1–9.
"Compensation." Mossell, 80.
"Dante." *A.M.E. Church Review* (Jan. 1885): 25.
Douglass, Frederick. *Oration by Frederick Douglass, delivered*

*on the occasion of the unveiling of the Freedmen's Monument
in memory of Abraham Lincoln, in Lincoln Park, Washington, D.C., April 14, 1876 with an Appendix* [includes
poem by Ray]. Washington, DC: Gibson Brothers,
Printers, 1876. 20–21.

"In Memoriam. Frederick Douglass." *Woman's Era* (Apr.
1895): 2–3.

"In Memoriam." Mossell, 81.

"Matin Idyll." *A.M.E. Church Review* 2 (1885–1886): 50.

"Niobe." *A.M.E. Church Review* 10 (1893–1894): 171.

"Quebec." *A.M.E. Church Review* 2 (1885–1886): 380.

"Sunset Picture." Mossell, 80–81.

Anthologies

Kerlin, Robert, ed. *Negro Poets and Their Poems.* Washington, DC: Associated Publishers, 1923.

Poems. In *Collected Black Women's Poetry.* Joan R. Sherman,
ed. Vol. 3. New York: Oxford University Press, 1988.

Robinson, William H., Jr., ed. *Early Black American Poets.*
Dubuque, IA: William C. Brown Company Publishers,
1969. 138–44.

Shockley, 330–32.

Stetson, Erlene, ed. *Black Sister: Poetry by Black American
Women, 1746–1980.* Bloomington: Indiana University
Press, 1981.

White, Newman Ivey, and Walter Clinton Jackson, eds. *An
Anthology of Verse by American Negroes.* New York: New
York University Press, 1972.

Wilson, Joseph Thomas. *Emancipation: Its Course and Progress, from 1481 B.C. to A.D. 1875.* Hampton, VA: Normal
School, 1881, 1882.

Writings about

Baker, Houston, Jr. *Long Black Song: Essays in Black American Literature and Culture.* Charlottesville: University Press of Virginia, 1972.

Brawley, *NG,* 68.

Brown, 169–75.

Bullock, 98.

Dann, 28.

Fauset, Jessie. *"Poems"* [Review]. *Crisis* 4 (1912): 183.

Flint, Allen. "Black Response to Colonel Shaw." *Phylon* 45.3 (1984): 210–19.

Frazier, Susan Elizabeth. "Some Afro-American Women of Mark." *A.M.E. Church Review* 9 (Apr. 1892): 378–86.

Hull, Gloria T. "Black Women Poets from Wheatley to Walker." *Negro American Literature Forum* 9 (1975): 91–96.

Mossell, 13, 15, 16, 79, 81.

"Our Literary Women." *Lancet* 19 (Oct. 1885): 1.

Porter, Dorothy. "The Organized Educational Activities of Negro Literary Societies, 1828–1846." *Journal of Negro Education* (1936). Reprinted in August Meier and Elliot Rudwick, eds. *The Making of Black America: Essays in Negro Life and History.* 2 vols. New York: Atheneum, 1969. 1: 276–88.

Rush, 613.

Sherman, xviii, xix, xxiv, xxvi, 129–35.

Shockley, 327–29.

Wesley, 4.

Sarah Parker Remond (1826–1894)

Writings by

The Negroes and Anglo-Africans as Freedmen and Soldiers. London: Emily Faithful, 1864.

"Colonization." *Freedman* (1 Feb. 1866): 162–63.

"Lecture on American Slavery by a Coloured Lady" [Paraphrase of Speech given by Remond]. *Warrington Times* (29 Jan. 1859). *(BAP)*.

"Miss Remond's First Lecture in Dublin." *London Anti-Slavery Advocate* (2 Apr. 1859).

"The Negroes in the United States of America" [Dorothy Porter, ed.]. *Journal of Negro History* (Apr. 1942): 216–18.

"New Year's Soirée of the Total Abstinence Society." *Scotsman* (2 Jan. 1861). *(BAP)*.

"Slavery in America" [Contains Excerpts and a Quotation of Remond from Matthew Davenport Hill, *Our Exemplars, Poor and Rich*]. *Derbyshire Courier* (13 Apr. 1861). *(BAP)*.

[Remond, Sarah Parker, et al.] "The Twenty-Eighth National Anti-Slavery Subscription Anniversary." *Liberator* (27 Dec. 1861). *(BAP)*.

———. "The Twenty-Ninth National Anti-Slavery Subscription Anniversary." *Liberator* (12 Dec. 1862). *(BAP)*.

Letters

"Disabilities of American Persons of Colour" [Letter to George Mifflin Dallas]. *Liberator* (17 Feb. 1860). *(BAP)*.

Letter to the American Minister. *National Anti-Slavery Standard* (28 Jan. 1860): 2.

Letter to Maria Weston Chapman. 6 Oct. 1859. Anti-Slavery Collections, Boston Public Library. *(BAP)*.

Letter to Mr. Dallas. *Liberator* (17 Feb. 1860): 25.

Letter to the Editor. *National Anti-Slavery Standard* (3 Nov. 1866): 2.

Letter to the Editor of the *London Daily News*. *Liberator* (22 Dec. 1865): 202.

Letter to Abby Kelley Foster. 21 Dec. 1858. Foster Papers, American Antiquarian Society. *(BAP)*.

Letter to a friend [from *London Anti-Slavery Advocate*]. *Liberator* (19 Nov. 1858): 186. *(BAP)*.

Letter to Mr. Garrison. *Liberator* (11 Nov. 1864): 183. *(BAP)*.

Letter to Mrs. William Ives. 28 Dec. 1858. Salem Female Anti-Slavery Society Papers, Essex Institute, Salem, MA. *(BAP)*.

Letter to Samuel May, Jr. 18 Oct. 1860. Anti-Slavery Collections, Boston Public Library. *(BAP)*.

Letter to Benjamin Moran. *National Anti-Slavery Standard* (28 Jan. 1860): 2.

Letter to Benjamin Moran. *National Principia* (28 Jan. 1860). *(BAP)*.

Letter to Benjamin Moran. *Liberator* (17 Feb. 1860): 25.

Letter to n. n. *Liberator* (20 Jan. 1860): 9.

Letter to n. n. *National Anti-Slavery Standard* (21 Jan. 1860): 4.

Letter to n. n. *National Anti-Slavery Standard* (3 Nov. 1866): 2.

Letter to n. n. *National Anti-Slavery Standard* (10 Oct. 1868): 2.

Letter to Wendell Phillips. 4 May 1860. Crawford Blagden Collection of the Papers of Wendell Phillips, Harvard University. *(BAP)*.

"Negro Character" [Letter to the Editor of the *London Daily News*]. *Liberator* (22 Dec. 1865). *(BAP)*.

"Slavery Still at Its Dirty Work" [Letter to the Editor of the *Scottish Press*]. *British Friend* (Jan. 1860). *(BAP)*.

Anthologies

Loewenberg, Bert J., and Ruth Bogin, eds. *Black Women in Nineteenth-Century American Life: Their Words, Their Thoughts, Their Feelings*. University Park: Pennsylvania State University Press, 1976. 222–33.

Writings about

"Abolition of Slavery in America." *Non-Conformist* (19 June 1861). *(BAP)*.

American and Foreign Anti-Slavery Society Annual Report (1853): 154.

"American Slavery." *Manchester Weekly Times* (17 Sept. 1859). *(BAP)*.

"American Slavery." *Warrington Standard* (29 Jan. 1859). *(BAP)*.

"American Slavery and African Colonisation." *Anti-Slavery Advocate* (1 Nov. 1859). *(BAP)*.

"Anti-Slavery Convention at Rochester, New York, February 10th and 11th." *National Anti-Slavery Standard* (21 Feb. 1857). *(BAP)*.

"Anti-Slavery Meeting in Manchester." *Non-Conformist* (21 Sept. 1859). *(BAP)*.

Bogin, Ruth. "Sara Parker Remond: Black Abolitionist from Salem." *Essex Institute Historical Collections* (Apr. 1974): 120–50.

DANB, 522–23.

Dannett, 1: 87, 88, 112–13.

Falk, Leslie A. "Black Abolitionist Doctors and Healers, 1810–1885." *Bulletin of the History of Medicine* 54.2 (1980): 258–72.

Forten, Charlotte. *A Free Negro in the Slave Era, The Journal of Charlotte L. Forten.* Ray Allen Billington, ed. New York: Dryden Press, 1953; Collier Books, 1961.

"Great Anti-Slavery Meeting in Wakefield." *Frederick Douglass' Paper* (17 Feb. 1860). *(BAP)*.

"The Lecture at the Lion Hotel." *Warrington Times* (4 Feb. 1859). *(BAP)*.

"Lecture by a Lady of Colour on American Slavery." *Scotsman* (6 Oct. 1860). *(BAP)*.

"Lecture on American Slavery." *Leeds Intelligencer* (24 Dec. 1859). *(BAP)*.

"Lecture on American Slavery by a Coloured Lady" [Paraphrase of Speech given by Remond]. *Warrington Times* (29 Jan. 1859). *(BAP)*.

"Lecture on Total Abstinence." *Dumfries and Galloway Courier* (22 Jan. 1861). *(BAP)*.

"Lectures on American Slavery." *Anti-Slavery Reporter* (July 1859). *(BAP)*.

"Leeds Young Men's Anti-Slavery Society." *Leeds Mercury* (24 Dec. 1859). *(BAP)*.

Liberator (7 Nov. 1856): 179; (11 Feb. 1859): 22–23; (18 Feb. 1859): 27; (8 Apr. 1859): 54; (20 May 1859): 77; (22 Dec. 1865): 202.

"Miss Remond at Bury." *Anti-Slavery Advocate* (1 Nov. 1859). *(BAP)*.

"Miss Remond in Bristol." *Anti-Slavery Advocate* (1 Sept. 1859). *(BAP)*.

"Miss Remond in Bristol." *Anti-Slavery Advocate* (1 Oct. 1859). *(BAP)*.

"Miss Remond in Edinburgh" [from the *Scotsman*]. *Anti-Slavery Advocate* (1 Nov. 1860). *(BAP)*.

"Miss Remond in Manchester." *Anti-Slavery Advocate* (1 Oct. 1859). *(BAP)*.

"Miss Remond's Anti-Slavery Lecture." *Liberator* (11 March 1859). *(BAP)*.

"Miss Remond's First Lecture in Dublin." *Anti-Slavery Advocate* (2 Apr. 1859). (*BAP*).

"Miss Remond's Lecture." Soulby's *Ulverston Advertiser* (19 Jan. 1861). *(BAP)*.

"Miss Remond's Second Lecture on Slavery." *Warrington Standard* (5 Feb. 1859). *(BAP)*.

"Miss Sarah P. Remond in London." *Anti-Slavery Advocate* (1 July 1859). *(BAP)*.

National Principia (28 Jan. 1860).

NAW, 136–37.

Porter, Dorothy B. "Sarah Parker Remond, Abolitionist and Physician." *Journal of Negro History* (July 1935): 287–93.

———. "The Remonds of Salem, Massachusetts: A Nineteenth-Century Family Revisited." *Proceedings of the American Antiquarian Society* 95.2 (1985): 259–95.

Quarles, Benjamin. *Black Abolitionists*. New York: Oxford University Press, 1969.

———. "Ministers Without Portfolio." *Journal of Negro History* (Jan. 1954): 27–42.

Sillen, Samuel. *Women Against Slavery*. New York: Masses & Mainstream, 1955.

"Slavery in America." *Derbyshire Courier* (13 Apr. 1861). *(BAP)*.

Stanton, Elizabeth Cady, et al., eds. *History of Woman Suffrage*. New York: Fowler and Wells, 1881. 1: 668.

"The Twenty-Seventh National Anti-Slavery Anniversary." *Anti-Slavery Advocate* (1 Nov. 1860). *(BAP)*.

"The Twenty-Sixth National Anti-Slavery Subscription Anniversary." *Anti-Slavery Advocate* (1 Sept. 1859). *(BAP)*.

Wallace, Sarah A., and Frances E. Gillespie, eds. *The Journal of Benjamin Moran, 1857–1865*. Chicago: University of Chicago Press, 1948–1949.

Wesley, 5.

Woodson, Carter G. *The Education of the Negro Prior to 1861*. New York: Arno Press, 1968.

Wyman, Lillie Buffum Chace, and Arthur Crawford Wyman. *Elizabeth Buffum Chace*. Boston: W. B. Clarke Co., 1914. 1: 196; 2: 42–43.

Letters

Chapman, Maria Weston. Letter to Sarah Parker Remond. 4 Sept. 1859. John B. and Mary A. Estlin Papers, Dr. Williams Library, London. *(BAP)*.

Moran, Benjamin. Letter to Sarah Remond. *Liberator* (17 Feb. 1860): 25.

———. Letter to Sarah Remond. *National Anti-Slavery Standard* (28 Jan. 1860): 2.

———. Letter to Sarah Remond. *National Principia* (28 Jan. 1860). *(BAP)*.

Mary Seacole (1800?–1899?)

Writings by

Wonderful Adventures of Mrs. Seacole in Many Lands. W.J.S., ed. London: James Blackwood, 1857.

Wonderful Adventures of Mrs. Seacole in Many Lands. Ziggi Alexander and Audrey Dewjee, eds. Bristol, England: Falling Wall Press, 1984.

Wonderful Adventures of Mrs. Seacole in Many Lands. Introduction by William L. Andrews. New York: Oxford University Press, 1988.

Letters

Letter to Lord Rokeby. Extract from *Daily Advertiser and Lawton's Commercial Gazette*. 10 Jan. 1857. [Vertical file on fiche] Schomburg Center, New York Public Library.

Writings about

"Mrs. Seacole in the Bankruptcy Court." Extract from *Daily Advertiser and Lawton's Commercial Gazette*. 9 Feb. 1857. [Vertical file on fiche] Schomburg Center, New York Public Library.

Phillips, T. S. *Mary Seacole (The Story of a Kingston Girl)*. [Kingston], Jamaica, 1932. No. 1 of a series, *Jamaicans Who Have Made Good*. [Vertical file on fiche] Schomburg Center, New York Public Library.

Scott, Thea. "The Identity of Mrs. Seacole: A Little Yellow Woman" [Letter to the Editor]. Extract from the *Gleaner* (5 Feb. 1938). Reprinted from *Sunday Times* [London] (16 Jan. [1938]). [Vertical file on fiche] Schomburg Center, New York Public Library.

Letters

Forrest, Sandford. Letter to the Editor. Extract from the *Gleaner* (9 Feb. 1938). [Vertical file on fiche] Schomburg Center, New York Public Library.

"Mrs. Mary Seacole" [Letter to the Editor from R. A. Wollcott]. *Gleaner* (27 July 1905). [Vertical file on fiche] Schomburg Center, New York Public Library.

Stewart, (Mrs.) K. "Jamaica's Florence Nightingale" [Letter to the Editor]. *Gleaner* (29 Aug. 1939). [Vertical file on fiche] Schomburg Center, New York Public Library.

Whitehorne, A. C. (Major). "Wore a dozen medals" [Letter to the Editor]. *Gleaner* (5 Feb. 1938). Reprinted from

Sunday Times [London] (16 Jan. [1938]). [Vertical file on fiche] Schomburg Center, New York Public Library.

Susan Isabella Lankford Shorter (1859–1912)

Writings by

Heroines of African Methodism. Xenia, OH: n.p., 1891.
"An Acrostic." *Christian Recorder* (13 Nov. 1890): 1.

Writings about

Brown, 205–7.
Bullock, 168.
Majors, 143–49.
Mossell, 16.
Scruggs, 162–64.
Wesley, 9.

Amanda Berry Smith (1837–1915)

Writings by

An Autobiography: The Story of the Lord's Dealings with Mrs. Amanda Smith, the Colored Evangelist; Containing an Account of Her Life Work of Faith, and Her Travels in America, England, Ireland, Scotland, India and Africa, as an Independent Missionary. Chicago: Meyer & Brother, 1893; The Christian Witness Co., 1921; Afro-Am Press, 1969.

An Autobiography: The Story of the Lord's Dealings with Mrs. Amanda Smith, the Colored Evangelist; Containing an Account of her Life Work of Faith, and Her Travels in America, England, Ireland, Scotland, India and Africa, as an Independent Missionary. Introduction by Jualynne E. Dodson. New York: Oxford University Press, 1988.

Anthologies

Loewenberg, Bert J., and Ruth Bogin, eds. *Black Women in Nineteenth-Century American Life: Their Words, Their Thoughts, Their Feelings*. University Park: Pennsylvania State University Press, 1976. 142–73.

Shockley, 228–32.

Writings about

Brown, 128–32.

Bullock, 165–66.

Cadbury, M. H. *The Life of Amanda Smith*. Birmingham, England: Cornish Bros., 1916.

Dannett, 1: 146.

Davis, 293.

Fitzpatrick, Kathleen. *Lady Henry Somerset*. Boston: Little Brown, 1923.

Grant, Abraham. *Deaconess Manual of the African Methodist Episcopal Church*. N.p.: African Methodist Episcopal Church, Bishop's Council, 1902.

Hardesty, Nancy. *Great Women of Faith: The Strength and Influence of Christian Women*. Grand Rapids, MI: Baker Book House, [c.1980].

Kerr, Alec C. *The City of Harvey, 1890–1962: History*. Harvey, IL: First National Bank, [c.1962].

Kletzing, H. F., and E. L. Kletzing. *Traits of Character Illustrated in Bible Light*. Naperville, IL: Kletzing Brothers, [c.1898].

Majors, 278–82.

Mossell, 15.

NAW, 3: 304–5.

Scruggs, 57–61.

Shockley, 225–28.

Taylor, Rev. Marshall W. *The Life, Travels, Labors, and Helpers of Mrs. Amanda Smith: The Famous Negro Missionary Evangelist.* Cincinnati: Cranston & Stowe, 1887.

Taylor, William. *The Flaming Torch in Darkest Africa.* New York: Eaton & Mains, 1898.

————. *Story of My Life.* New York: Hunt & Eaton, 1895.

Wesley, 5, 13.

Effie Waller Smith [Effie Waller] (1879–1960)

Writings by

The Collected Works of Effie Waller Smith. Introduction by David Deskins. New York: Oxford University Press, 1991.

Rhymes from the Cumberland. New York: Broadway Publishing Co., 1909.

Rosemary and Pansies. Boston: Richard G. Badger, The Gorham Press, 1909.

Songs of the Months. New York: Broadway Publishing Co., 1904.

"Autumn Winds." *Harper's Magazine* (Sept. 1917).

"Benignant Death." *Putnam's and the Reader* (Dec. 1908).

"The Faded Blossoms." *Independent* (20 July 1911).

"The Judgment of Roxenie." *Putnam's Monthly* (June 1909).

"The Shepherds' Vision." *Independent* (24 Dec. 1908).

"A Son of Sorrow." *Putnam's and the Reader* (Dec. 1908).

"The Tempting of Peter Stiles." *Putnam's Monthly* (Feb. 1908).

Writings about

Fraley, Jay. *Pike County News* (2 Apr. 1926).

Kinder, Alice. *Appalachian News Express* (1980).

Miller, James Wayne. *Open Eye* (Spring 1989).

Pipkin, Rev. J. J. *The History of a Rising Race: The Negro in Revelation, in History and in Citizenship*. N.p.: Thompson Publishing Co., 1902; Hallandale, FL: New World Book Manufacturing Co., 1971.

J. Pauline Smith

Writings by

Olive Prints, Selections from Robert Browning's Poems for Every Day in the Year. J. Pauline Smith, comp. Detroit: Press of William Graham Printing Co., 1903.

"Cries That Mount Upward." *Colored American Magazine* (Sept. 1908): 472.

"Golden Anniversary Lines." *Christian Recorder* (2 Sept. 1897): 1.

Rosetta Douglass Sprague [Rosetta Douglass] (1839–?)

Writings by

My Mother as I Recall Her. A paper read before Anna Murray Douglass Union, W.C.T.U., May 10, 1900. Published by Request. N.p.: n.p., 1900.

"Anna Murray Douglass: My Mother as I Recall Her." *Journal of Negro History* (Jan. 1923): 93–101.

"What Role Is the Educated Negro Woman to Play in the Uplifting of Her Race?" Culp, 167–71.

Anthologies

Sterling, Dorothy, ed. *Speak Out in Thunder Tones: Letters and Other Writings by Black Northerners, 1787–1865*. Garden City, NY: Doubleday, 1973. 180–82.

Writings about

Culp, 167.

Majors, 194–95.

Porter, Dorothy B. "Women Activists, Wives, Intellectuals, Mothers, and Artists." In *Candidates for Rediscovery: The Boston Version*. Proceedings of a Symposium at the Afro-American Studies Center, Boston University, 12 Apr. 1975. 76–84. Boston: Afro-American Studies Center, Boston University, 1975.

Quarles, Benjamin. "Frederick Douglass: Letters from the Haitian Legation." *Caribbean Quarterly* 4.1 (1955): 75–81.

Papers in Collections

My Mother as I Recall Her. A paper read before Anna Murray Douglass Union, W.C.T.U., May 10, 1900. Published by request. N.p.: n.p., 1900. Author's autographed presentation copy to E. B. Bruce. Schomburg Center, New York Public Library.

Maria W. Miller Stewart (1803–1879)

Writings by

Maria W. Stewart, America's First Black Woman Political Writer: Essays and Speeches. Marilyn Richardson, ed. Bloomington: Indiana University Press. 1987. [Includes selections from Stewart's major writings.]

Meditations From the Pen of Mrs. Maria W. Stewart. Boston: Garrison and Knapp, 1832.

Mediations From the Pen of Mrs. Maria W. Stewart (Widow of the late James W. Stewart), Now Matron of the Freedman's [sic] *Hospital, and Presented in 1832 to the First*

African Baptist Church and Society of Boston, Mass., First Published by W. Lloyd Garrison and Knap [sic], *Now Most Especially Dedicated to the Church Militant of Washington, D.C.* Washington, DC: Enterprise Publishing Co., 1879.

Productions of Mrs. Maria W. Stewart, Presented to the First African Baptist Church & Society, of the City of Boston. Boston: Friends of Freedom and Virtue, 1835.

Religion and the Pure Principles of Morality the Sure Foundation on Which We Must Build. Boston: Garrison and Knapp, 1831. Republished in *Early Negro Writing, 1760–1837.* Dorothy Porter, ed. Boston: Beacon Press, 1971. 460–71.

"Cause for Encouragement." *Liberator* (14 July 1832).

[Text of Speech delivered in Boston.] *Liberator* (28 Apr. 1832; 17 Nov. 1832; 27 Apr. 1833; 7 May 1833).

Anthologies

Bormann, Ernest G., ed. *Forerunners of Black Power; the Rhetoric of Abolition.* Englewood Cliffs, NJ: Prentice-Hall, [c.1971].

Loewenberg, Bert J., and Ruth Bogin, eds. *Black Women in Nineteenth-Century American Life: Their Words, Their Thoughts, Their Feelings.* University Park: Pennsylvania State University Press, 1976. 183–200.

Porter, Dorothy, ed. *Early Negro Writing, 1760–1837.* Boston: Beacon Press, 1971. 129–35, 136–40.

Productions of Mrs. Maria W. Stewart, Presented to the First African Baptist Church & Society, of the City of Boston. In *Spiritual Narratives.* Introduction by Sue E. Houchins. New York: Oxford University Press, 1988.

Writings about

Bullock, 47.

Flexner, Eleanor. *Century of Struggle: The Woman's Rights Movement in the United States*. Cambridge, MA: Belknap Press of Harvard University Press, 1959.

Giddings, Paula. *When and Where I Enter: The Impact of Black Women on Race and Sex in America*. New York: William Morrow, 1984. 49–54, 99–100, 105.

NAW, 3: 377–78.

O'Connor, Lillian. *Pioneer Women Orators: Rhetoric in the Ante-Bellum Reform Movement*. New York: Columbia University Press, 1954.

Porter, Dorothy B. "The Organized Educational Activities of Negro Literary Societies, 1828–1846." *Journal of Negro Education* (Oct. 1936): 555–76.

———. "Women Activists, Wives, Intellectuals, Mothers, and Artists." In *Candidates for Rediscovery: The Boston Version*. Proceedings of a Symposium at the Afro-American Studies Center, Boston University, 12 Apr. 1975. 76–84. Boston: Afro-American Studies Center, Boston University, 1975.

Quarles, Benjamin. *Black Abolitionists*. New York: Oxford University Press, 1969. 7, 50, 192.

Robinson, William H., Jr., ed. *Early Black American Prose*. Dubuque, IA: William C. Brown Company Publishers, 1971. xvii.

Sterling, Dorothy, ed. *Speak Out in Thunder Tones: Letters and Other Writings by Black Northerners, 1787–1865*. Garden City, NY: Doubleday, 1973. 67–68.

———. *We Are Your Sisters: Black Women in the Nineteenth Century*. New York: W. W. Norton, 1984. 153–59.

Wesley, 4.

Yellin, Jean Fagan. *Women and Sisters: The Antislavery Feminists in American Culture*. New Haven: Yale University Press, 1990.

Mary Still

Writings by

An Appeal to the Females of the African Methodist Episcopal Church, by Mary Still and Published by the Request of the Publication Society of the A.M.E. Church of Philadelphia. Philadelphia: Peter McKenna & Son, 1857.

Susie Baker King Taylor (1848–1912)

Writings by

Reminiscences of My Life in Camp with the 33rd United States Colored Troops, Late 1st S. C. Volunteers. Boston: the Author, 1902, 1904; New York: Arno Press, 1968.

Anthologies

Katz, William Loren. *Eyewitness: The Negro in American History*. New York: Pitman, 1967. 133, 215, 236.

Loewenberg, Bert J., and Ruth Bogin, eds. *Black Women in Nineteenth-Century American Life: Their Words, Their Thoughts, Their Feelings*. University Park: Pennsylvania State University Press, 1976. 89–94.

Merriam, Eve. *Growing Up Female in America*. Garden City, NY: Doubleday, 1971.

Reminiscences of My Life in Camp with the 33d United States Colored Troops Late 1st S. C. Volunteers. In *Collected Black Women's Narratives*. Introduction by Anthony G. Barthelemy. New York: Oxford University Press, 1988.

Shockley, 316–18.

Sterling, Dorothy, ed. *Speak Out in Thunder Tones: Letters and Other Writings by Black Northerners, 1787–1865.* Garden City, NY: Doubleday, 1973. 354–56.

Writings about

Booker, Simeon. *Susie King Taylor, Civil War Nurse.* New York: McGraw-Hill, 1969.

DANB, 581–82.

Dannett, 1: 166–73.

Dannett, Sylvia G. "No Bitterness for Susie King." *Civil War Times Illustrated* (May 1966): 15.

Fleming, John E. "Slavery, Civil War and Reconstruction: A Study of Black Women in Microcosm." *Negro History Bulletin* 38.6 (1975): 430–33.

McPherson, James M. *The Negro's Civil War: How American Negroes Felt and Acted During the War of the Union.* New York: Vintage Books, 1965.

Quarles, Benjamin. *The Negro in the Civil War.* Boston: Little, Brown, 1953.

Shockley, 312–16.

Papers in Collections

Reminiscences of My Life in Camp with the 33rd United States Colored Troops, Late 1st S. C. Volunteers. Boston: the Author, 1902. Author's autographed presentation copy to J.W.E. Bowen. Schomburg Center, New York Public Library.

Mary Eliza Church Terrell [Mrs. Robert H. Terrell] (1863–1954)

Writings by

A Colored Woman in a White World. Washington, DC: Ransdell Publishing Company, 1940; National Association of Colored Women's Clubs, Inc., 1968; New York: Arno Press, 1980.

Colored Women and World Peace [Pamphlet]. Washington, DC: Women's International League for Peace and Freedom, 1932.

Harriet Beecher Stowe; An Appreciation. Washington, DC: Murray Bros. Press, 1911. [Autographed copy, Schomburg Collection.]

The Progress of the Colored Women. An Address Before the National American Women's Suffrage Association, Washington, Feb. 18, 1898 on the occasion of its fiftieth anniversary. Washington, DC: Smith Bros., 1898.

"Announcement." *Woman's Era* (Aug. 1896): 3–4.

"Aunt Dinah and Dilsey Discuss the Problem." *Crisis* 25 (1923): 159.

"Club Work of Colored Women." *Southern Workman* 30 (1901): 435–38.

"The Disbanding of the Colored Soldiers." *Voice of the Negro* (Dec. 1906): 554.

"Graduates and Former Students of Washington Colored High School." *Voice of the Negro* (June 1904): 221.

"History of the High Schools for Negroes in Washington." *Journal of Negro History* (July 1917): 252–66.

"The International Congress of Women." *Voice of the Negro* (Oct. 1904): 454.

"An Interview with W. T. Stead on the Race Problem." *Voice of the Negro* (July 1907): 327.

"Lynching from a Negro's Point of View." *North American Review* (July 1904): 853–98.

"The Mission of Meddlers." *Voice of the Negro* (Aug. 1905): 566.

"Paul Laurence Dunbar." *Voice of the Negro* (Apr. 1906): 271.

"Peonage in the United States." *Nineteenth Century* (Aug. 1907).

"Plea for the White South by a Coloured Woman." *Nineteenth Century* (July 1906): 70–84.

"The Progress of Colored Women." *Voice of the Negro* (July 1904): 291–94.

"Prologue." *Woman's Era* (Nov. 1894): 4.

"Race Prejudice and Southern Progress." *Colored American Magazine* (Sept. 1906): 188–91.

"Samuel Coleridge-Taylor." *Voice of the Negro* (Jan. 1905): 665.

"Service Which Should be Rendered the South." *Voice of the Negro* (March 1905): 182.

"A Sketch of Mingo Saunders." *Voice of the Negro* (March 1907): 128.

"The Social Functions during Inauguration Week." *Voice of the Negro* (Apr. 1905): 237.

"Society among the Colored People of Washington." *Voice of the Negro* (Apr. 1904). 150.

"Solving the Colored Woman's Problem." In *World Fellowship of Faiths, International Congress, 1st, Chicago and New York, 1933–1934, Addresses.* New York: Liveright Publishing Co., 1935. 304–16.

"Susan B. Anthony. The Abolitionist." *Voice of the Negro* (June 1906): 411–16.

"Taft and the Negro Soldiers." *Independent* (July 1908).

"Washington." *Woman's Era* (Apr. 1895): 3–4; (July 1895): 3–4; (Jan. 1896): 14–15.

"The Washington Conservatory of Music." *Voice of the Negro* (Nov. 1904): 525.

"What Role Is the Educated Negro Woman to Play in the Uplifting of Her Race?" Culp, 172–77.

"Woman's Suffrage and the Fifteenth Amendment." *Crisis* (Aug. 1915).

Anthologies

Foner, Philip, ed. *Frederick Douglass on Women's Rights* [Terrell on Frederick Douglass]. Westport, CT: Greenwood Press, 1976. 175.

Writings about

Barton, Rebecca Chalmer. *Witnesses for Freedom*. New York: Harper, 1948. 68–79.

Boulware, Marcus H. *The Oratory of Negro Leaders: 1900–1968*. Westport, CT: Greenwood Press, 1969. 98–113.

Brawley, *NBH*, 261–62.

Brawley, Benjamin. *Women of Achievement*. Chicago: Women's Baptist Home Mission Society, 1919.

Brewer, William M. "Mary Church Terrell." *Negro History Bulletin* (Oct. 1954): 2.

Brown, Hallie Q. "Mrs. Mary Church Terrell at Cornell University." *Voice of the Negro* (Aug. 1905): 637.

Bullock, 67, 79, 82, 84, 97, 122, 127, 140, 168, 169–70, 192, 200, 217.

Campbell, Karlyn Kohrs. "Style and Content in the Rhetoric of Early Afro-American Feminists." *Quarterly Journal of Speech* 72.4 (1986): 434–45.

Chittenden, Elizabeth F. "As We Climb: Mary Church Terrell." *Negro History Bulletin* 38.2 (1975): 351–54.

Culp, 172.

DANB, 583–85.

Daniel, Constance. "Together Across New Frontiers." *Women United* (Oct. 1949).

Dannett, 1: 207–11.

Davis, 163–65.

["During a recent address in New York City on Abraham Lincoln, Mrs. M. C. Terrell of Washington, D. C. stated. . . ."] *Woman's Journal* (2 Apr. 1910).

Hunton, Addie W. "The Detroit Convention of the National Association of Colored Women." *Voice of the Negro* (Aug. 1906): 589.

Jones, Beverly W. "Before Montgomery and Greensboro: The Desegregation Movement in the District of Columbia, 1950–1953." *Phylon* 43.2 (1982): 144–54.

———. "Mary Church Terrell and the National Association of Colored Women, 1896 to 1901." *Journal of Negro History* 67.1 (1982): 20–33.

Majors, 321.

Marable, Manning. "Groundings with My Sisters: Patriarchy and the Exploitation of Black Women." *Journal of Ethnic Studies* 11.2 (1983): 1–39.

["M. C. Terrell makes first graduation speech by woman at Fisk."] *Woman's Journal* (July 1905).

["M. C. Terrell speaks and has reception in home of S. B. Anthony."] *Woman's Journal* (31 Dec. 1904).

Miller, M. Sammy. "Mary Church Terrell's Letters from Europe to Her Father." *Negro History Bulletin* 39.6 (1976): 615–18.

Mossell, 13, 16.

["Mrs. Mary Church Terrell delivered an eloquent. . . ."] *Weekly Call* (7 March 1896): 1.

["Mrs. Mary Church Terrell of Washington, D.C. . . ."] *Weekly Call* (7 May 1893): 1.

["Mrs. Mary Church Terrell was reported by the Associated Press. . . ."] *Woman's Journal* (23 Nov. 1907).

["Mrs. Terrell of the District of Columbia was among those who spoke from the floor."] *Woman's Journal* (16 Apr. 1904).

"The National Association of Colored Women." *Voice of the Negro* (July 1904): 310.

"No Capital Gains." *Time* (4 July 1949): 39–40.

Nolen, Anita. "The Feminine Presence: Women's Papers in the Manuscript Division." *Quarterly Journal of the Library of Congress* (Oct. 1975): 348–65.

[Obituary.] *Evening Star* (27 July 1954): A-12.

[Obituary.] *New York Times* (29 July 1954): 23.

[Obituary.] *Washington Post and Times Herald* (25 July 1954): 16.

[Obituary.] *Washington Sunday Star* (25 July 1954).

[Portrait.] *Voice of the Negro* (June 1904): frontispiece.

Quarles, Benjamin, and Dorothy Sterling. *Lift Every Voice: The Lives of Booker T. Washington, W.E.B. Du Bois, Mary Church Terrell, and James Weldon Johnson.* Garden City, NY: Doubleday, 1965.

Queen [*sic*] [Brown], Hallie E. "Mrs. Mary Church Terrell at Cornell University." *Voice of the Negro* (Sept. 1906): 637.

Render, Sylvia Lyons. "Afro-American Women: The Outstanding and the Obscure." *Quarterly Journal of the Library of Congress* (Oct. 1975): 306–21.

Robinson, 251.

Scruggs, 227–28.

Shepperd, Gladys Byram. *Mary Church Terrell, Respectable Person.* Baltimore: Human Relations Press, 1959.

"Southern View of Mrs. Terrell." *Colored American Magazine* (Dec. 1907): 412–13.

Sterling, Dorothy. *Black Foremothers: Three Lives.* Old Westbury, NY: Feminist Press, 1979. 60–117.

Stokes, O. P. "Women of Africa and African Descent." *International Journal of Religious Education* (Oct. 1967): 7.

Swift, Janet McKelvey. "Oberlin's Share." *Oberlin Alumni Magazine* (Sept. 1949).

Toppin, Edgar A. *A Biographical History of Blacks in America Since 1528*. New York: David McKay, 1971.

"The *Voice of the Negro* for 1905." *Voice of the Negro* (Dec. 1904).

Wesley, 5, 13, 17–18, 25–26, 38–40, 42–43, 44–47, 50, 59, 60–61, 63–64, 66–67, 70, 72, 87–89, 93, 98, 107, 110, 117, 120–21, 122, 127, 129, 145, 219, 311, 333, 357, 372, 500, 522.

Woman's Journal (20 May 1899; 13 Jan. 1900).

Papers in Collections

Boulware, Marcus H. "The Public Address of Colored Women." N.p., 1947. Typewritten manuscript. Fisk University Library.

Jones, Beverly Washington. "Quest for Equality: The Life of Mary Eliza Church Terrell, 1863–1954." Diss., University of North Carolina, Chapel Hill, 1980.

Mary Church Terrell clippings, Sophia Smith Collection, Smith College.

Mary Church Terrell Papers, Library of Congress.

Mary Church Terrell Papers, 1888–1976. Manuscript Collection, Moorland-Spingarn Research Center, Howard University.

Terrell, Mary Church. Letter to Carrie Chapman Catt. 9 Jan. 1919. Sophia Smith Collection, Smith College.

———. Letter to Carl Van Vechten. 12 Feb. 1950. Beinecke Library, Yale University.

———. Letter to Carl Van Vechten. 23 Feb. 1950. Beinecke Library, Yale University.

Clara Ann Thompson (1869–1949)

Writings by

A Garland of Poems. Boston: Christopher Publishing House, 1926.

Songs from the Wayside. Rossmoyne, OH: the Author, 1908.

What Means This Bleating of the Sheep? Rossmoyne, OH: n.p., 1921.

Anthologies

Songs from the Wayside. In *Collected Black Women's Poetry.* Joan R. Sherman, ed. Vol. 2. New York: Oxford University Press, 1988.

Stetson, Erlene, ed. *Black Sister: Poetry by Black American Women, 1746–1980.* Bloomington: Indiana University Press, 1981. 42.

Shockley, 322.

White, Newman Ivey, and Walter Clinton Jackson, eds. *An Anthology of Verse by American Negroes.* Durham, NC: Trinity College Press, 1924.

Writings about

Coyle, William. *Ohio Authors and Their Books; Biographical Data and Selective Bibliographies for Ohio Authors, Native and Resident, 1796–1950.* Cleveland: World Publishing Co., 1962.

Dabney, Wendell P. *Cincinnati's Colored Citizens: Historical, Sociological and Biographical.* Cincinnati: Dabney Publishing Co., 1926.

Sherman, 207, 249.

Shockley, 320–22.

Yenser, Thomas, ed. *Who's Who in Colored America: A Biographical Dictionary of Notable Living Persons of African*

Descent in America, 1930–1932. 3rd Edition. Brooklyn, NY: Thomas Yenser, 1933. 420.

Eloise Bibb Thompson (1878–1927)

Writings by

Africannus [Play]. Los Angeles: n.p., 1922.
Cooped up [Play]. N.p.: n.p., 1924. [Produced by Lafayette Players, New York, 1924.]
Poems. Boston: The Monthly Review Press, 1895.
"After Reading Bryant's Lines to a Waterfowl." *Opportunity* (March 1924): 83.
"Mademoiselle 'Tasie-A Story." *Opportunity* (Sept. 1925): 272–76.
"Masks." *Opportunity* (Oct. 1927): 300–302.

Anthologies
Poems. In *Collected Black Women's Poetry.* Joan R. Sherman, ed. Vol. 4. New York: Oxford University Press, 1988.
Shockley, 236–41.

Writings about

Abajian, James de T. *Blacks in Selected Newspapers, Censuses and Subjects.* Boston: G. K. Hall, 1977.
Beasley, Delilah L. *The Negro Trail Blazers of California, 1919.* Los Angeles: Times Mirror Printing & Binding House, 1919; New York: Negro Universities Press, 1969.
Loggins, 335, 454.
Scally, Sister Anthony. *Negro Catholic Writers, 1900–1943: A Bio-Bibliography.* Grosse Point, MI: Walter Romig, 1945.
Sherman, xviii, xxvi, 204–6.

Shockley, 233–35.

Who's Who of the Colored Race: A General Bibliographical Dictionary of Men and Women of African Descent. Chicago: n.p., 1915. 1: 262.

Priscilla Jane Thompson (1871–1942)

Writings by

Ethiope Lays. Rossmoyne, OH: the Author, 1900.

Gleanings of Quiet Hours. Rossmoyne, OH: the Author, 1907.

Anthologies

Ethiope Lays. In *Collected Black Women's Poetry.* Joan R. Sherman, ed. Vol. 2. New York: Oxford University Press, 1988.

Gleanings of Quiet Hours. In *Collected Black Women's Poetry.* Joan R. Sherman, ed. Vol. 2. New York: Oxford University Press, 1988.

Shockley, 308–11.

White, Newman Ivey, and Walter Clinton Jackson, eds. *An Anthology of Verse by American Negroes.* Durham, NC: Trinity College Press, 1924.

Writings about

Coyle, William. *Ohio Authors and Their Books; Biographical Data and Selective Bibliographies for Ohio Authors, Native and Resident, 1796–1950.* Cleveland: World Publishing Co., 1962.

Dabney, Wendell P. *Cincinnati's Colored Citizens, Historical, Sociological, and Biographical.* Cincinnati: Dabney Publishing Co., 1926.

Sherman, 207, 249.

Shockley, 304–8.

Yenser, Thomas, ed. *Who's Who in Colored America: A Biographical Dictionary of Notable Living Persons of African Descent in America, 1938–39–40.* 5th Edition. Brooklyn, NY: Thomas Yenser, 1940.

Katherine Davis Chapman Tillman
[Katie D. Chapman]

Writings by

Aunt Betsy's Thanksgiving. Philadelphia: A.M.E. Book Concern, n.d.

Fifty Years of Freedom, or From Cabin to Congress: A Drama in Five Acts. Philadelphia: A.M.E. Book Concern, 1910.

Heirs of Slavery. Philadelphia: A.M.E. Publishing House, 1909. [Unlocated.]

How to Live Well on a Small Salary. N.p.: n.p., [1895?]. [Unlocated.]

Lincoln's Proclamation. [Philadelphia: A.M.E. Book Concern?], 1902. [Unlocated.]

The Men Makers Club. [Philadelphia: A.M.E. Book Concern?], n.d. [Unlocated.]

Poems and Drama. N.p.: n.p., 1908. [Unlocated.]

Quotations from Negro Authors. Fort Scott, KS: n.p., 1921.

Recitations. Philadelphia: A.M.E. Book Concern, 1902.

The Spirit of Allen: A Pageant of African Methodism. N.p.: n.p., 1922.

Thirty Years of Freedom: A Drama in Four Acts. Philadelphia: A.M.E. Book Concern, 1902.

The Works of Katherine Davis Chapman Tillman. Claudia Tate, ed. New York: Oxford University Press, 1991.

"Afro-American Boy." *Christian Recorder* (24 June 1897): 1.

"Afro-American Poets and Their Verse." *A.M.E. Church Review* 14 (Apr. 1898): 421–28.

"Afro-American Women and Their Work." *A.M.E. Church Review* 11 (Apr. 1895): 477–99.

"Alexander Dumas, Père." *A.M.E. Church Review* 24 (Jan. 1907): 257–63.

"Alexander Sergeivich Pushkin." *A.M.E. Church Review* 25 (July 1909): 27–32.

"Allen's Army." *Christian Recorder* (7 Feb. 1895): 6.

Beryl Weston's Ambition: The Story of an Afro-American Girl's Life. *A.M.E. Church Review* 10 (July 1893): 173–91; 10 (Oct. 1893): 308–22.

Clancy Street. *A.M.E. Church Review* 15 (Oct. 1898): 643–50; 15 (Jan. 1899); 748–53; 15 (July 1899): 152–59; 15 (Oct. 1899): 241–51.

"Faith's Vision." *Christian Recorder* (29 July 1897): 1.

"The Glad New Year." *Christian Recorder* (10 Jan. 1893): 1.

"Heart-Keeping." *Christian Recorder* (12 March 1896): 1.

Heirs of Slavery: A Little Drama of To-day [Play]. *A.M.E. Church Review* 17 (Jan. 1901): 199–203.

"The Highest Life." *Christian Recorder* (8 Nov. 1900): 1.

"Lift Me Higher Master." *Christian Recorder* (26 Apr. 1894): 1.

"Lines to Ida B. Wells." *Christian Recorder* (5 July 1894): 1.

"Memory." *Christian Recorder* (12 July 1888): 1.

"Miles the Conqueror." *American Citizen* (20 Apr. 1894).

"My Queen." *Christian Recorder* (10 Sept. 1891): 5.

"The Negro Among Anglo-Saxon Poets." *A.M.E. Church Review* 14 (1898): 106–12.

"Only a Letter." *Christian Recorder* (9 Aug. 1888): 1.

"The Pastor." *Christian Recorder* (18 Oct. 1894): 1.

"Paying Professions for Colored Girls." *Voice of the Negro* (Jan.–Feb. 1907): 54–55.

"The Preacher at Hill Station." *A.M.E. Church Review* 19 (Jan. 1903): 634–43.

"A Psalm of the Soul." *Christian Recorder* (9 Jan. 1896): 1.

"A Rest Beyond." Mossell, 92–93.

"Some Girls That I Know." *A.M.E. Church Review* 9 (Jan. 1893): 288–92.

"Soul Visions." *Christian Recorder* (21 Aug. 1902): 1.

"The Superannuate." *Christian Recorder* (16 March 1899): 1.

"A Tribute to Negro Regiments." *Christian Recorder* (9 June 1898).

"The Warrior's Lay." *Christian Recorder* (22 Oct. 1902): 1.

"Which?" *Christian Recorder* (6 July 1899): 1.

Writings about

"Book List." *A.M.E. Church Review* (Apr. 1904): 418.

Bullock, 98, 129.

Dann, 66.

Dunnigan, Alice. "Early History of Negro Women in Journalism." *Negro History Bulletin* 28 (Summer 1965): 178.

"How to Live Well on a Small Salary" [Review]. *Christian Recorder* (31 Jan. 1895): 2.

Jones, Anna H. "Katherine D. Tillman, Chicago, IL." *National Association Notes* 8 (Oct. 1904): 3.

Majors, 322.

Mossell, 16, 27, 92–93.

Penn, 388–93.

Scruggs, 203–6.

Sherman, 245.

Margaret J. Murray Washington [Mrs. Booker T. Washington; Margaret J. Murray] (1865–1925)

Writings by

The Negro Home. Address by Mrs. Booker T. Washington at the Interracial Conference Held in Memphis, Tennessee, October 1920. Nashville: Woman's Missionary Council, Methodist Episcopal Church, 1925.

"Are We Making Good?" *Independent* (4 Oct. 1915): 22.

"Call to the National Federation of Afro-American Women." *Woman's Era* (Nov. 1895): 2–3.

"Club Work among Negro Women." In *Progress of a Race; or, the Remarkable Advancement of the American Negro, . . .* John W. Gibson and W. H. Crogman, eds. Naperville, IL: J. L. Nichols & Co., 1929. Republished in 1902 by J. W. Gibson and W. H. Crogman with title: *The Colored American from Slavery to Honorable Citizenship*.

"Gains in the Life of Negro Women." *Outlook* (30 Jan. 1904): 271–74.

[Letter from M. M. Washington.] *Woman's Journal* (11 Sept. 1897).

"Mrs. B. T. Washington's Illness." *Woman's Era* (Aug. 1896): 15.

"One Woman's Influence in Alabama's Black Belt." *Our Day* 16 (1886): 339.

"Separate Car Law." *Woman's Era* (Feb. 1896): 9.

"Social Improvement of the Plantation Woman." *Voice of the Negro* (July 1904): 288–90.

"The Songs of Our Fathers." *Colored American Magazine* (May 1905): 245–53.

"The Tuskegee Woman's Club." *Southern Workman* (Aug. 1920): 365.

"To the Women of the Country." *Woman's Era* (Aug. 1895): 16.

Writings about

[Article about N.A.C.W. Convention in Brooklyn.] *Woman's Journal* (5 Sept. 1908).

Brawley, *NBH*, 157, 261.

Brown, 225–30.

Bullock, 110, 116, 129, 170, 191.

Dannett, 1: 323.

Davis, 171–72.

Haynes, Elizabeth Ross. "Margaret Murray Washington." *Opportunity* (July 1925): 201.

Johnston, A. "Mrs. Booker Washington's Club for Women." *Harper's Bazaar* (March 1899): 186.

"The National Association of Colored Women." *Voice of the Negro* (July 1904): 310.

Neverdon-Morton, Cynthia. "Self-Help Programs as Educative Activities of Black Women in the South, 1895–1925; Focus on Four Key Areas." *Journal of Negro Education* 51.3 (1982): 207–21.

Scott, Emmet J. "Maggie J. Murray Washington's (Mrs. Booker Taliaferro Washington) Part in Husband's Work." *Ladies' Home Journal* (May 1907): 42.

Wesley, 21–22, 25, 29, 32, 34–36, 43, 45, 50, 59, 61, 63–64, 66–67, 70–72, 85–89, 91, 93, 102, 114, 218, 339, 344–45, 467, 486–87.

Woman's Journal (19 Sept. 1896; 23 Aug. 1902; 16 May 1903; 5 Sept. 1903; 5 Nov. 1904; 12 Nov. 1904; 9 Sept. 1905).

Papers in Collections

The Songs of Our Fathers; An Address Given on Fisk University Day, Louisiana Purchase Exposition in Festival Hall. July 6. Fisk University.

Washington, Margaret M. Letter to Ednah Dow Cheney. 1894. Sophia Smith Collection, Smith College.

————. Letter to Ednah Dow Cheney. 1899. Sophia Smith Collection, Smith College.

Ida Bell Wells-Barnett [Mrs. Ferdinand L. Barnett; pseud. Iola] (1862–1931)

Writings by

Crusade for Justice: The Autobiography of Ida B. Wells. Alfreda M. Duster, ed. Chicago: University of Chicago Press, 1970.

Mob Rule in New Orleans: Robert Charles and His Fight to the Death. Chicago: the Author, 1900.

On Lynchings: Southern Horrors, A Red Record, Mob Rule in New Orleans. New York: Arno Press, 1969.

The Reason Why the Colored American Is Not in the World's Columbian Exposition. Chicago: n.p., 1893.

A Red Record: Tabulated Statistics and Alleged Causes of Lynchings in the United States, 1892–1893–1894. Chicago: Donohue and Henneberry, 1895.

Selected Works of Ida B. Wells-Barnett. Trudier Harris, comp. New York: Oxford University Press, 1991.

Southern Horrors: Lynch Law in All Its Phases. New York: The New York Age Print, 1892. Published in Britain as *United States Atrocities. Lynch Law.* London: "Lux" Newspaper and Publishing Co., [1892?].

"How Enfranchisement Stops Lynchings." *Original Rights* (1910): 42–53.

"Lynching, Our National Crime." *National Negro Conference*. Proceedings. New York, 1909. 174–79.

"Lynching, the Excuse for It." *Independent* (16 May 1901).

"Lynching and the Excuse for It." In *Lynching and Rape: An Exchange of Views*. Bettina Aptheker, ed. AIMS Occasional Paper, no. 25. New York: American Institute for Marxist Studies, 1977.

"Lynch Law in All Its Phases." *Our Day* 9 (May 1893).

"Mrs. N. F. Mossell." Scruggs, 23–25.

"The Negro's Case in Equity." *Independent* (26 Apr. 1900): 1010.

"The Negro Problem from the Negro Point of View: IV. Booker T. Washington and His Critics." *World To-Day* (Apr. 1904): 511–23.

"Two Christmas Days: A Holiday Story." *A.M.E. Zion Church Quarterly* (Jan. 1894): 129–40.

Letters

Letter to *Chicago Tribune* (7 July 1919).

Letter to Mrs. Ridley. *Woman's Era* (July 1894): 4.

Anthologies

Aptheker, Herbert. *A Documentary History of the Negro People in the United States*. 2 vols. New York: Citadel Press, 1951, 1974.

Loewenberg, Bert J., and Ruth Bogin, eds. *Black Women in Nineteenth-Century American Life: Their Words, Their Thoughts, Their Feelings*. University Park: Pennsylvania State University Press, 1976. 252–62.

Shockley, 254.

Writings about

["Alas! Mrs. Ida B. Wells is being. . . ."] *Weekly Call* (30 June 1894): 1.

Aptheker, Bettina. "The Suppression of Free Speech: Ida B. Wells and the Memphis Lynchings, 1892." *San Jose Studies* (Nov. 1977): 34–40.

Bontemps, Arna, and Jack Conroy. *They Seek a City*. Garden City, NY: Doubleday, Doran and Co., 1945. 77–82.

Brawley, *NBH*, 261.

Bruce, John Edward. *Short Biographical Sketches of Eminent Negro Men and Women in Europe and the United States*. Yonkers, NY: Gazette Press, 1910.

Bullock, 74, 84, 97, 168.

Butterfield, Stephen. *Black Autobiography in America*. Amherst: University of Massachusetts Press, 1975.

DANB, 30–31.

Dann, 63.

Dannett. 1: 221; 2: 22–26.

Davis, 186.

["The defense of Miss Ida B. Wells. . . ."] *Weekly Call* (7 July 1894): 1.

Dunnigan, Alice E. "Early History of Negro Women in Journalism." *Negro History Bulletin* 28 (Summer 1965): 178.

Flexner, Eleanor. *Century of Struggle: The Woman's Rights Movement in the United States*. Cambridge, MA: Belknap Press of Harvard University Press, 1959.

Foner, Philip S., ed. *Frederick Douglass on Women's Rights*. Westport, CT: Greenwood Press, 1976.

Fox, Stephen R. *The Guardian of Boston: William Monroe Trotter*. New York: Atheneum, 1970. 168, 175, 223.

Giddings, Paula. *When and Where I Enter: The Impact of Black Women on Race and Sex in America*. New York: William Morrow, 1984. 19–31, 83, 89–93, 107–11, 115–17, 120, 125, 126, 127–28, 180–81.

Haley, James T., comp. *Sparkling Gems of Race Knowledge Worth Reading*. . . . Nashville: J. T. Haley and Co., 1897. 60 [portrait].

Hughes, Langston. *Famous Negro Heroes of America*. New York: Dodd, Mead, 1958.

"Ida B. Wells." *Weekly Call* (25 May 1895): 1.

["It Is Announced that Miss Ida B. Wells. . . ."] *Weekly Call* (15 June 1895): 1.

Kellogg, Charles Flint. *NAACP, A History of the National Association for the Advancement of Colored People*. Vol. 1, *1909–1920*. Baltimore: Johns Hopkins University Press, 1967.

Lerner, Gerda. *Black Women in White America: A Documentary History*. New York: Pantheon Books, 1972.

"Lynch Law Reviewed. Miss Wells' Masterly Discussion of Lynch Law.–Real Cause of Lawlessness." *Weekly Call* (27 Apr. 1895): 1.

Majors, 187–94.

Majors, Gerri, and Doris E. Saunders. *Black Society*. Chicago: Johnson Publishing Co., 1976.

Marable, Manning. "Groundings with My Sisters: Patriarchy and the Exploitation of Black Women." *Journal of Ethnic Studies* 11.2 (1983): 1–39.

Massa, Ann. "Black Women in the 'White City.' " *Journal of American Studies* (Dec. 1974): 319–37.

Meier, August. *Negro Thought in America, 1880–1915: Racial Ideologies in the Age of Booker T. Washington*. Ann Arbor: University of Michigan Press, 1963.

"Miss Ida Wells Explains." *Weekly Call* (1 Dec. 1894): 1.

["Miss Ida B. Wells, a companion. . . ."] *Weekly Call* (29 Sept. 1894): 1.

["Miss Ida B. Wells addressed. . . ."] *Weekly Call* (19 Jan. 1895): 1.

["Miss Ida B. Wells the great lynch law reformer. . . ."] *Weekly Call* (15 June 1895): 1.

["Miss Ida B. Wells' lecture at St. John's. . . ."] *Weekly Call* (15 June 1895): 1.

["Miss Ida B. Wells says the colored. . . ."] *Weekly Call* (30 March 1895): 1.

["Miss Ida B. Wells stopped. . . ."] *Weekly Call* (1 Sept. 1894): 4.

["Miss Ida B. Wells who took. . . ."] *Weekly Call* (9 March 1895): 4.

["Miss Ida B. Wells who took. . . ."] *Weekly Call* (23 March 1895): 4.

["Miss Ida B. Wells who took. . . ."] *Weekly Call* (30 March 1895): 4.

["Miss Ida B. Wells, whose name. . . ."] *Weekly Call* (25 May 1895): 1.

["Miss Ida B. Wells, the woman. . . ."] *Weekly Call* (1 June 1895): 1.

"Miss Wells and the Dispatch." *Weekly Call* (7 July 1894): 1.

Mossell, 15, 32–46.

["Mrs. Ida B. Wells, the great lecturer. . . ."] *Weekly Call* (6 July 1895): 1.

["Mrs. Ida B. Wells is meeting. . . ."] *Weekly Call* (16 June 1894): 1.

["Mrs. Ida B. Wells-Barnett is again speaking. . . ."] *Weekly Call* (14 Dec. 1895): 1.

["Mrs. Ida B. Wells-Barnett is at home. . . ."] *Weekly Call* (20 July 1895): 1.

["Mrs. Ida Wells-Barnett lectured in. . . ."] *Weekly Call* (7 Dec. 1895): 1.

NAW, 565–67.

Noble, Jeanne. *Beautiful, Also, Are the Souls of My Black Sisters: A History of the Black Woman in America*. Englewood Cliffs, NJ: Prentice-Hall, 1978.

"Our Literary Women." *Lancet* (10 Oct. 1885): 1.

Penn, 407–10.

Robinson, 48.

Robinson, William H., Jr., ed. *Early Black American Prose*. Dubuque, IA: William C. Brown Company Publishers, 1971. 159.

Rollins, Charlemae Hill. *They Showed the Way: Forty American Negro Leaders*. New York: Thomas Y. Crowell, 1964.

Rudwick, Elliott M., and August Meier. "Black Man [*sic*] in the 'White City': Negroes and the Columbian Exposition, 1893." *Phylon* (Winter 1965).

Scruggs, 33–39.

Sewell, George. "Ida B. Wells." *Black Collegian* (May/June 1976): 20–24.

Shockley, 248–53.

Spear, Allan H. *Black Chicago*. Chicago: University of Chicago Press, 1967.

Sterling, Dorothy. *Black Foremothers: Three Lives*. Old Westbury, NY: Feminist Press, 1979. 60–117.

Suggs, Henry Lewis. *The Black Press in the South, 1865–1979*. Westport, CT: Greenwood Press, 1983.

Tillman, Katherine, D. "Lines to Ida B. Wells." *Christian Recorder* (5 July 1894): 1.

Thornbrough, Emma Lou. "The National Afro-American League." *Journal of Southern History* (Nov. 1961).

Toppin, Edgar A. *A Biographical History of Blacks in America Since 1528.* New York: David McKay, 1971.

Tucker, David. "Miss Ida B. Wells and Memphis Lynching." *Phylon* 32 (1971): 112–22.

Wesley, 367.

Papers in Collections

Ida B. Wells-Barnett Papers, Sophia Smith Manuscript Collection, Smith College.

Thompson, Mildred. "Ida B. Wells-Barnett: An Exploratory Study of an American Black Woman, 1893–1930." Diss., George Washington University, 1979.

Phillis Wheatley [Phillis Peters] (c.1753–1784)

Note: The listing below, based on the work of William H. Robinson, presents Wheatley's major poems and her letters. It then lists the republication of her writings in black and antislavery journals and in selected anthologies. It also presents comment on Wheatley's life and work. For fuller bibliographic information, see William H. Robinson, *Phillis Wheatley: A Bio-bibliography.* Boston: G. K. Hall, 1981.

Writings by

Poems on Various Subjects, Religious and Moral. By Phillis Wheatley, Negro Servant to Mr. John Wheatley, of Boston, in New England. London: Printed for A. Bell, Bookseller, Aldgate; and sold by Messrs. Cox and Berry, King-Street, Boston, MDCCLXXIII. Nendeln, Liechtenstein: Kraus, 1970. [Thirty-nine poems, of which one is by a "JB" and the others are by Wheatley. Two versions of another London edition of this volume were published.]

Poems on Various Subjects, Religious and Moral. By Phillis Wheatley, Negro Servant to Mr. John Wheatley, of Boston, in New England. London, Printed. Philadelphia, reprinted, and sold by Joseph Crukshank in Market-Street Between Second and Third Streets, MDCCLXXXVI. [Another printing, 1789. Republished, New York: A. M. S. Press, 1976.]

Poems on Various Subjects, Religious and Moral. By Phillis Wheatley of Boston, in New England. Philadelphia: Printed by Joseph James in Chestnut Street, 1787, 1789.

Poems on Various Subjects, Religious and Moral. By Phillis Wheatley, Negro Servant to Mr. John Wheatley, of Boston, in New England. Albany: Reprinted from the London edition, by Barber & Southwick, for Thomas Spencer, Bookseller, 1793.

Poems on Various Subjects, Religious and Moral. By Phillis Wheatley, Negro Servant to Mr. John Wheatley, of Boston, in New England. Walpole, NH: Printed for Thomas & Thomas, by David Newhall, 1802.

Poems on Various Subjects, Religious and Moral. By Phillis Wheatley, Negro servant to the late Mr. John Wheatley, of Boston, Mass. Hartford, CT: Printed by Oliver Steele, 1804.

Poems on Various Subjects, Religious and Moral. By Phillis Wheatley, Negro Servant to Mr. John Wheatley, of Boston, in New England. London, Printed; reprinted in New England, 1816.

Also Published in:

Equiano, Olaudah. *The Interesting Narrative of the Life of Olaudah Equiano, or Gustavus Vassa, the African, Written by Himself.* Halifax, NS: J. Nicholson & Co., 1814;

M. Garlick, 1819. [Other editions of Equiano's *Narrative* (1789) do not include Wheatley's poems.]

Jackson, W. H., ed. *Poems on Various Subjects, Religious and Moral,* by Phillis Wheatley, Negro Servant to Mr. John Wheatley, of Boston, in New England, with Memoir by W. H. Jackson. Cleveland: Rewell, [c.1886]; Denver: W. H. Lawrence & Co., 1887.

Lavalle, Joseph. *The Negro Equalled by Few Europeans.* 2 vols. Philadelphia: William W. Woodward, 1801. 2: 169–244.

Micropublished in *History of Women.* New Haven: Research Publications, 1975.

Poems on Comic, Serious, and Moral Subjects. 2nd Edition, corrected. London: J. French, bookseller, 1773, 1787. [Evidently a reissue, with a new title page, of the 1773 *Poems on Various Subjects.*]

"A Beautiful Poem on Providence: Written by a Young Female Slave. To which is subjoined a Short Account of This Extraordinary Writer." Halifax, NS: printed by E. Gay, 1805. [A variant of "Thoughts on the Work of Providence" in the 1773 *Poems on Various Subjects.*]

"An elegiac poem. On the DEATH of that celebrated Divine and eminent Servant of Jesus Christ, the late Reverend, and pious GEORGE WHITEFIELD, chaplain to the Right Honourable the Countess of Huntington." 1770. [First published in Boston as a broadside of 62 lines. Then reprinted with differing headnotes four more times in Boston, twice in Newport, RI, once in New York, once in Philadelphia, and twice in London. Three versions of the text of this poem are known.]

"An Elegy, Sacred to the Memory of That Great Divine, the Reverend and Learned Dr. Samuel Cooper, Who Departed this Life December 29, 1783, Aetatis 59. By Phillis Peters." Boston: Printed and sold by E. Russell, in Essex-Street, near Liberty-Pole, MDCCLXXXIV. [A variant version exists.]

"An Elegy, to Miss Mary Moorhead, On the Death of her Father, the Reverend Mr. John Moorhead. Printed from the Original Manuscript, and sold by William M'Alpine, at his Shop in Marlborough-Street, 1773." Boston, 15 Dec. 1773. Broadside.

"Farewell to America to Mrs. S—W—." *Boston Evening Post* (10 May 1773): 2. [An early version of a poem in the 1773 volume.]

"Liberty and Peace. A Poem By Phillis Peters." Boston: Printed by Warden and Russell, at their office in Marlborough-Street, MDCCLXXXIV.

"An Ode, on the Birth Day of Pompey Stockbridge." N.p.: n.p., n.d. Broadside.

"An Ode of Verses on the much-lamented Death of the Rev. Mr. George Whitefield, Late Chaplain to the Countess of Huntington; Who departed this Life, at Newberry near Boston in New England, on the Thirtieth of September, 1770, in the Fifty-Seventh Year of his Age. Compos'd in America by a Negro Girl Seventeen Years of Age and sent over to a Gentleman of Character in London." 1771. [A variant of the eulogy of the death of Whitefield "Printed and sold for the Benefit of a poor Family burnt out a few weeks since near Shoreditch Church. . . ."]

"On the death of Dr. Samuel Marshall." *Boston Evening Post* (7 Oct. 1771). [Revised and published in 1773 volume.]

"On the death of J. C., an infant." *Philadelphia Magazine* (Sept. 1797). [A variant of the poem in the 1773 volume.]

"On Messrs. Hussey and Coffin." *Newport Mercury* [Rhode Island] (21 Dec. 1767): 3.

"Philis's [*sic*] Reply to the Answer in our Past by the Gentleman in the Navy." 2 Dec 1774. *Royal American Magazine* (11 Jan. 1775): 34–35.

"Recollection to Miss A— M—, humbly inscribed by the Authoress." [This poem is preceded by an undated letter from Wheatley to "Madam." Both poem and letter appeared in a letter signed "L," and dated "Boston, Jan. 1, 1772" in the *London Magazine; Or, the Gentleman's Monthly Intelligencer* 41 (March 1772): 134–35. Revised as "On Recollection," this poem was included in Wheatley's 1773 volume.]

"To a Gentleman in the Navy." Boston, 30 Oct., 1774. *Royal American Gazette* 1 (Dec. 1774): 473–74.

"To his excellency Gen. Washington." *Virginia Gazette* (20 March 1776): 1A. [Letter and poem; also in *Pennsylvania Magazine, or American Monthly Museum* 2 (Apr. 1776): 93.]

"To the Hon'ble Thomas Hubbard, Esq.: On the death of Mrs. Thankfull Leonard." Boston, 2 Jan. 1773. Broadside. [Revised as "To the Honourable H. T. Esq.: On the death of his daughter" in the 1773 volume.]

"To Mr. and Mrs. ——— On the Death of Their Infant Son. By Phillis Wheatley." *Boston Magazine* (Sept. 1784).

"To Mrs. Leonard on the Death of Her Husband." Boston, 1771. Broadside. [Apparently title and text were revised and published in the 1773 volume.]

"To the Rev. Mr. Pitkin, on the death of his lady." Boston, June 1772. Broadside. [Revised in the 1773 volume.]

"To the Right Honourable William Legge, Earl of Dartmouth, his Majesty's Secretary of State for America, &c.,

&c. . . ." *New York Journal* (3 June 1773). [A variant of a poem in the 1773 volume.]

Publications Presenting Additional Writings by Wheatley

Bates, Katherine. *American Literature*. New York: Macmillan, 1898. 78–79, 81. [Presents "Elegy on George Whitefield," a variant version.]

Brown, William Wells. *The Black Man*. 4th Edition. Boston: Robert F. Wallcut, 1865. Miami: Mnemosnye, [?]. 138–42. [Presents "On the death of a young girl," a variant of a poem in the 1773 volume.]

Deane, Charles. "Phillis Wheatley." *Proceedings of the Massachusetts Historical Society (1863–1864)*. 7: 165–67, 267–79, 303. [Presents "The following Thoughts on his excellency Major General Lee being betray'd into the hands of the enemy by the treachery of a pretended Friend; To the honourable James Bowdoin Esqr. are most respectfully inscrib'd, by his most obedient and devoted humble servant, Phillis Wheatley." Also presents seven letters from Wheatley to Obour Tanner.]

Duyckinck, Evert, and George Duyckinck. *Cyclopedia of American Literature*. 2 vols. New York: Charles Scribner, 1856. 1: 367–70. [Presents a group of Wheatley poems, sometimes in variant versions.]

Gillies, John. *Memoirs of the Life of the Reverend George Whitefield*. New Haven: Printed for Andrus & Starr, 1812. 192–93. ["Part of a poem on Mr. Whitefield, which is published . . . with this sermon preached Oct. 11, 1770, written by a Negro Servant Girl of seventeen years of age . . . belonging to Mr. J. Wheatley of Boston."]

Greene, Lorenzo J. *The Negro in Colonial New England, 1620–1776.* New York: Columbia University Press. Reprinted, New York: Atheneum, 1971. 245. [Presents "On Atheism," published from manuscript.]

Haskins, Elizabeth. *The Literary Remains of Joseph Brown Ladd, M.D.* . . . New York: H. C. Sleight, Clinton Hall, 1833. [Presents "To Maecenas," a variant fragment of a poem in the 1773 volume.]

Isani, Mukhtar Ali. "Early Versions of Some Works by Phillis Wheatley." *Early American Literature* 14 (Fall 1979): 149–55. [Presents "On the death of J. C., An Infant," a variant of a poem in the 1773 volume; and "To the Right Honourable Earl of Dartmouth, His Majesty's Secretary of State for America &c, &c," previously published in the *New York Journal* (3 June 1773).]

———. "An Elegy on Leaving——": A New Poem by Phillis Wheatley." *American Literature* 58 (Dec. 1986): 609–13.

———. " 'On the death of General Wooster': An Unpublished Poem by Phillis Wheatley." *Modern Philology* 77 (Feb. 1979): 306–9.

Kuncio. Robert C. "Some Unpublished Poems of Phillis Wheatley." *New England Quarterly* 43.2 (June 1970): 287–97. [Presents "To the King's most excellent Majesty in his repealing the american (*sic*) Stamp Act" (revised in the 1773 volume); "On the death of Mr. Snider Murder'd by Richardson"; "America"; "Atheism" (variant versions exist); "On Atheism" (variant versions exist); and "To the Honourable Commodore Hood on his pardoning a deserter."]

Lapsansky, Phil. " 'Deism', an Unpublished Poem by Phillis Wheatley." *New England Quarterly* 50 (Sept. 1977):

517–20. [Presents "Deism." A variant manuscript version exists.]

Ricketson, Daniel. *History of New Bedford, Bristol County, Massachusetts.* New Bedford, MA: the Author, 1858. 262–63. [Presents a variant of a Wheatley poem and identifies its subject.]

Robinson, William H., Jr., ed. *Early Black American Poets.* Dubuque, IA: William C. Brown Company Publishers, 1969. 111–12. ["On Friendship." Reprinted from a facsimile manuscript in the Moorland Collection at Howard University. The title "On Friendship" was among Wheatley's "1772 Proposed Titles."]

————. *Phillis Wheatley in the Black American Beginnings.* Detroit: Broadside Press, 1975. [This monograph presents the following four poems from manuscripts: "An Address to the Atheist, by P. Wheatley at the age of 14 years—1767" (one of Wheatley's "1772 Proposed Titles"; several versions exist); "Atheism" (one of Wheatley's "1772 Proposed Titles"; several versions exist); "An Address to the Deist—1767" (one of Wheatley's "1771 Proposed Titles"; two manuscript versions are known); "A poem on the death of Charles Eliot, aged 12 months" (a variant of a poem in the 1773 volume; various manuscript versions exist).]

————. "Phillis Wheatley in London." *CLA Journal* 21 (Dec. 1977): 187–201. [Presents "On the Decease of the Rev'd Dr. Sewell," 190–92, publication from manuscript of an early version of the poem in the 1773 volume; and "To the Right Honourable William, Earl of Dartmouth, His Majesty's Principal Secretary of State for North America &c., &c.," " an early version of a poem in the 1773 volume.]

Wilson, Armistead. *A Tribute for the Negro.* . . . Man-

chester, England: William Irvin, 1848; Westport, CT:
Negro Universities Press, 1970. 128–29, 332–48. [Pre-
sents variant versions of several of Wheatley's poems,
including "On the death of an Infant," "On the death of
a Young Gentleman," and "On the death of a lovely girl,
five years of age."]

Letters

Deane, Charles. *Letters of Phillis Wheatley. The Negro-Slave
Poet of Boston*. Boston: privately printed by J. Wilson &
Son, 1864. [Presents seven letters from Wheatley to
Arbour (Abour? Obour?) Tanner, an African-American
friend in Newport, RI: "Boston, May 19, 1772"; "Bos-
ton, July 19, 1772"; "Boston, Oct. 30, 1773"; "Boston,
Mar. 21, 1774"; "Boston, May 6, 1774"; "Boston, May
29, 1778"; "Boston, May 10, 1779".]

———. "Phillis Wheatley." *Proceedings of the Massachusetts
Historical Society (1863–1864)*. 7: 165–79, 303. [Pre-
sents a poem and seven letters from Wheatley to Arbour
(Abour? Obour?) Tanner, an African-American friend in
Newport, RI: "Boston, May 19, 1772"; "Boston, Oct.
30, 1773"; "Boston, Mar. 21, 1774"; "Boston, May 6,
1774"; "Boston, May 29, 1778"; "Boston, May 10,
1779".]

Isani, Mukhtar Ali. "Phillis Wheatley in London: An Unpublished Letter to David Wooster." *American Literature*
51 (May 1979): 255–60. [Presents letter dated "Boston,
18 Oct. 1773" to Col. David Worcester (*sic*) New Haven,
CT.]

Jackson, Sarah Dunlap. "Letters of Phillis Wheatley and
Susanna Wheatley." *Journal of Negro History* 57 (Apr.
1972): 211–15. [Includes a letter dated "London, June
27, 1773," to the Countess of Huntington, South Wales;

and a letter dated "July 17, 1773," to the Countess of Huntington, South Wales.]

"L." Signator of letter dated "Boston, Jan. 1, 1772," in the *London Magazine; Or, the Gentlemen's Monthly Intelligencer* 41 (March 1772): 134–35. [Presents Wheatley letter, to "Madam", undated. This appears with "Recollection to Miss A— M—, humbly inscribed by the authoress."]

"Providence, Oct. 26, 1775," to General George Washington, covering an enclosed poem. *Virginia Gazette* (20 March 1776): 1A. Also in *Pennsylvania Magazine, or American Monthly Museum* 2 (Apr. 1776): 93.

Quarles, Benjamin. "A Phillis Wheatley Letter." *Journal of Negro History* 34 (Oct. 1950): 462–64. [Letter dated "Boston, Feb. 9, 1774," to the Reverend Samuel Hopkins, Newport. This was originally published in the *Pennsylvania Freeman* (9 May 1839).]

Silverman, Kenneth. "Four New Letters by Phillis Wheatley." *Early American Literature* 7 (Winter 1974): 257–71. [All letters are from Wheatley in Boston to John Thornton in London: "Apr. 21, 1772"; "Dec. 1, 1773"; "Mar. 29, 1774"; "Oct. 30, 1770" (*sic;* actually 1774).]

Wagner, Jean. *Black Poets in the United States.* Translated by Kenneth Douglass. Urbana: University of Illinois Press, 1973. [Presents excerpt of letter dated "Boston, Feb. 11, 1774," from Wheatley to the Reverend Samson Occum in Connecticut.]

Edited Editions

Heartman, Charles Frederick, ed. *Poems and Letters.* With an appreciation by Arthur A. Schomburg. New York: C. F. Heartman, 1915; Miami: Mnemosyne Publishing Co., 1969. [The first collected edition.]

Mason, Julian D., Jr., ed. *The Poems of Phillis Wheatley.*
    Chapel Hill: University of North Carolina Press, 1966.
Memoir and Poems of Phillis Wheatley, a Native African and
    a Slave. Boston: G. W. Light, 1834. 2nd Edition.
    Boston: Light & Horton, 1835. 3rd Edition. Boston:
    Isaac Knapp, 1838; Miami: Mnemosyne Publishing Co.,
    1969. [The memoir by Margaretta Matilda Odell is the
    chief primary source for Wheatley's life.]
The Poems of Phillis Wheatley, as they were originally published
    in London, 1773. Philadelphia: R. R. and C. C. Wright,
    1909.
Renfro, G. Herbert, ed. *Life and Works of Phillis Wheatley.*
    Washington, DC: A. Jenkins, 1916; Miami: Mnemosyne
    Publishing Co., 1969; Plainview, NY: Books for Li-
    braries Press, 1970; Salem, NH: Ayer Co., 1984.
Robinson, William H., Jr., ed. *Phillis Wheatley and Her*
    Writings. New York: Garland, 1984. [Includes early
    poems extant in manuscripts and newspapers, a facsimile
    of *Poems on Various Occasions,* eight later poems, and
    twenty-five letters.]
Shields, John C., ed. *The Collected Works of Phillis Wheatley.*
    New York: Oxford University Press, 1988.
Six Broadsides Relating to Phillis Wheatley (Phillis Peters) with
    Portrait and Facsimile of her Handwriting. New York:
    Printed for Chas. Fred Heartman, 1915.
Wright, Charlotte Ruth, ed. *The Poems of Phillis Wheatley.*
    Philadelphia: the Wrights, 1930.
Works of Phillis Wheatley and Albert A. Whitman [Microfilm].
    New York: Public Library Collections.

Items Republished in Newspapers
"Church Review." *A.M.E. Church Review* (Jan. 1898): 332.
"A Farewell to America." *Liberator* (17 Nov. 1832): 184.

"A Funeral Poem on the Death of C. E., An Infant." *Liberator* (7 July 1832): 108.

"Goliath of Gath, I. Samuel, Ch. XVII." *Liberator* (28 Apr. 1832): 68.

"A Hymn to the Evening." *Liberator* (25 Feb. 1832): 32.

"Hymn to Humanity." *Freedom's Journal* (9 Nov. 1827): 140.

"A Hymn to Humanity." *Liberator* (1 Sept. 1832): 140.

"Hymn to Morning." *Freedom's Journal* (9 Nov. 1827): 140.

"A Hymn to the Morning." *Liberator* (19 May 1832): 80.

"Isaiah Ixiii, 1–8." *Liberator* (26 May 1832): 84.

Letter to Rev. Mr. Samuel Hopkins. *Pennsylvania Freeman* (9 May 1839): 1.

"Niobe in Distress for Her Children, Slain by Apollo." *Liberator* (22 Dec. 1832): 204.

"On Being Brought from Africa to America." *Liberator* (17 March 1832): 44.

"On the Death of J. C., An Infant." *Liberator* (20 Oct. 1832): 168.

"On the Death of Mr. Samuel Marshall, 1771." *Liberator* (14 July 1832): 112.

"On the Death of the Rev. Dr. Sewell, 1759." *Liberator* (24 March 1832): 48.

"On the Death of the Rev. Mr. George Whitefield, 1770." *A.M.E. Church Review* (Jan. 1898): 331.

"On the Death of the Rev. Mr. George Whitefield, 1770." *Liberator* (7 Apr. 1832): 56.

"On the Death of a Young Gentleman." *Liberator* (31 March 1832): 52.

"On the Death of a Young Lady of Five Years of Age." *Liberator* (14 Apr. 1832): 66.

"On Imagination." *Liberator* (9 June 1832): 92.

"On Recollection." *Liberator* (2 June 1832): 88.

"On Virtue." *A.M.E. Church Review* (Jan. 1898): 331.

"On Virtue." *Liberator* (18 Feb. 1832): 28.

"Recollection." *London Magazine* (March 1772): 134–35.

"The Tears of a Slave." *Liberator* (10 March 1832): 40.

"Thoughts on the Works of Providence." *A.M.E. Church Review* (Jan. 1898): 332.

"Thoughts on the Works of Providence." *Liberator* (8 Dec. 1832): 196.

"To Captain H———D, of the LXV Regiment." *Liberator* (18 Aug. 1832): 132.

"To a Clergyman, on the Death of His Lady." *Liberator* (12 May 1832): 76.

"To a Gentleman on His Voyage to Great Britain for the Recovery of His Health." *Liberator* (13 Oct. 1832): 164.

"To His Honor the Lieutenant Governor, on the Death of His Lady—March 24, 1773." *Liberator* (25 Aug. 1832): 136.

"To the Hon. T. H., Esq. on the Death of His Daughter." *Liberator* (28 July 1832): 120.

"To the King's Most Excellent Majesty, 1768." *Liberator* (10 March 1832): 40.

"To a Lady and Her Children, on the Death of Her Son and Their Brother." *Liberator* (22 Sept. 1832): 152.

"To a Lady, on the Death of Her Husband." *Liberator* (21 Apr. 1832): 66.

"To a Lady, on the Death of Three Relations." *Liberator* (5 May 1832): 72.

"To the Lady, on Her Coming to North America with Her Son, for the Recovery of Her Health." *Liberator* (15 Sept. 1832): 148.

"To a Lady on Her Remarkable Preservation in a Hurricane in North Carolina." *Liberator* (11 Aug. 1832): 128.

"To Maecenas." *Liberator* (11 Feb. 1832): 24.

"To the Rev. Dr. Thomas Amory." *Liberator* (8 Sept. 1832): 144.

"To the Right Hon. William, Earl of Dartmouth, His Majesty's Principal Secretary of State for North America." *Liberator* (29 Sept. 1832): 156.

"To S. M., a Young African Painter, on Seeing His Works." *Liberator* (21 July 1832): 116.

"To the University of Cambridge in New England." *Liberator* (3 March 1832): 36.

Washington, George. Letter. *Anti-Slavery Record* 1 (1835): 170.

———. Letter to Phillis Wheatley [Extract]. *Pennsylvania Freeman* (24 May 1838): 2.

———. Letter to Phillis Wheatley. *Pennsylvania Freeman* (19 Feb 1846): 1.

"Ye martial pow'rs, and all ye tuneful mine, . . ." [on Goliath of Gath]. *A.M.E. Church Review* (Jan. 1898): 333.

Anthologies

Allen, William G. *Wheatley, Banneker, and Horton; with Selections from the Poetical Works of Wheatley and Horton and the Letter of Washington to Wheatley, and of Jefferson to Banneker.* Boston: Press of Daniel Laing, 1849.

Barksdale, Richard, and Keneth Kinnamon. *Black Writers of America: A Comprehensive Anthology.* New York: Macmillan, 1972. 38–44.

Brawley, Benjamin Griffith. *Early Negro American Writers: Selections with Biographical and Critical Introductions.* Chapel Hill: University of North Carolina Press, 1935; Freeport, NY: Books for Libraries Press, 1968; New York: Dover Publications, 1970.

Brown, Sterling A., Arthur P. Davis, and Ulysses Lee, eds. *The Negro Caravan: Writings by American Negroes*. New York: Dryden Press, 1941; Arno Press, 1970. 283–86.

Calverton, V. F., ed. *An Anthology of American Literature*. New York: Modern Library, 1929.

Chambers, Bradford, and Rebecca Moon, eds. *Right On! An Anthology of Black Literature*. New York: New American Library, 1970.

Child, Lydia Maria, ed. *The Freedmen's Book*. Boston: Ticknor and Fields, 1865.

Davis, Arthur P., and J. Saunders Redding, eds. *Cavalcade: Negro American Writing from 1760 to the Present*. Boston: Houghton Mifflin, 1971. 8–16.

Eleazer, Robert B., comp. *Singers in the Dawn*. 7th Edition. Atlanta: Commission on Interracial Cooperation, 1942, 1943.

Faderman, Lillian, and Barbara Bradshaw, eds. *Speaking for Ourselves*. Glenview, IL: Scott, Foresman, 1969.

Ford, Nick Aaron, ed. *Black Insights: Significant Literature by Black Americans, 1760 to the Present*. Waltham, MA: Ginn, 1971.

Haslam, Gerald W., ed. *Forgotten Pages of American Literature*. Boston: Houghton Mifflin, 1970.

Hayden, Robert, ed. *Kaleidoscope*. New York: Harcourt, Brace & World, 1967.

Hughes, Langston, and Arna Bontemps, eds. *The Poetry of the Negro, 1746–1970*. Revised ed. Garden City, NY: Doubleday, 1970.

Lomax, Alan, and Raoul Abdul, eds. *3000 Years of Black Poetry*. New York: Dodd, Mead, 1970.

Long, Richard A., and Eugenia W. Collier, eds. *Afro-American Writing: An Anthology of Prose and Poetry*. New

York: New York University Press, 1972. 2nd and Enlarged Edition. University Park: Pennsylvania State University Press, 1985.

Miller, Ruth, ed. *Blackamerican Literature: 1760–Present*.
Beverly Hills, CA: Glencoe Press, 1971. 33–39.

Patterson, Lindsay. *Introduction to Black Literature in America*. New York: Publishers Co., 1968.

Porter, Dorothy, ed. *Early Negro Writing 1760–1837*. Boston: Beacon Press, 1971. 532–34.

Randall, Dudley, ed. *The Black Poets*. New York: Bantam
Books, 1971.

Robinson, William H., Jr., ed. *Early Black American Poets*.
Dubuque, IA: William C. Brown Company Publishers,
1969. 97–112, 257.

––––––. *Early Black American Prose*. Dubuque, IA: William
C. Brown Company Publishers, 1970. 3–10.

Shockley, 22–25.

Spurgeon, Charles, ed. *Ebony and Topaz*. Freeport, NY:
Books for Libraries Press, 1971.

Sterling, Dorothy, ed. *Speak Out in Thunder Tones: Letters
and Other Writings by Black Northerners, 1787–1865*.
Garden City, NY: Doubleday, 1973. 42–44, 382.

Untermeyer, Louis, ed. *American Poetry from the Beginning
to Whitman*. New York: Harcourt, Brace, [c.1931].

White, Newman Ivey, and Walter Clinton Jackson, eds. *An
Anthology of Verse by American Negroes*. Durham, NC:
Moore, 1968. 3, 4–5, 27–28, 220–25, 230–31, 235.

Bibliographies

Heartman, Charles Frederick. *Phillis Wheatley (Phillis Peters): A Critical Attempt and a Bibliography of her Writings*.
New York: the Author, 1915.

Myers, Carol Fairbanks. *Women in Literature: Criticism of the Seventies*. Metuchen, NJ: Scarecrow Press, 1976. 202.

Porter, Dorothy B. "Early American Negro Writings: A Bibliographical Study." *The Papers of the Bibliographical Society of America* 30 (Third Quarter 1945): 192–270. [For Wheatley, see pp. 261–67.]

————. *North American Negro Poets: A Bibliographical Checklist of Their Writings, 1760–1944*. Hattiesburg, MS: Book Farm, 1945.

Robinson, William H., Jr. *Phillis Wheatley: A Bibliography*. Boston: G. K. Hall, 1981.

Rush, 752–58.

Schomburg, Arthur Alfonso, comp. *A Bibliographical Checklist of American Negro Poetry*. New York: C. F. Heartman, 1916.

Writings about

Ahuma, S.R.B. *Memoirs of West African Celebrities, Europe, &c. (1700–1850) With Special Reference to the Gold Coast*. Liverpool: D. Marples, 1905.

Akers, Charles W. "Our Modern Egyptians: Phillis Wheatley and the Whig Campaign against Slavery in Revolutionary Boston." *Journal of Negro History* (Apr. 1975): 397–410.

Applegate, Ann. "Phillis Wheatley: Her Critics and Her Contribution." *Negro American Literature Forum* 9 (1975): 123–26.

Armistead, Wilson A. *A Tribute for the Negro*. Manchester, England: William Irvin, 1848; Westport, CT: Negro Universities Press, 1970.

Bacon, Martha Sherman. *Puritan Promenade*. Boston: Houghton Mifflin, 1964.

Baker, Houston, Jr. *Long Black Song: Essays in Black Amer-*

ican Literature and Culture. Charlottesville: University Press of Virginia, 1972.

Baker, Thomas Nelson. "The Negro Women." *Alexander's Magazine* (15 Dec. 1906).

Bardolph, Richard. *The Negro Vanguard.* New York: Random House, 1961. 32–34, 54, 83, 184.

——. "Social Origins of Distinguished Negroes 1770–1865." *Journal of Negro History* (July 1955): 226.

Baskin, Wade, and Richard Runes. *Dictionary of Black Culture.* New York: Philosophical Library, 1973. 468.

Belock, M. "Biographical Sketches of Men of Color." *Educational Forum* (Jan. 1970): 212–13.

Bennett, M. W. "Negro Poets." *Negro History Bulletin* (May 1946): 171–72.

Bergman, Peter M. *The Chronological History of the Negro in America.* New York: Harper & Row, 1969. 28, 38, 54, 59.

Borland, Kathryn Kilby, and Helen Ross Speicher. *Phillis Wheatley: Young Colonial Poet.* Indianapolis: Bobbs-Merrill, 1968. [A biography for children.]

Brawley, *NBH*, 19–24.

Brawley, *NG*, 17–19, 28–32, 73, 90.

Brawley, *NLA*, 10–32, 73, 75, 103.

Brawley, Benjamin Griffith. "Phillis Wheatley." *Voice of the Negro* (Jan. 1906): 55.

Brown, 5–10.

Brown, Sterling. *Negro Poetry and Drama and the Negro in American Fiction.* New York: Arno Press, 1969. Republication of *Negro Poetry and Drama.* Washington, DC: The Associates in Negro Folk Education, 1937; and *The Negro in American Fiction.* Washington, DC, The Associates in Negro Folk Education, 1937.

Brown, William Wells. *The Black Man, His Antecedents, His*

Genius, and His Achievements. New York: Thomas Hamilton; Boston: R. F. Wallcut, 1863; New York: Johnson Reprints, 1968.

———. *The Rising Son; or, the Antecedents and Advancement of the Colored Race*. Boston: A. G. Brown & Co., 1874.

Bruce, John Edward. *Short Biographical Sketches of Eminent Negro Men and Women in Europe and the United States*. Vol 1. Yonkers, NY: Gazette Press, 1910.

———. *Tracts for the People* [Tract no. 13]. Yonkers, NY: n.p., [18?].

Butcher, Margaret Just. *The Negro in American Culture* [c.1956]. New York: Mentor, 1971. 24, 96, 170.

Clarke, John Henrik. "The Origin and Growth of Afro-American Literature." *Journal of Human Relations* 16.3 (1968): 368–84.

Collins, Terence. "Phillis Wheatley; the Dark Side of the Poetry." *Phylon* 36 (1975): 77–88.

Cook, Mercer, and Stephen E. Henderson. *The Militant Black Writer in Africa and the United States*. Madison: University of Wisconsin Press, 1969.

Cromwell, John Wesley. *The Negro in American History; Men and Women Eminent in the Evolution of the American of African Descent*. Washington, DC: The American Negro Academy, [c.1914].

DANB, 640–42.

Dannett, 1: 32–39.

Davis, Arthur P. "Personal Elements in the Poetry of Phillis Wheatley." *Phylon* 13 (1953): 191–98.

Davis, John P., ed. *The American Negro Reference Book*. Englewood Cliffs, NJ: Prentice-Hall, 1966. 23, 766, 850–51.

Delany, Martin Robinson. *The Condition, Elevation, Immigration, and Destiny of the Colored People of the United*

States. Philadelphia: the Author, 1852; New York: Arno Press, 1968. 87–90.

Dobbler, Lavinia G., and Edgar A. Toppin. *Pioneers and Patriots: The Lives of Six Negroes of the Revolutionary Era*. Garden City, NY: Doubleday, 1965. 30–50.

Du Bois, W.E.B. *The Gift of Black Folk, The Negroes in the Making of America*. Boston: Stratford, 1924.

Eppse, Merl R. *The Negro, Too, in American History*. Chicago: National Educational Publisher, 1939.

Erkkila, Betsy. "Revolutionary Women." *Tulsa Studies in Women's Literature* (Fall 1987): 189–223.

Fabre, Michel. "Phyllis [*sic*] Wheatley, poetesse noire de l'independance." In *La France et l'esprit de 76*. Daniel Royot, ed. Clermont-Ferrand: Assn. pour les Pubs. de la Faculté des Lett. et. Sciences Humaines. 1977. 149–62.

"Facing Facts to Be Celebrated During Negro History Week." *Negro History Bulletin* (Feb. 1939): 38.

Fauset, Arthur Huff. *For Freedom; A Biographical Story of the American Negro*. Philadelphia: Franklin Publishing and Supply Co., [c.1927].

Fishel, Leslie H., and Benjamin Quarles. *The Black in America: A Documentary History*. 3rd Edition. Glenview, IL: Scott, Foresman, [c.1976].

Frazier, Susan Elizabeth. "Some Afro-American Women of Mark." *A.M.E. Church Review* (Apr. 1892): 378–86.

Gayle, Addison. *Black Expression*. New York: Weybright and Talley, 1969.

Graham, Shirley. *The Story of Phillis Wheatley*. New York: J. Messner, 1949.

———. "The Story of Phillis Wheatley." *Negro Digest* (Dec. 1949): 85–97.

Grant, Abraham. *Deaconess Manual of the African Methodist Episcopal Church*. N.p.: African Methodist Episcopal Church, Bishop's Council, 1902.

Greene, Lorenzo Johnston. *The Negro in Colonial New England*. New York: Atheneum, 1968.

Gregoire, Henri. *An Enquiry Concerning the intellectual and moral faculties and literature of Negroes; followed with an account of the life and works of fifteen negroes and mulattoes, distinguished in science, literature and the arts*. D. B. Warden, trans. Brooklyn, NY: Thomas Kirk, 1918. [Originally published as *De la litterature des Negres. . . .* Paris: Maradan, 1808.]

Griswold, Rufus Wilmot. *The Female Poets of America*. Philadelphia: Carey and Hart, 1849.

Hammon, Jupiter. *An Address to Miss Phillis Wheatley, an Ethiopian Poetess in Boston Who Came from Africa at Eight Years of Age, and Soon Became Acquainted with the Gospel of Jesus Christ*. Hartford, CT: the Author, 1778. [Widely republished.]

Happer, Emily Foster. *The First Negro Poet of America*. [Detached from *Literary Collector* (July 1904).] Greenwich, CT: Literary Collector Press, [c.1904].

Harris, Trudier, ed. *Afro-American Writers Before the Harlem Renaissance. Dictionary of Literary Biography*. Vol. 50. Detroit: Gale, 1986.

Haviland, Laura S. *A Women's Life-Work: Labors and Experiences of Laura S. Haviland*. Cincinnati: Walden and Stowe, 1881, 1882; Chicago: C. V. Waite and Co., 1887; Publishers Association of Friends, 1889; Miami: Mnemosyne Publishing Co., 1969.

Haynes, Elizabeth Ross. *Unsung Heroes*. New York: DuBois and Dill, 1921.

Holmes, Wilfred. "Phyllis [*sic*] Wheatley." *Negro History Bulletin* (Feb. 1943): 117–18.

Horton, Luci. "The Legacy of Phillis Wheatley." *Ebony* (March 1974): 94–102.

Hughes, Langston. *Famous American Negroes*. New York: Dodd, Mead, 1954.

Hull, Gloria T. "Black Women Poets from Wheatley to Walker." In *Sturdy Black Bridges: Visions of Black Women in Literature*. Roseann P. Bell, Bettye J. Parker, and Beverly Guy-Sheftall, eds. Garden City, NY: Anchor Press, Doubleday, 1979.

"Intelligent Negroes." *Chamber's Miscellany of Useful and Entertaining Tracts*. Edinburgh: W. & R. Chambers, 1946. 7: 63.

Isaacs, Harold R. *The New World of Negro Americans*. New York: John Day Co., 1963.

Isani, Mukhtar Ali. "The British Reception of Wheatley's *Poems on Various Subjects*." *Journal of Negro History* (Summer 1981): 144–49.

———. "The First Proposed Edition of *Poems on Various Subjects* and the Phillis Wheatley Canon." *American Literature* (March 1977): 97–103.

———. "Gambia on My Soul: Africa and the African in the Writings of Phillis Wheatley." *MELUS* 6 (1979): 64–72.

Jackson, Blyden. *The Waiting Years: Essays in American Negro Literature*. Baton Rouge: Louisiana State University Press, 1976.

Jensen, Marilyn. "Boston's Poetic Slave." *New-England Galaxy* 18.3 (1977): 22–29.

Johnson, Allen, and Dumas Malone, eds. *Dictionary of American Biography*. 20 vols. New York: Scribner's, 1928–1937. Seven Supplements, 1944–1965.

Johnson, James Weldon. *Black Manhattan*. New York: Knopf, 1930.

Johnson, Lonnell Edward. "Portrait of the Bondslave in the

Bible: Slavery and Freedom in the Works of Four Afro-American Poets." *Dissertation Abstracts International* 47 (1987): 3038A.

Jordan, June. "The Difficult Miracle of Black Poetry in America; or, Something Like a Sonnet for Phillis Wheatley." *Massachusetts Review* (Summer 1986): 252–62.

Kaplan, Sidney. *The Black Presence in the Era of the American Revolution, 1770–1800.* Greenwich, CT: New York Graphic Society in association with the Smithsonian Institution Press, 1973.

Klinkowitz, Jerome. "Early Writers: Jupiter Hammon, Phillis Wheatley, and Benjamin Banneker." In *Black American Writers: Bibliographical Essays, I: The Beginnings through the Harlem Renaissance and Langston Hughes.* Thomas M. Inge, Maurice Duke, and Jackson R. Bryer, eds. New York: St. Martin's Press, 1978. 1–20.

Koike, Sekio. "Phillis Wheatley: Her Place in American Slave Literature." *Kyushu American Literature* (Fukuoka, Japan) 18 (1977): 33–39.

Le Cointe-Marsillac. *Le More-Lack, ou essai sur les moyens les plus doux et les pins équitables d'abolir.* . . . London and Paris: Pranit, 1789.

Levernier, James A. "Wheatley's 'On Being Brought from Africa to America.'" *Explicator* (Fall 1981): 25–26.

Levernier, James A., and Douglas R. Wilmes, eds. *American Writers before 1800: A Biographical and Critical Dictionary.* 3 vols. Westport, CT: Greenwood Press, 1983.

Literature of the Revolution, 1765–1787. Vol. 3. Library of American Literature. New York: Webster, 1891.

"Life and Works of Phillis Wheatley." G. Herbert Renfro, comp. [Review.] *Crisis* 13 (1917): 287.

Loggins, 5, 14, 16–29, 43, 55, 93, 97, 105, 110, 116,

179, 232, 238, 239, 248, 336, 341, 342, 344, 353, 369, 370, 371, 372, 373, 409–10, 411.

Lossing, Benson John. *Eminent Americans: Comprising Brief Biographies of Three Hundred and Thirty Distinguished Persons*. New York: Mason Brothers, [c.1856].

Low, W. A., and Virgil A. Clift, eds. *Encyclopedia of Black America*. New York: McGraw-Hill, 1981.

Majors, 17–23.

Mather, Samuel. *Who Was Who in America: Historical Volume (H) 1607–1896*. Chicago: Marquis, 1963. 338.

Matson, R. Lynn. "Phillis Wheatley—Soul Sister?" *Phylon* (Fall 1972): 222–30.

Mays, Benjamin E. *The Negro's God as Reflected in His Literature*. Boston: Chapman and Grimes, 1938.

Miller, Kelly. "The Artistic Gifts of the Negro." *Voice of the Negro* (Apr. 1906): 252.

Montgomery, Gregory. "The Spirit of Phillis Wheatley." *Opportunity* (June 1924): 181–82.

Morrison, Allen. "Phylis [*sic*] Wheatley." *Ebony* (Aug. 1966): 90.

NAW, 3: 573–74.

Negro History Bulletin (Feb. 1938): 6; (Apr. 1940): 107; (Nov. 1940): 46.

"Negro Poets, Singers in the Dawn." *Negro History Bulletin* (Nov. 1938): 10.

Nell, William C. *The Colored Patriots of the American Revolution*. Boston: Robert F. Wallcut, 1855; New York: Arno Press, 1968. 64–73.

[Obituary.] *Boston Magazine* (Dec. 1784): 619–20, 630.

Ogude, S. E. "Slavery and the African Imagination: A Critical Perspective." *World Literature Today* (Winter 1981): 21–25.

O'Neale, Sondra. "A Slave's Subtle War: Phyllis [*sic*]

Wheatley's Use of Biblical Myth and Symbol." *Early American Literature* (Fall 1986): 144–65.

Ovington, Mary White. *Phillis Wheatley* [Play]. New York: Schulte Press, [c.1932].

Oxley, Thomas L. G. "Survey of Negro Literature, 1760–1926." *Messenger* (Feb. 1927): 37–39.

Parks, Carole A. "Phillis Wheatley Comes Home. . . ." *Black World* (Feb. 1974): 92–97.

Parton, James. "Phillis Wheatley, the Negro Poetess." *Wood's Household Magazine* (July 1872): 7–9.

Person, James E., Jr., ed. *Literary Criticism from 1400–1800*. Vol. 3. Detroit: Gale, 1986.

Phyllis [sic] *Wheatley* [Pamphlet]. Denver: Lawrence and Co., 1887.

Pinkney, Alphonso. *Black American*. Englewood Cliffs, NJ: Prentice-Hall, 1969.

"The Poems of Phillis Wheatley. Charlotte Ruth Wright, ed." [Review.] *Crisis* 37 (1930): 321.

"The Poems of Phillis Wheatley." *Crisis* (Dec. 1911): 49.

"The Poems of Wheatley." *A.M.E. Church Review* (Jan. 1910): 282–85.

Porter, Dorothy B. "Women Activists, Wives, Intellectuals, Mothers, and Artists." In *Candidates for Rediscovery: The Boston Version*. Proceedings of a Symposium at the Afro-American Studies Center, Boston University, 12 Apr. 1975. Boston: Afro-American Studies Center, Boston University, 1975. 76–84.

Quarles, Benjamin. *Black Abolitionists*. New York: Oxford University Press, 1969. 35

———. "Black History's Early Advocates." *Negro Digest* (Feb. 1970): 4–9.

Rawley, James A. "The World of Phillis Wheatley." *New England Quarterly* (Dec. 1977): 666–77.

Redding, J. Saunders. *They Came in Chains*. Philadelphia: J. B. Lippincott, 1950.

————. *To Make a Poet Black*. Chapel Hill: University of North Carolina Press, 1939.

Remond, Charles Lenox. "Phillis Wheatley." *Negro History Bulletin* (Feb. 1938): 6.

Renfro, G. Herbert. "A Discourse on the Life and Poetry of Phillis Wheatley." *A.M.E. Church Review* (July 1891): 76–109.

Richmond, Merle A. *Bid the Vassal Soar: Interpretive Essays on the Life and Poetry of Phillis Wheatley and George Moses Horton*. Washington, DC.: Howard University Press, 1974.

Ricketson, Daniel. *The History of New Bedford, Bristol County, Massachusetts*. New Bedford, MA: the Author, 1858.

Rigsby, Gregory. "Form and Content in Phillis Wheatley's Elegies." *CLA Journal* 19.2 (1975): 248–57.

Robinson, 37.

Robinson, William H., Jr. *Black New England Letters: The Uses of Writings in Black New England*. NEH Learning Library Program, no. 2. Boston: Boston Public Library, 1977.

————, ed. *Critical Essays on Phillis Wheatley*. Boston: G. K. Hall, 1982.

————. *Early Black American Prose*. Dubuque, IA: William C. Brown Company Publishers, 1971. 3.

————. *Phillis Wheatley and Her Writings*. New York: Garland, 1984.

————. "Phillis Wheatley in London." *CLA Journal* 21 (1977): 187–201.

Rogal, Samuel J. "Phillis Wheatley's Methodist Connection." *Black American Literature Forum* (Spring–Summer 1987): 85–95.

Rollins, Charlemae, ed. *Famous American Negro Poets*. New York: Dodd, Mead, 1965.

————. *They Showed the Way: Forty American Negro Leaders*. New York: Thomas Y. Crowell, 1964.

Roy, J. H. "Know Your History." *Negro History Bulletin* (Jan. 1958): 87.

Rubin, Louis D. "The Search for a Language, 1746–1923." In *Black Poetry in America: Two Essays in Historical Interpretation*. Blyden Jackson and Louis D. Rubin, Jr. Baton Rouge: Louisiana State University Press, 1974. 1–35.

Rush, 752–53.

Scheick, William J. "Phillis Wheatley and Oliver Goldsmith: A Fugitive Satire." *Early American Literature* (Spring 1984): 82–84.

Scruggs, 265.

Scruggs, Charles. "Phillis Wheatley and the Poetical Legacy of Eighteenth-Century England." *Studies in Eighteenth-Century Culture* 10 (1981): 279–95.

Seeber, Edward D. "Phillis Wheatley." *Journal of Negro History* (July 1939): 259–62.

Sherman, 252–53.

Shields, John C. "Phillis Wheatley and Mather Byles: A Study in Literary Relationship." *CLA Journal* (June 1980): 377–90.

————. "Phillis Wheatley's Poetics of Ascent." *Dissertation Abstracts International* 39 (1979): 4948A.

————. "Phillis Wheatley's Use of Classicism." *American Literature* 52.1 (1980): 97–111.

Shockley, 17–22.

Shockley, Ann Allen. "The Negro Woman in Retrospect: A Blueprint for the Future." *Negro History Bulletin* (Dec. 1965): 55–56.

Shurtleff, N. S. "Phillis Wheatley, The Negro-Slave Poet."

Proceedings of the Massachusetts Historical Society (1864). 7: 270–72.

Sistrunk, Albertha. "Phillis Wheatley: An Eighteenth-Century Black American Poet Revisited." *CLA Journal* 23 (1980): 391–98.

Steele, Thomas J., S.J. "The Figure of Columbia: Phillis Wheatley Plus George Washington." *New England Quarterly* (June 1981): 264–66.

Stephen, Leslie, and Sidney Lee, eds. *Dictionary of National Biography*. 21 vols., 1 supplement. London: Oxford University Press, 1882–1900. 7 Supplements, 1901–1970.

Tasker, William W. "Panorama of American Literature." *Daye* (1947): 46–47.

Thatcher, Benjamin Bussey. *Memoir of Phillis Wheatley, a Native African and a Slave*. Boston: G. W. Light; New York: Moore and Payne, 1834.

Thorpe, Earl E. "African Thought in Negro Americans." *Negro History Bulletin* (Oct. 1959): 5.

Toppin, Edgar A. *A Biographical History of Blacks in America Since 1528*. New York: David McKay, 1971.

Turner, Darwin T. *Black American Literature: Essays, Poetry, Fiction, Drama*. Columbus, OH: Charles E. Merrill, 1970.

Turner, Lorenzo Dow. "Anti-Slavery Sentiments in American Literature." *Journal of Negro History* (Oct. 1949): 388–89.

Wegelin, Oscar. *Was Phillis Wheatley America's First Negro Poet?* [Detached from *Literary Collector* (Aug. 1904).] Greenwich, CT: Literary Collector Press, [c.1904].

Weight, Glenn S. "Anniversary of Phillis Wheatley Remains an Inspiration to All." *Negro History Bulletin* 25.4 (1962): 91–92.

Wesley, 42.

Wheatley, Hannibal Parish. *Genealogy of the Wheatley or Wheatleigh Family*. Farmington, NH: E. H. Thomas, 1902.

Williams, George W. *History of the Negro Race, 1619–1800*. Vol. 1. New York: G. P. Putnam's Sons, 1883; Arno Press, 1968.

Williams, Kenny J. *They Also Spoke: An Essay on Negro Literature in America, 1787–1930*. Nashville: Townsend, 1970.

Williams, Ora. *American Black Women in the Arts and Sciences*. Metuchen, NJ: Scarecrow Press, 1973.

Wilson, G. R. "The Religion of the American Negro Slave: His Attitude Towards Death." *Journal of Negro History* (Jan. 1923): 44–45.

Women and Literature (Fall 1976): 85–86.

Woodson, Carter G., ed. "Phillis Wheatley." In *The Mind of the Negro as Reflected in Letters Written During the Crisis 1800–1860*. Washington, DC: Association for the Study of Negro Life and History, 1926; New York: Negro Universities Press, 1969. xvi–xxi.

Workman, W. D. "Historical Group Aids the Negro." *Negro History Bulletin* (Apr. 1961): 159.

Yeocum, Rev. William H. "Phillis Wheatley, the First African Poetess." *A.M.E. Church Review* (Jan. 1890): 329–33.

Papers in Collections

[Biographical Articles.] Sophia Smith Collection, Smith College.

"Boston, Oct. 25th 1770." To the Countess of Huntington. Countess of Huntington Papers, Cambridge University. [Covers an enclosed version of Wheatley's eulogy on Whitefield.]

"Boston, May 6, 1774." To the Reverend Samuel Hopkins in Newport, RI. Manuscript collections, Boston Public Library.

"Boston N.E., Oct. 10, 1772." To the Earl of Dartmouth, covering the enclosed manuscript poem, "To the Right Honourable William Earl." Massachusetts Historical Society. [A variant version of the poem was published in the *New York Journal* (June 3, 1773).]

Copy of inscriptions to Thomas Wallcott. 26 March 1774. In *The Importance of Early Piety*. John Lathrop. Boston: n.p., 1771. Beinecke Library, Yale University.

Latimer, C., comp. *Bibliography on the Contribution of Negro Women to American Civilization* [Typescript]. February 1940; additions February 1942. Schomburg Center, New York Public Library.

"Queenstreet, Boston, July 15th 1778." to "Madam" [Mrs. Mary Clap Wooster] in New Haven. Library of Congress.

Robinson, Sylvia Blanche. "Salute to Phillis Wheatley" [Poem]. Archives, Robert W. Woodruff Library, Atlanta University.

Shenstone, William. *The Works, in Verse and Prose, of William Shenstone, esq.: Containing Letters to Particular Friends, from the Year 1739 to 1763.* 3rd Edition. London: Printed for J. Dodsley, 1773. Wheatley's inscribed copy. Schomburg Center, New York Public Library.

Stevens, Thomas. *Commonplace Book: Holograph, Consisting of Verse, Hymns and Anecdotes of Dissenting Ministers, with Table of Contents.* 1779–1781. Beinecke Library, Yale University.

Wheatley, Phillis. "To the University of Cambridge, 1767" [Photostat]. Manuscript Collection, Robert W. Woodruff Library, Atlanta University.

Writers' Program of the Work Projects Administration. *Negroes of New York*. New York, 1938–1941. [Microfilm.] Schomburg Center, New York Public Library.

Frances Anne Rollin Whipper [pseud. Frank A. Rollin] (1845/1847?–1901)

Writings by

Life and Public Services of Martin R. Delany. Boston: Lee and Shepard, 1868, 1883.

Anthologies

Life and Public Services of Martin R. Delany. In *Two Biographies by African-American Women*. Introduction by William L. Andrews. New York: Oxford University Press, 1991.
Shockley, 127.

Writings about

Loggins, 183, 259, 384, 390, 427, 428, 441.
Major, Gerri, and Doris E. Saunders. *Black Society*. Chicago: Johnson Publishing Co., 1976.
Shockley, 123–26.
Sterling, Dorothy. *The Making of an Afro-American: Martin Robison Delany, 1812–1885*. New York: Doubleday, 1971.
Ullman, Victor. *Martin R. Delany: The Beginning of Black Nationalism*. Boston: Beacon Press, 1971.
Williamson, Joel. *After Slavery: The Negro in South Carolina During Reconstruction, 1861–1877*. Chapel Hill: University of North Carolina Press, 1965.

*Elizabeth Wicks

Writings by

Address Delivered Before the African Female Benevolent Society of Troy, on Wednesday, February 12, 1834 . . . to which is Annexed an Eulogy on the Death of Mrs. Jane Lansing, With an Address by Eliza A. T. Dungy. Troy, NY: R. Buckley, 1834.

Fannie Barrier Williams (1855–1944)

Writings by

Present Status and Intellectual Progress of Colored Women. Address delivered by Fannie Barrier Williams before the Congress of Representative Women, World's Congress Auxiliary of the World's Columbian Exposition. Chicago, May, 1898. Chicago: n.p., 1898.

"After Many Days, A Christmas Story." Colored American Magazine (Dec. 1902): 140–53.

[Article.] Woman's Era (1 June 1894): 5.

[Article on Women's Suffrage.] Woman's Journal (7 March 1896).

"Chicago's Provident Hospital and Training School—Social Matters." Woman's Era (Oct.–Nov. 1986): 13–14.

"The Club Movement among the Colored Women." Voice of the Negro (March 1904): 99.

"The Club Movement among Colored Women in America." In A New Negro for a New Century. John E. MacBrady, ed. Chicago: American Publishing House, 1900; Miami: Mnemosyne Publishing Co., 1969. 379–405.

"Club Movement among Negro Women." In The Colored American from Slavery to Honorable Citizenship. J. W. Gibson and W. H. Crogman, eds. Atlanta: J. L. Nichols

& Co., [c. 1902]. [Revised and Enlarged Editions published 1902, 1912, and 1929 with title: *Progress of a Race; or, the Remarkable Advancement of the American Negro.*]

"The Clubs and Their Location in All the States of the National Association of Colored Women and Their Mission." In *A New Negro for a New Century*. John E. MacBrady, ed. Chicago: American Publishing House, 1900; Miami: Mnemosyne Publishing Co., 1969. 406–28.

"The Colored Girl." *Voice of the Negro* (June 1905): 400–403.

"The Colored Woman and Her Part in Race Regeneration." In *A New Negro for a New Century*. John E. MacBrady, ed. Chicago: American Publishing House, 1900.

"A Colored Woman's Tribute." *Woman's Journal* (9 March 1907).

"Colored Women of Chicago." *Southern Workman* (Oct. 1914): 564–66.

"The Frederick Douglas [*sic*] Centre." *Voice of the Negro* (Dec. 1904): 601–4.

"The Frederick Douglas [*sic*] Center." *Southern Workman* (June 1906): 334–36.

"An Extension of the Conference Spirit." *Voice of the Negro* (July 1904): 300–303.

"Great Britain's Compliment to American Colored Women." *Woman's Era* (Aug. 1894): 1.

"Illinois." *Woman's Era* (Apr. 1895): 4–5; (May 1895): 4–5; (June 1895): 4–5; (July 1895): 5–6; (Aug. 1895): 21–22; (Nov. 1895): 7–8; (Jan. 1896): 15–16; (Feb. 1896): 13–14.

"The Importance of Employment for Negro Women." *Hampton Negro Conference*. Proceedings. Vol. 7. Hampton, VA: Hampton Institute Press, 1898–1903.

"Industrial Education: Will It Solve the Negro Problem?" *Colored American Magazine* (July 1904): 491–95.

"The Influence of Art on Home Life." *Woman's Era* (May 1896): 13–14.

"The Need of Organized Womanhood." *Colored American Magazine* (Jan. 1909): 652–53.

"The Negro and Public Opinion." *Voice of the Negro* (Jan. 1904): 31.

"The New Colored Woman." In *Sparkling Gems of Race Knowledge Worth Reading*. . . . James T. Haley, comp. Nashville: J. T. Haley and Co., 1897.

"A New Method of Dealing with the Race Problem." *Voice of the Negro* (July 1906): 502.

"A Northern Negro's Autobiography." *Independent* (14 July 1904).

["The one thing that should appeal most strongly to our hearts. . . ."] In *Sparkling Gems of Race Knowledge Worth Reading*. . . . James T. Haley, comp. Nashville: J. T. Haley and Co., 1897. 110–11.

"Opportunities and Responsibilities of Colored Women." In *Afro-American Encyclopedia*. . . . James T. Haley, comp. Nashville: Haley & Florida, 1895. 141–61.

"Perils of the White Negro." *Colored American Magazine* (Dec. 1907): 421–23.

"Refining Influence of Art." *Voice of the Negro* (March 1906): 211.

"Religious Duty to the Negro." In *World's Parliament of Religions, Chicago, 1893*. John Wesley Hanson, ed. Chicago: n.p., 1896.

"The Smaller Economies." *Voice of the Negro* (May 1904): 184.

"Social Bonds in the 'Black Belt' of Chicago." *Charities* (7 Oct. 1905): 1–96. Reprinted in *Charities—The Negro in the Cities of the North*. New York: Charity Organization

Society, 1905. Also in *The Survey. The Negro in the Cities of the North*. New York: Charity Organization Society, [c. 1905].

["The Sweetest Flower that Blows. . . ."] *Colored American Magazine* (Dec. 1901): 3.

"The Timely Message of the Simple Life." *Voice of the Negro* (March 1905): 160.

"The Trained Nurse and Negro Homes." *Southern Workman* (Sept 1901): 481.

["We are scarcely willing to admit the fact that our own prejudices. . . ."] In *Sparkling Gems of Race Knowledge Worth Reading. . . .* James T. Haley, comp. Nashville: J. T. Haley and Co., 1897. 104.

"Vacation Values." *Voice of the Negro* (Dec. 1905): 863.

Wesley, 2, 12, 26, 35–36, 44, 46, 76.

"The Woman's Part in a Man's Business." *Voice of the Negro* (Nov. 1904): 543–47.

"Women in Politics." *Woman's Era* (Nov. 1894): 12–13.

"Work Attempted and Missed in Organized Club Work." *Colored American Magazine* (May 1908): 281–85.

Anthologies

Ammons, Elizabeth, comp. *Short Fiction by Black Women, 1900–1920*. New York: Oxford University Press, 1991.

Loewenberg, Bert J., and Ruth Bogin, eds. *Black Women in Nineteenth-Century American Life: Their Words, Their Thoughts, Their Feelings*. University Park: Pennsylvania State University Press, 1976. 263–80.

Stein, Leon, comp. *Fragments of Autobiography: An Original Anthology*. New York: Arno Press, 1974.

Writings about

Bullock, 97, 115, 122, 129, 192.

DANB, 656–57.

Dannett, 1: 327.

Davis, 266–67.

Martin, Charlotte Elizabeth. *The Story of Brockport for One Hundred Years*. Brockport, NY: n.p., 1929.

McClellan, G. M. "The Negro as a Writer." Culp, 279.

Meier, August. *Negro Thought in America, 1880–1915: Racial Ideologies in the Age of Booker T. Washington*. Ann Arbor: University of Michigan Press, 1963.

Mossell, 16, 21, 30.

"Mrs. Fannie Barier [*sic*] Williams in Boston." *Woman's Era* (June 1896): 3.

["Mrs. Fannie Barrier Williams of Chicago. . . ."] *Weekly Call* (23 Nov. 1895): 1.

["Mrs. Fannie Barrier Williams of the Editorial Staff. . . ."] *Weekly Call* (7 Sept. 1895): 1.

NAW, 3: 620–22.

Spear, Allen H. *Black Chicago*. Chicago: University of Chicago Press, 1967. 25, 66, 69–70, 83, 101.

Terrell, Mary Church. "The Social Functions during Inauguration Week." *Voice of the Negro* (Apr. 1904): 237.

Thornbrough, Emma Lou. *T. Thomas Fortune: Militant Journalist*. Chicago: University of Chicago Press, 1972.

"The *Voice of the Negro* for March." *Voice of the Negro* (Feb. 1905).

"The *Voice of the Negro* for 1905." *Voice of the Negro* (Dec. 1904).

Papers in Collections

Photograph, Sophia Smith Collection, Smith College.

Harriet E. Adams Wilson (c.1807/1808–1870)

Writings by

Our Nig; or, Sketches from the Life of a Free Black, In a Two-Story White House, North. Showing That Slavery's Shadows Fall Even There by "Our Nig." Boston: Printed by George C. Rand & Avery, 1859.

Our Nig; or, Sketches from the Life of a Free Black, In a Two-Story White House, North. Showing That Slavery's Shadows Fall Even There by "Our Nig." Henry Louis Gates, Jr., ed. New York: Random House, Vintage Books, 1983.

Anthologies

Gilbert, Sandra M., and Susan Gubar, eds. *The Norton Anthology of Literature by Women: The Tradition in English.* New York and London: W. W. Norton, 1985. 834–38.

Shockley, 88–95.

Writings about

Ammons, Elizabeth. "Stowe's Dream of the Mother-Savior: *Uncle Tom's Cabin* and American Women Writers before 1920." In *New Essays on Uncle Tom's Cabin.* Eric J. Sundquist, ed. Cambridge: Cambridge University Press, 1986. 155–95.

Foster, Frances Smith. "Adding Color and Contour to Early American Self-Portraitures: Autobiographical Writings of Afro-American Women." In *Conjuring: Black Women, Fiction, and Literary Tradition.* Marjorie Pryse and Hortense J. Spillers, eds. Bloomington: Indiana University Press, 1985.

Jones, Jacqueline. *"Our Nig; or, Sketches from the Life of a Free Black, In a Two-Story White House, North. Showing*

That Slavery's Shadows Fall Even There" [Review]. *Journal of Southern History* (Aug. 1984): 481–82.

Shockley, 84–88.

Watson, Carole McAlpine. *Prologue: The Novels of Black American Women, 1891–1965*. Westport, CT: Greenwood Press, 1985.

Viola Mae Young (1887–?)

Writings by

Little Helps for Pastors and Members. Rosebud, AL: the Author, 1909.

Phillis Wheatley.
From *Poems on Various Subjects, Religious and Moral* (1773).

Jarena Lee. From *Religious Experience and Journal of Mrs. Jarena Lee,
Giving an Account of Her Call to Preach the Gospel* (1849).

Frances E. W. Harper.
From *Homespun Heroines and other Women of Distinction* (1926) by Hallie Q. Brown.

Elleanor Eldridge.
Courtesy Dorothy Sterling.

Sarah Parker Remond.
Courtesy Dorothy Sterling.

Harriet Tubman. Courtesy Dorothy Sterling.

Elizabeth Keckley.
From *Homespun Heroines and other Women of Distinction* (1926) by Hallie Q. Brown.

Gertrude E. H. Bustill Mossell and children.
From *The Work of the Afro-American Woman* (1894).

Lucy A. Delaney. From *From the Darkness
Cometh the Light or Struggles for Freedom* (c. 1891).

Annie L. Burton. From *Memories of Childhood's Slavery Days* (1909).

Priscilla Jane Thompson. From *Ethiope Lays* (1900).

Ida B. Wells-Barnett.
Courtesy Dorothy Sterling.

Alice Dunbar-Nelson.
From *The Works of Alice
Dunbar-Nelson*.

Anna J. Cooper, Charlotte Forten Grimké, seated;
Ella D. Barrier (sister of Fannie Barrier Williams), Rev. Francis
Grimké, Fannie Shippen Smythe, standing, left to right.
Courtesy Dorothy Sterling.

PART II

Writings by and about
African-American Women Who Had Been
Held in Slavery and Whose Dictated Narratives
or Biographies Were Published
before the End of 1910

Note: Asterisk indicates writers identified in the process of compiling this listing, hence not searched in all the resources listed at the end of this volume.

Margaret Jane Blake (1811–1880)

Dictated Narrative/Biography

Memoirs of Margaret Jane Blake, Related to Sarah R. Levering, Baltimore Whose Father Owned Jane Blake. Philadelphia: Innes and Son, 1897.

Jane Brown

Dictated Narrative/Biography

Narratives of Jane Brown and Her Two Children, Related to the Reverend G. W. Offley. Hartford, CT: G. W. Offley, 1860.

Ellen Craft [and William Craft] (c.1826–c.1897)

Dictated Narrative/Biography

Running a Thousand Miles for Freedom; or the Escape of William and Ellen Craft from Slavery. London: William Tweedie, 1860; Miami: Mnemosyne Publishing Co., 1969; New York: Arno Press, 1969.

Writings by

Letter. *Liberator* (29 Nov. 1851). Reprinted in *The Mind of the Negro as Reflected in Letters Written during the Crisis, 1800–1860.* Carter Woodson, ed. Washington, DC: Association for the Study of Negro Life and History, 1926. 262–64. New York: Negro Universities Press, 1969.

Letter. *National Anti-Slavery Standard* (23 Dec. 1852): 123.

Letter to *Anti-Slavery Advocate*. *Pennsylvania Freeman* (23 Dec. 1852): 207.

Letter to the Editor. *Anti-Slavery Advocate* (Dec. 1852). *(BAP)*. Reprinted in *The British Isles, 1830–1865. The Black Abolitionist Papers*. C. Peter Ripley, ed. Vol. 1. Chapel Hill: University of North Carolina Press, 1985. 330–31.

Letter to John Bishop Estlin. 14 March 1853. Boston Public Library, Anti-Slavery Collections. *(BAP)*.

Letter to "Sir." *Liberator* (17 Dec. 1852). Reprinted in *The Mind of the Negro as Reflected in Letters Written during the Crisis, 1800–1860*. Carter Woodson ed. Washington, DC: Association for the Study of Negro Life and History, 1926. 262–64. New York: Negro Universities Press, 1969.

Craft, Ellen, and William Craft et al. "Address of the London Emancipation Committee to the Rev. George B. Cheever, D.D." 1 Aug. 1860. John Rylands Library, Manchester, England. *(BAP)*.

Craft, William, and Ellen Craft. Letter to "My Dear Friend." *Liberator* (2 Jan. 1852): 2. *(BAP)*.

Anthologies

Bontemps, Arna. *Great Slave Narratives*. Boston: Beacon Press, 1969.

Loewenberg, Bert J., and Ruth Bogin, eds. *Black Women in Nineteenth-Century American Life: Their Words, Their Thoughts, Their Feelings*. University Park: Pennsylvania State University Press, 1976. 104–24.

Robinson, William H., Jr., ed. *Early Black American Prose*. Dubuque, IA: William C. Brown Company Publishers, 1971. 141–56.

Sterling, Dorothy, ed. *Speak Out in Thunder Tones: Letters and Other Writings by Black Northerners, 1787–1865.* Garden City, NY: Doubleday, 1973. 156–60.

Writings about

"Account of Anti-Slavery Meeting at Bristol with Quotes." *Inquirer* (19 Apr. 1851). *(BAP).*

Anti-Slavery Meeting, Bristol, Eng., 1851. Bristol, England: James Ackerland, 1851.

Anti-Slavery Reporter [London] (1 July 1863): 155–56; (1 Sept. 1864): 18.

Blackett, R.J.M. "Fugitive Slaves in Britain: The Odyssey of William and Ellen Craft." *Journal of American Studies* [Great Britain] 12.1 (1978): 41–62.

Bowditch, Vincent Y. *Life and Correspondence of Henry Ingersoll Bowditch.* Vol 2. Boston and New York: Houghton Mifflin, 1902.

Brown, William Wells. *The American Fugitive in Europe. Sketches of Places and People Abroad.* Boston: J. P. Jewett and Co., 1855; New York: Sheldon, Lampont and Blakeman, 1855.

Butterfield, Stephen. *Black Autobiography in America.* Amherst: University of Massachusetts Press, 1975.

Commager, Henry Steele. *Theodore Parker.* Boston: Little, Brown, 1936.

Child, Lydia Maria. *Freedmen's Book.* Boston: Ticknor and Fields, 1865. 179–204.

DANB, 139–40.

Dannett, 1: 126–31.

Doyle, Mary Ellen. "The Slave Narratives as Rhetorical Art." In *The Art of the Slave Narrative: Original Essays in Criticism and Theory.* Macomb: Western Illinois University, 1982.

Franklin, H. Bruce. *The Victim as Criminal and Artist*. New York: Oxford University Press, 1978.

Freedman [London] (1 Dec. 1865): 110–11; (1 July 1866): 276–78; (1 March 1867): 117–18; (1 Apr. 1867): 137; (1 May 1867): 151.

Frothingham, Octavius B. *Theodore Parker: A Biography*. Boston: J. R. Osgood and Co., 1874.

[May, Samuel.] *The Fugitive Slave Law and Its Victims* [Pamphlet]. New York: American Anti-Slavery Society, 1856, 1861; Freeport, NY: Books for Libraries Press, 1970.

McDougall, Marion Gleason. *Fugitive Slaves (1619–1865)*. Boston: Fay House Monographs No. 3, 1891.

National Anti-Slavery Standard (18 Sept. 1869).

National Anti-Slavery Standard (20 Nov. 1869).

NAW, 1: 396–98.

Porter, Dorothy. "Women Activists, Wives, Intellectuals, Mothers, and Artists." In *Candidates for Rediscovery: The Boston Version*. Proceedings of a Symposium at the Afro-American Studies Center, Boston University, 12 Apr. 1975. Boston: Afro-American Studies Center, Boston University, 1975. 76–84.

Quarles, Benjamin. *Black Abolitionists*. New York: Oxford University Press, 1969. 62, 63, 134, 135, 137, 148, 150, 202, 203.

Report of *The Great Anti-Slavery Meeting, Held April 9, 1851, in the Public Rooms, Broadmead, Bristol, to Receive the Fugitive Slaves, William and Ellen Craft* [Pamphlet]. Bristol, England, 1851.

Robinson, 69–70.

Siebert, Wilbur H. "The Vigilance Committee of Boston." *Bostonian Society Proceedings* (27 Jan. 1953): 26–28.

Singular Escapes from Slavery. Leeds, England: n.p., n.d.

Special Report of the Anti-Slavery Conference Held in Paris (1867). London, 1869.

Sterling, Dorothy. *Black Foremothers: Three Lives*. Old Westbury, NY: Feminist Press, 1979. 2–59.

Still, William. *The Underground Railroad. . . .* Philadelphia: Porter & Coates, 1872.

"Story of Ellen Crafts [*sic*]." *Wisconsin Free Democrat* (11 July 1849). *(BAP)*.

Weiss, John. *Life and Correspondence of Theodore Parker*. Vol. 2. New York, 1864; London: Longman, Green, Longman, Roberts, and Green, 1863; New York: D. Appleton & Co., 1864.

Williams, Kenny J. *They Also Spoke: An Essay on Negro Literature in America, 1787–1930*. Nashville: Townsend, 1970.

Collections

Report of the Great Anti-Slavery Meeting Held . . . In the Public Room, Broadmead, Bristol, To Receive the Fugitive Slaves William and Ellen Craft. 9 Apr. 1851. Printed by James' Ackland, Dolphin St., Bristol, England, 1851. Presscopy, Bibliothèque Nationale, Paris.

Starling, Marion Wilson. "The Slave Narrative, Its Place in American Literary History." Diss., New York University, 1946.

Silvia Dubois (c.1768–?)

Dictated Narrative/Biography

Larison, C. W., M.D. *Silvia Dubois, (Now 116 Years Old.) A Biografy of The Slav who Whipt Her Mistress and Gand Her Fredom*. Ringos, NJ: C. W. Larison, 1883.

———. *Silvia Dubois. A Biografy of the Slav Who Whipt*

Her Mistres and Gand Her Fredom. Jared C. Lobdell, ed. and trans. New York: Oxford University Press, 1988.

Anthologies

Loewenberg, Bert J., and Ruth Bogin, eds. *Black Women in Nineteenth-Century American Life: Their Words, Their Thoughts, Their Feelings*. University Park: Pennsylvania State University Press, 1976. 39–47.

Elleanor Eldredge (1785–?)

Dictated Narratives/Biographies

McDougall, Frances Harriet (Whipple) Green. *Elleanor's Second Book*. Providence, RI: B. T. Albro, Printer, 1839, 1841, 1842.

————. *Memoirs of Elleanor Eldridge*. Providence, RI: B. T. Albro, Printer, 1840, 1841, 1842, 1843, 1846, 1847.

————. *Memoirs of Elleanor Eldridge: Woman of Colour*. Austin and New York: The Pemberton Press, 1969. [Reprint of the 1842 edition.]

Anthologies

Loewenberg, Bert J., and Ruth Bogin, eds. *Black Women in Nineteenth-Century American Life: Their Words, Their Thoughts, Their Feelings*. University Park: Pennsylvania State University Press, 1976. 78–88.

Writings about

Dannett, 1: 67–69.

Elizabeth (1766–1866)

Dictated Narratives/Biographies

Elizabeth, A Colored Minister of the Gospel, Born in Slavery.
Philadelphia: Tract Association of Friends, 1889. Tract
Association of Friends, no. 170, Schomburg Center, New
York Public Library.

Memoir of Old Elizabeth, a Coloured Woman. Philadelphia:
Collins, Printer, 1863.

Anthologies

Loewenberg, Bert J., and Ruth Bogin, eds. *Black Women in
Nineteenth-Century American Life: Their Words, Their
Thoughts, Their Feelings.* University Park: Pennsylvania
State University Press, 1976. 127–34.

Memoir of Old Elizabeth, A Coloured Woman. In *Six Women's
Slave Narratives.* Introduction by William L. Andrews.
New York: Oxford University Press, 1988.

Mattie J. Jackson

Dictated Narrative/Biography

Thompson, Dr. L. S. *The Story of Mattie J. Jackson.* Lawrence, KS: Sentinel Office, 1866.

Anthologies

Thompson, Dr. L. S. *The Story of Mattie J. Jackson.* In *Six
Women's Slave Narratives.* Introduction by William L.
Andrews. New York: Oxford University Press, 1988.

*Phebe Ann Jacobs

Dictated Narrative/Biography

Upham, Mrs. T. C. *Narrative of Phebe Ann Jacobs.* London:
W. & F. G. Cash, [1850?].

Louisa Picquet (1828–?)

Dictated Narrative/Biography

Mattison, Rev. H., A.M. *Louisa Picquet, The Octoroon: A Tale of Southern Slave Life* [or *Inside Views of Southern Domestic Life*]. New York: the Author, 1861.

Anthologies

Loewenberg, Bert J., and Ruth Bogin, eds. *Black Women in Nineteenth-Century American Life: Their Words, Their Thoughts, Their Feelings*. University Park: Pennsylvania State University Press, 1976. 54–69.

Mattison, Rev. H., A.M. *Louisa Picquet, The Octoroon: A Tale of Southern Slave Life*. In *Collected Black Women's Narratives*. Introduction by Anthony G. Barthelemy. New York: Oxford University Press, 1988

Mary Prince

Dictated Narrative/Biography

Ferguson, Moira, ed. *The History of Mary Prince, a West Indian Slave, Related by Herself*. London and New York: Pandora Press, 1987.

Pringle, Thomas, ed. *The History of Mary Prince, a West Indian Slave. To which is added, The Narrative of Asa-Asa, a Captured African*. Edinburgh: Waugh & Innes; London: F. Westley and A. H. Davis, 1831.

Anthologies

Pringle, Thomas, ed. *The History of Mary Prince, a West Indian Slave. To which is added, The Narrative of Asa-Asa, a Captured African*. In *Classic Slave Narratives*.

Introduction by Henry Louis Gates, Jr. New York: Mentor, 1987.

———. *The History of Mary Prince, a West Indian Slave. To which is added, The Narrative of Asa-Asa, a Captured African.* In *Six Women's Slave Narratives.* Introduction by William L. Andrews. New York: Oxford University Press, 1988.

Chloe Spear (c.1749/50–1815)

Dictated Narrative/Biography

Webb, Mary C. *Memoir of Mrs. Chloe Spear, A Native of Africa, Who Was Enslaved in Childhood, and Died in Boston, January 3, 1815 . . . Aged 65 Years. By a Lady of Boston.* Boston: James Loring, 1832.

Writings about

Loggins, 97, 418.

Lavinia Still

Dictated Narrative/Biography

Pickard, [Mrs.] Kate E. *The Kidnapped and the Ransomed. Being the Personal Recollections of Peter Still and His Wife "Vina," after Forty Years of Slavery.* Syracuse: W. T. Hamilton; New York and Auburn, NY: Miller, Orton and Mulligan, 1856; New York: Negro Publication Society of America, 1941; Negro Universities Press, 1968.

———. *The Kidnapped and the Ransomed. Being the Personal Recollections of Peter Still and His Wife "Vina," after Forty Years of Slavery.* Maxwell Whiteman, ed. Philadelphia: Jewish Publication Society of America, 1970.

Writings about

Bleby, Henry. *The Stolen Children*. London: Wesleyan Conference, 1872.

Criterion (14 June 1856): 101.

National Anti-Slavery Standard (16 Aug. 1856).

Still, William. *The Underground Railroad*. . . . Philadelphia: Porter & Coates, 1872.

Sojourner Truth [Isabella Van Wagener] (1797–1883)

Dictated Narratives/Biographies

Gilbert, Olive. *Narrative of Sojourner Truth; A Bondswoman of Olden Time, Emancipated by the New York Legislature in the Early Part of the Present Century; With a History of Her . . . Last Sickness and Death*. Boston: published for the Author, 1875; Battle Creek, MI, 1878; Review and Herald Office, 1884; Chicago: Johnson Publishing Co., [c.1970], [reprint of 1878 edition].

————. *Narrative of Sojourner Truth; A Northern Slave, Emancipated from Bodily Servitude by The State of New York, in 1828*. Boston: published for the Author, 1850; New York: the Author, 1853.

Narrative of Sojourner Truth; A Bondswoman of Olden Time, With a History of Her Labors and Correspondence Drawn from Her "Book of Life." Introduction by Jeffrey C. Stewart. New York: Oxford University Press, 1991.

Writings by

Note: Although this subject was illiterate, the following items are attributed to her. We assume they were dictated.

Letter to the Editor. *Liberator* (2 Nov. 1833). *(BAP)*.

Letter to the Editor. *National Anti-Slavery Standard* (12 May 1866): 2; (27 Apr. 1867): 2; (19 Oct. 1867): 3. *(BAP)*.

Letter to a Friend. *Liberator* (23 Dec. 1864): 206.

Letter to William Lloyd Garrison. 28 Aug. 1851. Boston Public Library, Anti-Slavery Collections. *(BAP)*.

Letter to William Lloyd Garrison. 11 Apr. 1864. Boston Public Library, Anti-Slavery Collections. *(BAP)*.

Letter to Oliver Johnson. *National Anti-Slavery Standard* (13 Feb. 1864): 2. *(BAP)*.

Letter to Rowland Johnson. *National Anti-Slavery Standard* (17 Dec. 1864): 2. *(BAP)*.

Letter to Mr. A. M. Powell. *National Anti-Slavery Standard* (4 March 1871): 6.

Letter to the Reunion Subscription Festival. *National Anti-Slavery Standard* (20 May 1871): 5.

[With Charles L. Remond.] "Proceedings at the Anti-Slavery Celebration at Farmingham, 4 July 1854." *Liberator* (14 July 1854). *(BAP)*.

Speech at Akron, Ohio, 29 May 1851 ["Reminiscences by Frances D. Gage"]. In *History of Woman Suffrage*. Elizabeth Cady Stanton et al., eds. New York: Fowler and Wells, 1881. 1: 115–17.

Speech at New York City, 9 May 1867. In *History of Woman Suffrage*. Elizabeth Cady Stanton et al., eds. New York: Fowler and Wells, 1881. 2: 193–94.

Speech at New York City, 10 May 1867. In *History of Woman Suffrage*. Elizabeth Cady Stanton et al., eds. New York: Fowler and Wells, 1881. 2: 222.

Speech by Sojourner Truth. *National Anti-Slavery Standard* (11 July 1863). *(BAP)*.

Two Addresses in *Proceedings of the First Anniversary of the*

American Equal Rights Association Held at the Church of the Puritans, New York (9, 10 May 1867): 63, 66–68.

Anthologies

Brentano, Frances Isabella (Hyams), ed. *Nation Under God: A Religious-Patriotic Anthology.* Great Neck, NY: Channel Press, 1964.

Loewenberg, Bert J., and Ruth Bogin, eds. *Black Women in Nineteenth-Century American Life: Their Words, Their Thoughts, Their Feelings.* University Park: Pennsylvania State University Press, 1976. 234–44.

Mark, Irving, and Eugene L. Schwaab, eds. *The Faith of Our Fathers: An Anthology Expressing the Aspirations of the American Common Man, 1790–1860.* New York: Knopf, 1952. 33–34.

Sterling, Dorothy, ed. *Speak Out in Thunder Tones: Letters and Other Writings by Black Northerners, 1787–1865.* Garden City, NY: Doubleday, 1973. xi, 128–29, 143–44, 172–74, 330–31, 381.

Stetson, Erlene, ed. *Black Sister: Poetry by Black American Women, 1746–1980.* Bloomington: Indiana University Press, 1981. 24.

Writings about

[Account of Women's Rights Convention.] *Anti-Slavery Bugle* (21 June 1851). *(BAP)*.

"Ain't I a Woman?" *American Heritage* (Aug. 1976).

Armstrong, James W. "Candace Anderson's Sampler of Michigan Women." *Michigan History* 70.2 (1986): 16–23.

Bennett, Lerone. "Pioneers in Protest: Sojourner Truth." *Ebony* (19 Oct. 1964): 62–70.

Bernard, Jacqueline. *Journey Toward Freedom; the Story of Sojourner Truth*. New York: W. W. Norton, 1967.

Boulware, Marcus H. *The Oratory of Negro Leaders: 1900–1968*. Westport, CT: Negro Universities Press, 1969.

Brawley, *NBH*, 73–79.

Brawley, *NG*, 7, 261.

Brawley, *NLA*, 69, 84.

Brown, 13–17.

Campbell, Karlyn Kohrs. "Style and Content in the Rhetoric of Early Afro-American Feminists." *Quarterly Journal of Speech* (Nov. 1986): 434–45.

Collins, Helen, and Bruce Bliven. *A Mirror for Greatness: Six Americans*. New York: McGraw-Hill, 1975.

Collins, Kathleen. "Shadow and Substance: Sojourner Truth." *History of Photography* (July–Sept. 1983).

Cromwell, John Wesley. *The Negro in American History; Men and Women Eminent in the Evolution of the American of African Descent*. Washington, DC: The American Negro Academy, [c.1914].

Crosthwaite, Jane. "Women and Wild Beasts: Versions of the Exotic in Nineteenth Century American Art." *Southern Humanities Review* (Spring 1985): 97–114.

DANB, 605–6.

Dannett, 1: 95–101.

Davis, 249–54.

Fauset, Arthur Huff. *For Freedom; a Biographical Story of the American Negro*. Philadelphia: Franklin Publishing and Supply Co., [c.1927].

———. *Sojourner Truth: God's Faithful Pilgrim* [Biography]. Chapel Hill: University of North Carolina Press, 1938; New York: Russell & Russell, 1971.

Fleming, John E. "Slavery, Civil War and Reconstruction:

A Study of Black Women in Microcosm." *Negro History Bulletin* 38.6 (1975): 430–33.

Garrison, William Lloyd. *Christian Register* (7 March 1895).

Harlowe, Marie. "Sojourner Truth, the First Sit-in." *Negro History Bulletin* 29 (Fall 1966): 173–74.

Hauser, Elizabeth J. *Woman's Journal* (24 Aug. 1912)

Haviland, Laura S. *A Woman's Life-Work: Labors and Experiences of Laura S. Haviland*. Cincinnati: Walden and Stowe, 1881, 1882; Chicago: C. V. Waite and Co., 1887; Publishers Association of Friends, 1889; Miami: Mnemosyne Publishing Co., 1969.

Haynes, Elizabeth Ross. *Unsung Heroes*. New York: DuBois and Dill, 1921.

Irwin, Inez (Haynes). *Angels and Amazons, A Hundred Years of American Women*. Garden City, NY: Doubleday, Doran & Company, [c.1933].

Koike, Seiko. "Sojourner Truth: Her Thought and Literary Activities." *Kyushu American Literature* (Fukuoka, Japan) 14 (1972): 50–67.

Lebedun, Jean. "Harriet Beecher Stowe's Interest in Sojourner Truth, Black Feminist." *American Literature* 46.3 (1974): 359–63.

"Lecture by Sojourner Truth." *National Anti-Slavery Standard* (10 Dec. 1853). *(BAP)*.

Loggins, 219–22, 233, 434, 439.

Mabee, Carleton. "Sojourner Truth and President Lincoln." *New England Quarterly* 41.4 (1988): 519–29.

———. "Sojourner Truth, Bold Prophet: Why Did She Never Learn to Read?" *New York History* (1988): 55–77.

Majors, 184–85.

McDade, Thomas M. "Matthias, Prophet Without Honor."

New-York Historical Society Quarterly 62.4 (1978): 311–34.

Montgomery, Janey Weinhold. *A Comparative Analysis of the Rhetoric of Two Negro Women Orators: Sojourner Truth and Frances E. Watkins Harper*. Fort Hays: Fort Hays Kansas State College, 1968.

Mossell, 28–29.

NAW, 3: 479–81.

Ortiz, Victoria. *Sojourner Truth, a Self-Made Woman*. New York: J. B. Lippincott, 1974.

Pauli, Hertha Ernestine. *Her Name Was Sojourner Truth*. New York: Appleton-Century-Crofts, 1962.

Porter, Dorothy B. "Anti-Slavery Movement in Northampton." *Negro History Bulletin* 24.2 (1960): 33–34, 41.

———. "Sojourner Truth Calls Upon the President: An 1864 Letter." *Massachusetts Review* 13.1/2 (1972): 297–99.

"Proceedings of the Rhode Island State Anti-Slavery Society". *National Anti-Slavery Standard* (28 Nov. 1850). *(BAP)*.

Quarles, Benjamin. *Black Abolitionists*. New York; Oxford University Press, 1969. 121, 179.

Redding, J. Saunders. *The Lonesome Road . . . the Story of the Negro's Part in America*. Mainstream of America Series. Garden City, NY: Doubleday, [c.1958].

Ritter, E. Jay. "Sojourner Truth." *Negro History Bulletin* (May 1963): 254.

Robinson, 130–31.

Scruggs, 48.

Shafer, Elizabeth. "Sojourner Truth: A Self-Made Woman." *American History Illustrated* 8.9 (1974): 34–39.

Sherman, Caroline E. Letter to Gerrit Smith. 25 June 1863. Gerrit Smith Papers, Syracuse University. *(BAP)*.

Sillen, Samuel. *Women Against Slavery*. New York: Masses & Mainstream, 1955.

Smith, B. M. Letter to Sojourner Truth. *National Anti-Slavery Standard* (4 March 1871): 6.

Smith, Gerrit. Letter to Sojourner Truth. *National Anti-Slavery Standard* (26 Dec. 1868): 3.

Smith, Grace Ferguson. "Sojourner Truth—Listener to the Voice." *Negro History Bulletin* (March 1973): 63–65.

"Sojourner Truth." *Pacific Appeal* (27 Feb. 1864). *(BAP)*.

Sojourner Truth. Washington, DC: Youth Pride, 1968.

Speech by Sojourner Truth. *National Anti-Slavery Standard* (11 July 1863). *(BAP)*.

Stanton, Elizabeth Cady, et al., eds. *History of Woman Suffrage*. New York: Fowler and Wells, 1881. 1: 220, 224, 668, 824; 2: 183.

Stone, William Leete. *Matthias and His Impostures*. New York: Harper Brothers, 1835.

Stowe, Harriet Beecher. "Sojourner Truth, The Libyan Sibyl." *Atlantic Monthly* (Apr. 1863): 473–81.

Terry, Esther. "Sojourner Truth: The Person Behind the Libyan Sibyl." *Massachusetts Review* (Summer–Autumn 1985): 425–44.

Tomkins, Fred. *Jewels in Ebony*. London: S. W. Partridge, [186?].

Toppin, Edgar A. *A Biographical History of Blacks in America Since 1528*. New York: David McKay, 1971.

Vale, Gilbert. *Fanaticism; Its Source and Influence, Illustrated by the Simple Narrative of Isabella in the Case of Matthias . . . A Reply to W. L. Stone*. New York: the Author, 1835.

Wesley. 2–3, 4.

White, W. "Sojourner Truth: Friend of Freedom." *New Republic* (24 May 1948): 15–18.

Whitton, Mary Ormsbee. *These Were the Women; U.S.A. 1776–1860*. New York: Hastings House, [c.1954].

Woodward, Helen Beal. *The Bold Women*. New York: Farrar, Straus and Young, [c.1953].

Wyman, Lillie Buffum Chace. *American Chivalry*. Boston: W. B. Clarke Co., 1913.

———. "Sojourner Truth." *New England Magazine* (24 March 1901): 59–66.

Yellin, Jean Fagan. *Women and Sisters: The Antislavery Feminists in American Culture*. New Haven: Yale University Press, 1990. Chapter 4.

Papers in Collections

Boulware, Marcus H. "The Public Address of Colored Women." [Typewritten.] 1947. Fisk University.

Garrison, Ellen W. Letter to Maria (Mott) Davis. 28 Jan. 1875. Sophia Smith Collection, Smith College.

Garrison, George T. Letter to H. C. Wright. 2 May 1857. Sophia Smith Collection, Smith College.

Garrison, William Lloyd. Letter to Ellen W. Garrison. 6 Aug. 1870. Sophia Smith Collection, Smith College.

Information regarding Sojourner Truth in Joanne Hamlin Manuscript Collection, Schlesinger Library, Radcliffe College.

Photographs of Sojourner Truth. 1864. Sophia Smith Collection, Smith College.

Whiting, N. H. Letter to F.J.G. 28 Apr. 1886. Sophia Smith Collection, Smith College.

Writers' Program of the Work Projects Administration. *Negroes of New York*. New York, 1938–1941. [Microfilm.] Schomburg Center, New York Public Library.

Harriet Tubman [Davis] (1821?–1913)

Dictated Narratives/Biographies

Bradford, Sarah Elizabeth (Hopkins). *Harriet: The Moses of Her People*. New York: George R. Lockwood & Son, 1886; Corinth Books, 1961.

———. *Scenes in the Life of Harriet Tubman*. Auburn, NY: W. J. Moses, 1869.

Anthologies

Loewenberg, Bert J., and Ruth Bogin, eds. *Black Women in Nineteenth-Century American Life: Their Words, Their Thoughts, Their Feelings*. University Park: Pennsylvania State University Press, 1976. 219–21.

Sterling, Dorothy, ed. *Speak Out in Thunder Tones: Letters and Other Writings by Black Northerners, 1787–1865*. Garden City, NY: Doubleday, 1973. xi, 221, 274, 277, 282–83, 353–54, 356, 381–82.

Writings about

Adams, Samuel Hopkins. *Grandfather Stories*. . . . New York: New American Library, 1959.

Bennett, Lerone. "Harriet Tubman." *Ebony* (Nov. 1964): 148.

Brawley, *NBH*, 67–72.

Brawley, *NG*, 6, 324.

Brawley, *NLA*, 83.

Brawley, Benjamin Griffith. *Women of Achievement*. Chicago: Women's American Baptist Home Mission Society, [c. 1919].

Brown, 55–68.

Brown, William Wells. *The Rising Son; or, the Antecedents*

and Advancement of the Colored Race. Boston: A. G. Brown & Co., 1874.

Buckmaster, Henrietta. *Women Who Shaped History*. New York; Coules, 1858; Collier Books, 1966.

Bullock, 193.

Clarke, James B. "An Hour with Harriet Tubman." *Christophe: A Tragedy in Prose of Imperial Haiti*. William Edgar Easton. Los Angeles: Press Grafton Publishing Co., 1911.

Conrad, Earl. *Harriet Tubman*. Washington, DC: Associated Publishers, 1943; New York: Eriksson Press, 1969.

———. *Harriet Tubman: Negro Soldier and Abolitionist*. New York: International Press, 1968.

———. "I Bring You General Tubman." *Black Scholar* (Jan.–Feb. 1970).

DANB, 606–7.

Dannett, 1: 132–39.

Davis, 254–62.

Davis, Sue. "Harriet Tubman: The Moses of Her People." *Women: A Journal of Liberation* (Spring 1970): 12–15.

Dennis, Charles. "The Work of Harriet Tubman." *Americana* (6 Nov. 1911): 1067–72.

Dictionary of American Biography. New York: Scribner's, 1936. [1964] 10: 27.

Epstein, Sam, and Beryl Epstein. *Harriet Tubman: Guide to Freedom*. New York: Garrard, 1968.

Eusebius, Sister Mary. "Modern Moses: Harriet Tubman." *Journal of Negro Education* (Winter 1950): 16–27.

Falk, Leslie A. "Black Abolitionist Doctors and Healers, 1810–1885." *Bulletin of the History of Medicine* 54.2 (1980): 258–72.

Foner, Philip S., ed. *Frederick Douglass on Women's Rights.* Westport, CT: Greenwood Press, 1976.

Fordham, Monroe. "The Harriet Tubman Home and Museum, Auburn, New York." *Afro-Americans in New York Life and History* 1.1 (1977): 105–10.

Haviland, Laura S. *A Woman's Life-Work: Labors and Experiences of Laura S. Haviland.* Cincinnati: Walden and Stowe, 1881, 1882; Chicago: C. V. Waite and Co., 1887; Publishers Association of Friends, 1889; Miami: Mnemosyne Publishing Co., 1969.

Haynes, Elizabeth Ross. "Harriet Tubman the Moses of Her People." Davis, 254–62.

———. *Unsung Heroes.* New York: DuBois and Dill, 1921.

Hughes, Langston. *Famous American Negroes.* New York: Dodd, Mead, [c.1954].

———. *Famous Negro Heroes of America.* New York: Dodd, Mead, [c.1958].

Lawrence, Jacob. *Harriet and the Promised Land.* New York: Windmill Books, Simon and Schuster, 1968.

"Liberator, Harriet Tubman Helped Run the Underground Railroad." *Life* (22 Nov. 1968): 101.

Loggins, 259, 399, 440.

Matthews, Victoria Earle. "Harriet Tubman." *Woman's Era* (June 1896): 8.

McGovern, Ann. *Runaway Slave: The Story of Harriet Tubman.* New York: Four Winds Press, 1965.

Metcalf, George R. *Black Profiles.* New York: McGraw-Hill, 1968. 169–94.

Mossell, 28.

NAW, 3: 481–83.

Newton, James E. "The Underground Railroad in Delaware." *Negro History Bulletin* 40.3 (1977): 702–3.

Nies, Judith. *Seven Women: Portraits from the American Radical Tradition*. New York: Viking Press, 1977.

Parrish, Anne. *A Clouded Star*. New York: Harper, 1948.

Petry, Ann. *The Girl Called Moses; the Story of Harriet Tubman*. London: Methuen & Co., 1960.

————. *Harriet Tubman, Conductor of the Underground Railroad*. New York: Thomas Y. Crowell, 1955.

Quarles, Benjamin. *Black Abolitionists*. New York: Oxford University Press, 1969. 146, 157, 239.

Robinson, 131.

Rollins, Charlemae Hill. *They Showed the Way: Forty American Negro Leaders*. New York: Thomas Y. Crowell, 1964.

Roy, J. H. "Know Your History." *Negro History Bulletin* (22 Nov. 1958): 38–40; (24 Jan. 1961): 93–94.

Ryder, Georgia A. "Black Women in Song: Some Socio-Cultural Images." *Negro History Bulletin* 39.5 (1976): 601–3.

Schwab. (Mrs.) George. *Harriet Tubman, Who Led Slaves to Freedom. . . .* London: Sheldon Press, [19?].

Scruggs, 65.

Scruggs, Otey. "The Meaning of Harriet Tubman." In *Remember the Ladies: New Perspectives on Women in American History. Essays in Honor of Nelson Manfred Blake*. Carol V. R. George, ed. Syracuse: Syracuse University Press, 1975. 110–21.

Sickels, Eleanor Maria. *In Calico and Crinoline, True Stories of American Women, 1608–1865*. New York: Viking Press, 1935.

Siebert, Wilbur H. *The Underground Railroad*. New York: Macmillan, [c.1898]; Arno Press, 1968.

Sillen, Samuel. *Woman Against Slavery*. New York: Masses & Mainstream, 1955.

Small, Sasha. *Heroines*. New York: Workers Library Publishers, n.d.

Sterling, Dorothy. *Freedom Train: The Story of Harriet Tubman*. Garden City, NY: Doubleday, 1954.

Sterling, Philip. *Four Took Freedom: The Lives of Harriet Tubman, Frederick Douglass, Robert Smalls, and Blanche K. Bruce*. Garden City, NY: Doubleday, [c.1967].

Still, William. *The Underground Railroad*. . . . Philadelphia: Porter & Coates, 1872.

Swift, Hidegard Hoyt. *The Railroad to Freedom: A Story of the Civil War*. New York: Harcourt, Brace, 1932.

Taylor, Robert W. *Harriet Tubman, the Heroine in Ebony*. Boston: George H. Ellis, Printer, 1901.

Thompson, Priscilla. "Harriet Tubman, Thomas Garrett, and the Underground Railroad." *Delaware History* 22.1 (1986): 1–21.

Toppin, Edgar A. *A Biographical History of Blacks in America Since 1528*. New York: David McKay, 1971.

Wesley, 4, 38, 71, 302.

Whiting, Helen Adele. "Slave Adventures: Harriet and Her Caravans." *Negro History Bulletin* (Apr. 1956) 164.

Woman's Journal (1 Aug. 1908)

Woodward, Helen Beal. *The Bold Women*. New York: Farrar, Straus and Young, [c.1953].

Wyman, Lillie Buffum Chace. "Harriet Tubman." *New England Magazine* (14 March 1896): 110–18.

Collections

Diaries of Martha C. Wright, Sophia Smith Collection, Smith College.

Diary of William Lloyd Garrison, II. [14 March 1869; 14 Apr. 1897.] Sophia Smith Collection, Smith College.

Garrison, Agnes. Letter to Ellen Wright Garrison. 25 Nov.

1899. [Letter missing; Tubman reference in Index Folder I–21.] Sophia Smith Collection, Smith College.

———. Letter to Ellen Wright Garrison. 26 Nov. 1899. [Letter missing; Tubman reference in Index Folder I–21.] Sophia Smith Collection, Smith College.

Garrison, Eleanor. Letter to MSG. 10 Nov. 1948. Sophia Smith Collection, Smith College.

Garrison, Ellen Wright. Letter to William Lloyd Garrison, II. 12 June 1894. Sophia Smith Collection, Smith College.

———. Letter to William Lloyd Garrison, II. 22 Oct. 1906. Sophia Smith Collection, Smith College.

———. Letter to L. McKim. 16 Nov. 1861. Sophia Smith Collection, Smith College.

———. Letter to David Wright. 30 May 1895. Sophia Smith Collection, Smith College.

———. Letter to Martha Coffin Wright. 23 Apr. 1866; 26 Dec. 1868; 19 Dec. 1869; 3 Feb. 1872; 4 Nov. 1872; 14 Oct. 1873.

Garrison, George. Letter to William Lloyd Garrison, II. 10 Feb. 1864. Sophia Smith Collection, Smith College.

Mott, Lucretia. Letter to Martha Coffin Wright. 1 Jan. 1867. Sophia Smith Collection, Smith College.

———. Letter to Martha Coffin Wright. 1 Sept. 1867? [Fragment], Sophia Smith Collection, Smith College.

Papers in Florence (Woolsey) Hazzard Manuscript Collection, Schlesinger Library, Radcliffe College.

[Photograph.] Sophia Smith Collection, Smith College.

Wright, David. Letter to Martha Coffin Wright. 24 Dec. 1834[?]; 9 Feb. 1861; 3 Apr. 1866. Sophia Smith Collection, Smith College.

Wright Martha Coffin. Letter to Ellen Wright Garrison. 30 Dec. 1860; 9 Apr. 1866; 1 Nov. 1866; 19 May 1867;

6 Sept. 1867; 9 Feb. 1868; 22 March 1868; 8 Oct. 1868; 16 Dec. 1868; 20 Oct. 1869; 22 Dec. 1869; 5 May 1870; 2 Oct. 1872; 2 Oct. 1873; 9 Oct. 1873. Sophia Smith Collection, Smith College.

————. Letter to Anna and Patty Lord. 11 Sept. 1868. Sophia Smith Collection, Smith College.

————. Letter to Mariana Pelham Mott. 7 Nov. 1865. Sophia Smith Collection, Smith College.

————. Letter to Sisters. 31 July 1868; 8 Oct. 1868. Sophia Smith Collection, Smith College.

————. Letter to David Wright. 2 Apr. 1866; 22 March 1867; 27 Jan. 1869; 7 March 1869. Sophia Smith Collection, Smith College.

————. Letter to Fanny Pelham Wright. 6 Feb. 1869; 29 Nov. 1871. Sophia Smith Collection, Smith College.

————. Letter to Frank Wright. 28 May 1862; 12 Apr. 1866. Sophia Smith Collection, Smith College.

————. Letter to William Pelham Wright. 19 Jan. 1868; 5 Feb. 1868; 24 Feb. 1868. Sophia Smith Collection, Smith College.

Writers' Program of the Work Projects Administration. *Negroes of New York*. New York: 1938–1941. [Microfilm.] Schomburg Center, New York Public Library.

Wyman, Lillie. Letter to FJG. 24 November [?]. Sophia Smith Collection, Smith College.

Bethany Veney

Dictated Narrative/Biography

The Narrative of Bethany Veney: A Slave Woman. Worcester, MA: Press of George H. Ellis, Boston, 1889.

Anthologies

The Narrative of Bethany Veney: A Slave Woman. In *Collected Black Women's Narratives.* Introduction by Anthony G. Barthelemy. New York: Oxford University Press, 1988.

*Sally Williams

Dictated Narrative/Biography

Williams, Rev. Isaac. *Aunt Sally; or the Cross the Way of Freedom; The Narrative of the Slave-Life and Purchase of the Mother of Reverend Isaac Williams, of Detroit, Michigan.* Cincinnati: The American Reform Tract and Book Society, 1858, 1862; Miami: Mnemosyne Publishing Company, 1969.

PART III

*Writings by and about
African-American Women Whose Works
Appeared in Periodicals and Collections and
Whose Earliest Publications Appeared
before the End of 1910*

Note: Asterisk indicates writers identified in the process of compiling this listing, hence not searched in all the resources listed at the end of this volume.

Maria Louise Baldwin (1856–1922)

Writings by

"The Changing Ideal of Progress." *Southern Workman* (Jan. 1900).

Letter. *Woman's Era* (1 May 1894): 4.

"A Night Watch." *Woman's Era* (Sept. 1894).

"The Working Value of Educational Ideals." *Hampton Negro Conference*. Vol. 5. Hampton, VA: Hampton Institute Press, 1898–1903.

Writings about

Brawley, *NBH*, 277–79.

Brown, 182–93.

Bullock, 189.

Crisis (Apr. 1917): 281.

DANB, 21–22.

Dannett, 1: 219; 2: 39.

Du Bois, W.E.B. *Crisis* (Apr. 1922): 248–49.

Forbes, George. *AME Church Review* (Apr. 1922): 216–20, 229–30.

League of Women for Community Service. *Souvenir Program of the Dedication of the Maria L. Baldwin Memorial Library* (Dec. 20, 1923).

Mossell, 11.

NAW, 1: 86–88.

[Obituary.] *Southern Workman* (March 1922).

Porter, Dorothy B. "Maria Louise Baldwin." *Journal of Negro Education* (Winter 1952): 94–96.

Solomons, Olivia S. *Negro History Bulletin* (Oct. 1941): 19–21.

Southern Workman (Jan. 1890): 11; (Aug. 1899): 284.

[Tributes and Obituaries.] *Boston Evening Transcript* (10, 11, 17 Jan.); (18 March 1922.)

Wesley, 26, 32, 41.

Papers in Collections

Announcement of Baldwin Memorial 1922. Manuscript collection, Schlesinger Library, Radcliffe College.

Charlotte Hawkins Brown manuscript collection, Schlesinger Library, Radcliffe College.

Saturday Morning Club manuscript collection, Schlesinger Library, Radcliffe College.

Ariel Serena Bowen (?–1904)

Writings by

"Is the Young Negro an Improvement, Morally, on his Father?" Culp, 264–69.

Writings about

Culp, 264.

Dannett, 1: 227.

Davis, 27, 43, 45, 49, 50.

"Mrs. Ariel Serena Bowen" [Obituary]. *Voice of the Negro* (Aug. 1904): 301.

"A Tribute to Mrs. J.W.E. Bowen." *Voice of the Negro* (Aug. 1904): 335.

Rosa D. Bowser

Writings by

"Report of the Committee on Domestic Economy." *Hampton Negro Conference*. Vol. 4. Hampton, VA: Hampton Institute Press, 1898–1903.

"Report of the Committee on Domestic Science." *Hampton Negro Conference*. Vol. 6. Hampton, VA: Hampton Institute Press, 1898–1903.

"Virginia." *Woman's Era* (Apr. 1895): 14–15; (May 1895): 15; (June 1895): 9–10; (July 1895): 10–11; (Nov. 1895): 13–14.

"What Role Is the Educated Negro Woman to Play in the Uplifting of Her Race?" Culp, 177–82.

Writings about

Bullock, 192.
Culp, 177.
Dannett, 1: 229.
Majors, 149–51.
Scruggs, 283.
Wesley, 38.

Mary E. Britton [pseud. Aunt Peggy]

Writings by

"Women's Suffrage as an Important Factor in Public Reforms." *American Catholic Tribune* (1877).

Writings about

Dann, 66.
Dunnigan, Alice E. "Early History of Negro Women in

Journalism." *Negro History Bulletin* 28 (Summer 1965): 178.

Majors, 216–17.

Mossell, 16.

"Our Literary Women." *Lancet* 10 (Oct. 1885): 1.

Penn, 415, 417 [portrait].

Scruggs, 303.

Lucy Hughes Brown

Writings by

"A Retrospect." Mossell, 90–91.

"Thoughts on Retiring." Mossell, 89–90.

Writings about

Bullock, 174.

Mossell, 16, 93.

Scruggs, 265.

Sherman, 245.

*Gertrude Dorsey Browne [Gertrude H. Dorsey; Gertrude Dorsey Brown; Gertrude Hayes Brown]

Writings by

"The Better Looking." *Colored American Magazine* (March 1905): 146–50.

"Blood Moneys of La Petei'." *Colored American Magazine* (Oct. 1905): 567–70.

"A Case of Measure for Measure" [Serial]. *Colored American Magazine* (Apr. 1906): 253–58; (May 1906): 301–4; (July 1906): 25–28; (Aug. 1906): 97–100; (Sept. 1906): 167–72; (Oct. 1906): 281–84.

"An Equation." *Colored American Magazine* (Aug. 1902): 278–83.

"Scrambled Eggs." *Colored American Magazine* (Jan. 1905): 31–38; (Feb. 1905): 79–86.

"The Untold." *Colored American Magazine* (Sept. 1907): 187–88.

"The Voice of the Rich Pudding." *Colored American Magazine* (Oct. 1907): 305–9.

Anthologies

Ammons, Elizabeth, comp. *Short Fiction by Black Women, 1900–1920*. New York: Oxford University Press, 1991.

Writings about

Colored American Magazine (Jan. 1906).

Josephine B. Bruce [Mrs. Blanche K. Bruce]

Writings by

"The After Glow of the Women's Convention." *Voice of the Negro* (Nov. 1904): 541–43.

"The Farmer and the City Folk." *Voice of the Negro* (June 1904): 237.

"The Ladies' Auxiliary." *Woman's Era* (Oct.–Nov. 1896): 9.

"They Entertained the Federation and Promoted the Success of the Convention." *Woman's Era* (Aug. 1896): 5–6.

"What Has Education Done for Colored Women?" *Voice of the Negro* (July 1904): 294–98.

Writings about

Bullock, 129.
Davis, 43.

Hunton, Addie W. "The Southern Federation of Colored
    Women." *Voice of the Negro* (Dec. 1905): 850.
Wesley, 25, 35, 38, 45, 47, 59, 61, 63–64.

*Edith Estelle Bulkley

Writings by

"The Balance of Power." *Colored American Magazine* (Jan.
    1905): 8–12; (Feb. 1905): 68–74.

Anthologies

Ammons, Elizabeth, comp. *Short Fiction by Black Women,
    1900–1920*. New York: Oxford University Press, 1991.

A. E. Chancellor

Writings by

"Death a Refuge." *Weekly Anglo-African* (21 Apr. 1860): 1.
"I Weep for Thee." *Weekly Anglo-African* (14 Apr. 1860):
    1.
"Lines Inspired by a Cold Interview with an Abolitionist."
    Weekly Anglo-African (16 June 1860): 1.
"Lines, to the Memory of John I. Gaines." *Weekly Anglo-
    African* (17 Dec. 1859): 4.

Writings about

Loggins, 211.
Sherman, 245.

Mary Virginia Cook [pseud. Grace Ermine]

Writings by

"Nothing but Leaves." *American Baptist*. [Kentucky] [1886?]
    Excerpted in Penn, 373.

"Woman's Work." In *The Negro Baptist Pulpit: A Collection of Sermons and Papers by Colored Baptist Ministers*. Edward M. Brawley, comp. Philadelphia: American Baptist Publication Society, 1890; Freeport, NY: Books for Libraries Press, 1971.

Writings about

Bullock, 168.

Dann, 64.

Dunnigan, Alice E. "Early History of Negro Women in Journalism." *Negro History Bulletin* 28 (Summer 1965): 178.

Majors, 195–96.

Mossell, 11.

Penn, 367–74.

Scruggs, 120.

Smith, Lucy W. "Women as Journalists." *Indianapolis Freeman* (23 Feb. 1889). Reprinted in Dann, 61–67.

*Julia Ringwood Coston

Writings by

"In Memoriam." *Christian Recorder* (9 Dec. 1897): 3.

Writings about

Bullock, 168–69.

DANB, 136.

Majors, 251–58. [Portrait, 252.]

Mossell, 15.

NAW, 1: 251–58.

Scruggs, 140–43, 383.

Grace E. Mapps Douglass

Writings by

"Lines." *Anglo-African Magazine* (Nov. 1859): 345–46. *(BAP)*.

"Lines." Mossell, 96–97.

Letters

[With Sarah Douglass.] Letter to "Brother Garrison." *Liberator* (21 June 1839): 98. *(BAP)*.

[————.] Letter to Charles Stuart Weld. 28 Sept. 1840. Weld-Grimké Papers, Clements Library, University of Michigan. *(BAP)*.

"Open Letter to the Anti-Slavery Societies and Friends of the Oppressed Generally from Philadelphia Anti-Slavery Society." *National Enquirer* (19 Nov. 1836). *(BAP)*.

Writings about

Mossell, 47, 96–97.

Quarles, Benjamin. *Black Abolitionists*. New York: Oxford University Press, 1969. 27, 28, 38, 44, 105.

Sherman, 242.

Sarah Mapps Douglass Douglass [pseud. Sophronisba] (1806–1882)

Writings by

"An Address." *Liberator* (21 July 1832). *(BAP)*.

"Announcement of Second Annual Fair by the Women's Association." *North Star* (5 Sept. 1850). *(BAP)*.

"Dialogue between a Mother and Her Children on the Precious Stones." *Repository of Religion and Literature and of Science and Art* (Oct. 1858).

[Douglass, Sarah M., et al.] "Announcement of the Nineteenth Annual Anti-Slavery Fair of Pennsylvania." *Pennsylvania Freeman* (30 March 1854). *(BAP)*.

[————.] "Appeal of the Philadelphia Association." *North Star* (7 Sept. 1849). *(BAP)*.

[————.] "Appeal of the Woman's Association of Philadelphia." *North Star* (13 July 1849). *(BAP)*.

[————.] "An Article Regarding the Woman's Association Constitution." *North Star* (9 March 1849). *(BAP)*.

[————.] "Fourteenth Annual Anti-Slavery Fair of Pennsylvania." *Pennsylvania Freeman* (20 .Sept. 1849). *(BAP)*.

[————.] Nineteenth Annual Anti-Slavery Fair of Pennsylvania." *National Anti-Slavery Standard* (23 Sept. 1854). *(BAP)*.

[————.] "Notice to the Abolitionists of Eastern Pennsylvania." *National Anti-Slavery Standard* (25 Apr. 1844). *(BAP)*.

[————.] "Pennsylvania Anti-Slavery Fair." *National Anti-Slavery Standard* (20 Dec. 1849). *(BAP)*.

"A Good Habit Recommended." *Anglo-African Magazine* (May 1859). *(BAP)*.

"Resolution of Philadelphia Female Anti-Slavery Society." *Pennsylvania Freeman* (21 June 1838). *(BAP)*.

Letters

Barnes, Gilbert, and Dwight Dumond, eds. *Letters of Theodore Dwight Weld, Angelina Grimké Weld, and Sarah Grimké, 1822–44*. New York and London: Appleton-Century Co., 1934. 467–71, 480–83, 829–32.

[With Grace Mapps Douglass.] Letter to "Brother Garrison." *Liberator* (21 June 1839): 98. *(BAP)*.

[————.] Letter to Charles Stuart Weld. 28 Sept. 1840.

Weld-Grimké Papers, Clements Library, University of Michigan. *(BAP)*.

[Douglass, Sarah M., et al.] Letter Announcing the Annual Anti-Slavery Fair. *Pennsylvania Freeman* (18 Nov. 1847). *(BAP)*.

[———.] "Letter to the Managers and Patrons of the Musical Fund Bazaar." *Pennsylvania Freeman* (16 Dec. 1847). *(BAP)*.

Letter to William Bassett. Dec. 1837. [Copy] Anti-Slavery Collections, Boston Public Library. *(BAP)*.

Letter to Samuel E. Cornish with Enclosure of a poem by "Ella." *Colored American* (20 Jan. 1838). *(BAP)*.

Letter to the Editor of *Friend*. Sept. 1840. Weld-Grimké Papers, Clements Library, University of Michigan. *(BAP)*.

Letter to Abby Kelley Foster. 18 May 1838. Abby Kelley and Stephen S. Foster Papers, American Antiquarian Society. *(BAP)*.

Letter to Abby Kelley [Foster]. 19 March 1839. Abby Kelley and Stephen S. Foster Papers, American Antiquarian Society. *(BAP)*.

Letter to William Lloyd Garrison. 29 Feb. 1832. Anti-Slavery Collections, Boston Public Library. *(BAP)*.

Letter to William Lloyd Garrison. *Liberator* (6 Oct. 1837): 162. *(BAP)*.

Letter to William Lloyd Garrison and Isaac Knapp. 6 Dec. 1832. Anti-Slavery Collections, Boston Public Library. *(BAP)*.

Letter to the *Pennsylvania Freeman*. *Pennsylvania Freeman* (21 June 1838): 2.

Letter to Charles Whipple. 26 Apr. 1841. Anti-Slavery Collections, Boston Public Library. *(BAP)*.

[Sophronisba.] Letter to William Lloyd Garrison. *Liberator* (14 July 1832). 2: 110.

Anthologies

Lerner, Gerda, ed. *Black Women in White America*. New York: Pantheon Books, 1972. 85–87, 362–65.

Writings about

Barnes, Gilbert, and Dwight Dumond, eds. *Letters of Theodore Dwight Weld, Angelina Grimké Weld, and Sarah Grimké, 1822–44*. New York and London: Appleton-Century Co., 1934. 829–32.

Bracey, John H., comp. *Blacks in the Abolitionist Movement*. Belmont, CA: Wadsworth Publishing Co., 1971.

Bullock, 47, 61.

Cadbury, Henry J. "Negro Membership in the Society of Friends." *Journal of Negro History* (Apr. 1936): 151–213.

Coppin, Fanny J. *Reminiscences of School Life, and Hints on Teaching*. Philadelphia: A.M.E. Book Concern, 1913. 148–49.

DANB, 186–87.

Dannett, 1: 79–81, 83.

Drake, Thomas E. *Quakers and Slavery in America*. New Haven: Yale University Press, 1950.

Holly, James Theodore. "A General View of Hayti" [Letter]. *Liberator* (19 June 1863): 99. *(BAP)*.

Lerner, Gerda. *The Grimké Sisters from South Carolina*. Boston: Houghton Mifflin, 1967; New York: Schocken Books, 1971. 129–30, 133, 159–60, 173, 241, 256.

Mossell, 103.

NAW, 1: 511–13.

Nell, William C. *Colored Patriots of the American Revolution*. Boston: Robert F. Wallcut, 1855; New York: Arno Press, 1968. 346–47, 351.

Pease, Elizabeth. *Society of Friends in the U.S.: Their Views of the Anti-Slavery Question and Treatment of the People of Color*. Darlington, England: J. Wilson, 1840.

Porter, Dorothy B. "The Organized Educational Activities of Negro Literary Societies 1828–1846." *Journal of Negro Education* (1936). Republished in *The Making of Black America: Essays in Negro Life and History*. August Meier and Elliot Rudwick, eds. New York: Atheneum, 1969. 276–88.

Quarles, Benjamin. *Black Abolitionists*. New York: Oxford University Press, 1969. 26, 27, 28, 38, 44, 73, 134.

Smith, Anna Bustill. "The Bustill Family." *Journal of Negro History* (Oct. 1925): 638–44.

Sterling, Dorothy, ed. *Speak Out in Thunder Tones: Letters and Other Writings by Black Northerners, 1787–1865*. Garden City, NY: Doubleday, 1973. 75, 96–97, 375.

Wesley, 4.

Letters

Letter from William Lloyd Garrison. 5 March 1832; 18 March 1842. Anti-Slavery Collections, Boston Public Library. *(BAP)*.

Letter from Angelina Grimké. 28 March 1859. Miscellaneous Manuscripts, Library of Congress. *(BAP)*.

Letter from Angelina E. Grimké and Sarah M. Grimké. 3 Apr. 1837. Weld-Grimké Papers, Clements Library, University of Michigan. *(BAP)*.

Letter from Sarah Grimké. 22 Oct. 1837. In *Letters of Theodore Dwight Weld, Angelina Grimké Weld, and Sarah Grimké, 1822–44*. Gilbert Barnes and Dwight Dumond, eds. New York and London: Appleton-Century Co., 1934. 467–71. *(BAP)*.

Letter from Sarah Grimké. 23 Nov. 1837. In *Letters of*

Theodore Dwight Weld, Angelina Grimké Weld, and Sarah Grimké, 1822–44. Gilbert Barnes and Dwight Dumond, eds. New York and London: Appleton-Century Co., 1934. 480–83. *(BAP).*

Letter from Sarah Grimké. 21 Nov. 1844; 27 Apr. 1861; 19 June [n.d.]. Miscellaneous Manuscripts, University of Chicago. *(BAP).*

Letter from Sarah M. Grimké. 8 Sept. 1839; 10 Oct. 1839; 16 July 1848. Weld-Grimké Papers, Clements Library, University of Michigan. *(BAP)*

Letters from Angelina Grimké Weld. 25 Feb. 1838; 21 March 1839; 13 Sept. 1839; 4 Oct. 1839. Weld-Grimké Papers, Clements Library, University of Michigan. *(BAP).*

Letter from Theodore Dwight Weld. 16 July 1848. Weld-Grimké Papers, Clements Library, University of Michigan. *(BAP).*

Papers in Collections

Conyers, Charlene Fay. "A History of the Cheyney State Teachers College 1837–1951." Diss., New York University, 1960.

Letter to Elizabeth Margaret Chandler. 1 March 1833. Elizabeth Chandler Papers, Bentley Library, University of Michigan.

Sarah Louisa Forten [pseuds. Ada; Magwasca]

Writings by

[Ada.] "An Appeal to Woman." *Liberator* (1 Feb. 1834): 20.

[———.] "The Farewell." *Liberator* (30 June 1832).

[———.] "Farewell to New England." *Liberator* (11 Oct. 1839): 166.

[Ada.] "The Grave of the Slave." *Liberator* (22 Jan. 1831): 14. *(BAP)*.

[———.] "Hours of Childhood." *Liberator* (18 Jan. 1834): 12.

[———.] "Legislation No. I." *Liberator* (14 Apr. 1837): 69.

[———.] "Legislation—No. II." *Liberator* (16 June 1837): 100.

[———.] "Legislation. It Was Not All a Dream." *National Enquirer* (1 July 1837). *(BAP)*.

[———.] "Life." *Liberator* (3 Aug. 1833): 122.

[———.] "Lines." *Liberator* (5 Oct. 1838): 160.

[———.] "Lines, Suggested on Reading 'An Appeal to the Christian Women of the South' [by A. E. Grimké]." *Liberator* (29 Oct. 1836): 176.

[———.] "To the Memory of J. Horace Kimball, late editor of the Herald of Freedom." *Liberator* (4 May 1838): 72. *(BAP)*.

[———.] "A Mother's Crying." *Liberator* (7 July 1832): 106.

[———.] "A Mother's Grief." *Liberator* (7 July 1832). *(BAP)*.

[———.] "My Country." *Liberator* (4 Jan. 1834): 4.

[———.] ["Not for a single Pleiad. . . ."] *Liberator* (24 March 1837): 52.

[———.] ["Not for a single Pleiad. . . ."] *National Enquirer* (22 March 1837).

[———.] ["Our Country latest at the goal. . . ."] *Pennsylvania Freeman* (30 Aug. 1838). *(BAP)*.

[———.] "Past Joys." *Liberator* (19 March 1831): 1. *(BAP)*.

[———.] "Prayer." *Liberator* (26 March 1831): 50. *(BAP)*.

[———.] ["The Scroll is open—Many a name is written. . . ."] *Liberator* (11 Feb. 1837): 28.

[————.] "The Separation." *Liberator* (21 Dec. 1833): 203.

[————.] "The Slave." *Liberator* (16 Apr. 1831): 62. *(BAP)*.

[————.] "The Slave." *Liberator* (11 March 1837): 44.

[————.] "The Slave Girl's Address to Her Mother." *Liberator* (29 Jan. 1831): 18. *(BAP)*.

[————.] "The Slave Girl's Farewell." *Liberator* (27 June 1835): 104.

[————.] "To the Hibernia." *Liberator* (25 May 1833): 84. *(BAP)*.

[————.] "The United States Come Last." *Liberator* (1 March 1839): 36.

[————.] ["Oh, when this earthly tenement. . . ."] *Liberator* (29 March 1839): 52. *(BAP)*.

"Farewell to New England." *Pennsylvania Freeman* (3 Oct. 1839). *(BAP)*.

"The Grave of the Slave." Mossell, 74–75.

"The Grave of the Slave." *Philanthropist* (11 March 1836). *(BAP)*.

"On the Abandonment of Prejudice." Mossell, 75.

"A Prayer." *Philanthropist* (11 March 1836). *(BAP)*.

["We are thy sisters . . ."] Epigraph. *Appeal to the Women of the Nominally Free States. . . ."* Angelina Grimké. New York, 1837.

Letters

[Forten, Sarah, et al.] "Open Letter to the Anti-Slavery Societies and Friends of the Oppressed Generally from the Philadelphia Anti-Slavery Society." *National Enquirer* (19 Nov. 1836). *(BAP)*.

Letter to Angelina E. Grimké. 15 Apr. 1837. Weld-Grimké Papers, Clements Library, University of Michigan. *(BAP)*. Reprinted in *Letters of Theodore Dwight Weld, Angelina*

Grimké Weld, and Sarah Grimké, 1822–44. Gilbert Barnes and Dwight Dumond, eds. New York and London: Appleton-Century Co., 1934.

Letter to Elizabeth H. Whittier. 23 March 1835; 25 Dec. 1836. Whittier Papers, Central Michigan University. *(BAP)*.

Anthologies

Eaton, Clement, ed. *In the Leaven of Democracy*. New York: Braziller, [c. 1963].

Sterling, Dorothy, ed. *Speak Out in Thunder Tones: Letters and Other Writings by Black Northerners, 1787–1865*. Garden City, NY: Doubleday, 1973. 79–80, 86–87, 375.

Stetson, Erlene, ed. *Black Sister: Poetry by Black American Women, 1746–1980*. Bloomington: Indiana University Press, 1981. 17–21.

Writings about

Dannett, 1: 82–83.

Litwack, Leon. "The Emancipation of the Negro Abolitionist." In *The Abolitionists*. Richard O. Curry, ed. Hinsdale, IL: Dryden Press, 1973.

Majors, 194.

Mossell, 74–75.

Nell, William C. *Colored Patriots of the American Revolution*. Boston: Robert F. Wallcut, 1855; New York: Arno Press, 1968. 346–47, 351.

Quarles, Benjamin. *Black Abolitionists*. New York: Oxford University Press, 1969. 25, 27, 41.

Robinson, 82–85.

Sherman, 245.

Stevenson, Brenda. Introduction. In *The Journals of Charlotte Forten Grimké*. Brenda Stevenson, ed. New York: Oxford University Press, 1988.

Wesley, 4.

Whittier, John G. "To the Daughters of James Forten." Reprinted in *A Life for Liberty: Anti-Slavery and Other Letters of Sallie Holley*. Sallie Holley. New York and London: G. P. Putnam's Sons, 1899.

Mamie Eloise Fox

Writings by

"Bishop Payne." *Christian Recorder* (15 March 1900): 1.

"Easter." *Christian Recorder* (2 Apr. 1896): 3.

"Hiding Christ." *Christian Recorder* (13 June 1895): 1.

"In Memoriam." *Christian Recorder* (21 Oct. 1897): 1.

"Intemperance." *Christian Recorder* (5 Sept. 1895): 1.

"Laudate Dominum." *Christian Recorder* (10 Dec. 1896): 1.

"Lead Thou Me On." *Christian Recorder* (23 June 1898): 1.

"The Right Will Triumph." *Christian Recorder* (19 Dec. 1895): 1; (23 July 1896): 1.

"Sowing and Reaping." *Christian Recorder* (2 March 1899): 1.

"Thanksgiving Hymn." *Christian Recorder* (24 Nov. 1898): 6.

["O! Watchman, Aloft in the Tower of Zion. . . ."] *Christian Recorder* (9 Sept. 1897); 1.

"What God Hath Wrought." *Christian Recorder* (8 Oct. 1896): 1.

"What Shall We Do With Christ?" *Christian Recorder* (17 Oct. 1895): 1.

Writings about
Majors, 125–28, 365.
Rush, 307.
Sherman, 245.

*Susan Elizabeth Frazier

Writings by
"Mrs. William E. Matthews." *Woman's Era* (1 May 1894):
     1.
"Some Afro-American Women of Mark." *A.M.E. Church
     Review* (Apr. 1892): 378–86.

Writings about
Brown, 222–24.
Dannett, 1: 255.

Miss Garrison

Writings by
"A Ray of Light." *A.M.E. Church Review* 6 (July 1889–
     Apr. 1890): 74–489.

Anthologies
Shockley, 153–61.

Writings about
Shockley, 151–53.

Nora Antonia Gordon (1866–?)

Writings by
"Miss Packard's Birthday." Scruggs, 221–22.

Writings about

Brawley, Benjamin Griffith. *Women of Achievement*. Chicago: Women's American Baptist Home Mission Society, [c.1919]. 43–58.

Dannett, 1: 259.

Gibson, J. W., and William Henry Crogman, eds. *Progress of a Race: Or, the Remarkable Advancement of the American Negro*. Harrisburg, PA: The Minter Company, 1902. 406.

Scruggs, 217.

*Maude K. Griffin

Writings by

"Guests Unexpected, A Thanksgiving Story." *Colored American Magazine* (Nov. 1908): 614–16.

Anthologies

Ammons, Elizabeth, comp. *Short Fiction by Black Women, 1900–1920*. New York: Oxford University Press, 1991.

Josephine B. C. Jackson

Writings by

"April." Mossell, 86–87.

"Gone Before: In Memoria of Mrs. Bishop Payne." *Christian Recorder* (12 Sept. 1889): 1.

"Thankful." *Christian Recorder* (27 March 1890): 5.

Writings about

Mossell, 86.

Sherman, 245.

Lena Terrell Jackson

Writings by

"History of Fisk University for Twenty-Five Years." Scruggs, 135–39.
"The Negro as a Laborer." Culp, 304–8.

Writings about

Culp, 304.
Dannett, 1: 56.

Ida F. Johnson

Writings by

"God's Children—The Fatherless." *Howard's American Magazine* (Nov. 1899): 51.
"God's Children—The Fatherless." Mossell, 91–92.

Writings about

Mossell, 91, 93.
Sherman, 245.

Anna Holland Jones

Writings by

"The Century's Progress of the American Colored Woman." *Voice of the Negro*, pt. 1 (Sept. 1905): 631–33; "The American Colored Woman." *Voice of the Negro*, pt. 2 (Oct. 1905): 692–94.
"Frederick J. Loudin—An Appreciation." *Voice of the Negro* (May 1905): 326.

"Katherine D. Tillman, Chicago, IL." *National Association Notes* 8 (Oct. 1904): 3.
"Missouri." *Woman's Era* (Jan. 1896): 14.

Writings about

Majors, 147.
Mossell, 12.
Scruggs, 295.
Wesley, 36, 38, 47, 60, 71, 394, 399.

Molly E. Lambert

Writings by

A.M.E. Church Review 1.2 (1885): 170–72, 284–85.
"Christ Is Risen." Mossell, 78–79.
"A Dream of Heaven." *Christian Recorder* (13 May 1877): 1.
"Musings." *Christian Recorder* (8 May 1869): 57.
"My Dream. Hymn to the New Year." *A.M.E. Church Review* [n.d.].

Writings about

Bullock, 98, 168.
Dann, 67.
Majors, 335.
Mossell, 15, 78–79.
"Our Literary Women." *Lancet* 10 (Oct. 1885): 1.
Penn, 427.
Schomburg, Arthur A., comp. *A Bibliographical Checklist of American Negro Poetry*. Bibliographica Americana: A Series of Monographs, Charles F. Heartman, ed. New York: Charles F. Heartman, 1916. 2: 27.

Sherman, 241.
Shockley, 118.

Lucy Craft Laney (1854–1933)

Writings by

"The Burden of the Educated Colored Woman." *Hampton Negro Conference*. Vol. 3. Hampton, VA: Hampton Institute Press, 1898–1903.

[Progress Report from the "Founder of the Haines Normal Institute in Atlanta."] *The Church at Home and Abroad* (Aug. 1893): 140.

Letter. *Woman's Era* (Aug. 1895): 11.

Anthologies

Loewenberg, Bert J., and Ruth Bogin, eds. *Black Women in Nineteenth-Century American Life: Their Words, Their Thoughts, Their Feelings*. University Park: Pennsylvania State University Press, 1976. 283–95.

Writings about

Abbott's Monthly (June 1931).

Brawley, *NBH*, 279–82, 285.

DANB, 380.

Daniel, 1–27.

Dannett, 1: 200, 281.

Feger, H. V. "A Girl Who Became a Great Woman." *Negro History Bulletin* (March 1942): 123.

Griggs, A. C. "Lucy Craft Laney." *Journal of Negro History* (Jan. 1934): 97–102.

"Haines Normal and Industrial Institute." In *Afro-American Encyclopedia*. . . . James T. Haley, comp. Nashville: Haley & Florida, 1895. 110–11.

Hunting, Harold Bruce. *Pioneers of Goodwill*. New York: Friendship Press, 1929.

Journal of Negro History 19 (1934): 97–102.

Majors, 325.

McCrorey, Mary Jackson. "Lucy Laney." *Crisis* (June 1934): 161.

"Miss Lucy Laney." In *Afro-American Encyclopedia*. . . . James T. Haley, comp. Nashville: Haley & Florida, 1895. 108–9.

Mossell, 11, 30.

NAW, 365–67.

Ovington, Mary White. *Portraits in Color*. New York: Viking Press, [c.1927].

Rowe, George Clinton. "Our Heroes." *Our Heroes*. N.p., 1890.

Wesley, 292, 295.

Yenser, Thomas, ed. *Who's Who in Colored America: Dictionary of Notable Living Persons of African Descent in America, 1930–1932*. 3rd Edition. Brooklyn, NY: Thomas Yenser, 1933. 261.

*Mary E. Ashe Lee [Mrs. B. F. Lee]

Writings by

"Afmerica." Mossell, 83–85.

"Afmerica." *Negro* [Boston] (July 1886): 5–9.

"Afmerica." *Southern Workman* (Oct. 1886): 107.

"Easter." *Christian Recorder* (18 Apr. 1889): 4.

"I Care Not When I Die." *Christian Recorder* (28 Nov. 1889): 6.

"In Memoriam—Mrs. Amy McNeely." *Christian Recorder* (13 Aug. 1891): 1.

"Lead Thou Me." *Christian Recorder* (12 Feb. 1891): 5.

"Long She Suffered Here in Pain." *Christian Recorder* (29 Apr. 1875): 5.

"The Ode of the Class of '73." *Christian Recorder* (10 July 1873): 1.

"Sea and Sky." *Christian Recorder* (4 Sept. 1890): 1.

"Tawawa" [Excerpt]. Mossell, 82.

"These Two of Our Fathers." *Christian Recorder* (19 Sept. 1889): 1.

"Thoughts on Good Friday." *Christian Recorder* (10 Apr. 1890): 1.

"To Hallie Q. Brown." *Christian Recorder* (24 Apr. 1890): 1.

"To Mrs. N. F. Mossell on Her Book, *The Work of Afro-American Women*" [sic]. *Christian Recorder* (10 Jan. 1895): 1.

Writings about
Davis, 56.
Majors, 257, 311–12.
Mossell, 16, 81–85.
"Our Literary Women." *Lancet* 10 (Oct. 1885): 1.
Scruggs, 277–80.

Ida Evans Luckie

Writings by
"The Poet." *Woman's Era* (July 1896): 13–14.

Writings about
Majors, 327.
Sherman, 245.

Azalia Edmonia Martin

Writings by

"Alice of Long Ago." *Colored American Magazine* (Feb. 1904): 95.

"August." *Voice of the Negro* (July 1905): 577.

"Autumn's Lullaby." *Voice of the Negro* (Oct. 1905): 684.

"The Curse of Gold." *Voice of the Negro* (March 1906): 174.

"A December Day." *Voice of the Negro* (Dec. 1905): 866.

"Ecstasy." *Voice of the Negro* (Jan. 1907): 43.

"Little Maid." *Voice of the Negro* (May 1905): 317.

"Meditation." *Voice of the Negro* (Sept. 1905): 627.

"A Mother's Lullaby." *Voice of the Negro* (Oct. 1906): 418.

"November." *Voice of the Negro* (Nov. 1905): 770.

"The Ocean's Mass." *Voice of the Negro* (Apr. 1906): 270.

"Phantoms." *Voice of the Negro* (July 1905): 469.

"The Protest." *Voice of the Negro* (Dec. 1906): 551.

"The Roll Call of the Great." *Colored American Magazine* (Apr. 1904): 258.

"A Song." *Voice of the Negro* (July 1906): 486.

"A Song to Afric's Great." *Colored American Magazine* (Nov. 1903): 823.

"A Song to the Flowers." *Voice of the Negro* (May 1905): 385.

"Spring." *Voice of the Negro* (Apr. 1905): 233.

"The Stream of Life." *Voice of the Negro* (July 1904): 340.

"The Sun and the Storm King." *Voice of the Negro* (Aug. 1906): 582.

"The Sun and the Storm Queen." *Voice of the Negro* (July 1906): 482.

"Twilight." *Voice of the Negro* (Sept. 1904): 370.

"Winter." *Voice of the Negro* (Feb. 1905): 233.

Writings about
Bullock, 112, 133.

Lena Mason

Writings by
"The Negro and Education." Culp, 445–46.
"A Negro in It." Culp, 447–48.

Writings about
Culp, 445.
Dannett, 1: 287.

Emma Frances Grayson Merritt (1860–1933)

Writings by
"American Prejudice—Its Cause, Effect and Possibilities."
    Voice of the Negro (July 1905): 466.
"Douglas [*sic*] Day." *Voice of the Negro* (Apr. 1906): 279.

Writings about
Bullock, 129.
Crisis (Sept. 1930).
DANB, 431–32.
Dannett, 1: 291.
Journal of Negro History (Apr. 1932): 351–54.
Taylor, Estelle W. "Emma Frances Grayson Merritt: Pioneer
    in Negro Education." *Negro History Bulletin* (Aug.–Sept.
    1975).
Terrell, Mary Church. "Graduates and Former Students of
    Washington Colored High School." *Voice of the Negro*
    (June 1904): 223.

Wesley, 38.

Woodson, Carter G. "Emma Frances Grayson Merritt." *Opportunity* (Aug. 1930): 244–45.

Yenser, Thomas, ed. *Who's Who in Colored America: Dictionary of Notable Living Persons of African Descent in America, 1930–1932.* 3rd Edition. Brooklyn, NY: Thomas Yenser, 1933. 301–2.

*Violette Neatly-Blackwell

Writings by

"Childhood's Memory." *Colored American Magazine* (Dec. 1901): 100.

Writings about

"Here and There." *Colored American Magazine* (March 1902): 393.

*Frances Nordstrom

Writings by

"The Gift of the Storm." *Colored American Magazine* (Apr. 1905): 190–93.

Anthologies

Ammons, Elizabeth, comp. *Short Fiction by Black Women, 1900–1920.* New York: Oxford University Press, 1991.

Fannie A. Parker

Writings by

"Fleeting Years." Mossell, 87–88.

Writings about
Mossell, 93.
Sherman, 245.

Sarah Dudley Pettey [Mrs. C. C. Pettey]

Writings by
"What Role Is the Educated Negro Woman to Play in the
    Uplifting of Her Race?" Culp, 182–85.

Writings about
Culp, 182.
Dannett, 1: 303.
Majors, 57–64.

*Lelia Plummer

Writings by
"The Autobiography of a Dollar Bill." *Colored American
    Magazine* (Dec. 1904): 726–28.

Anthologies
Ammons, Elizabeth, comp. *Short Fiction by Black Women,
    1900–1920*. New York: Oxford University Press, 1991.

Lucy Terry Prince (1730–1821)

Writings by
Anthologies
History of Western Massachusetts. Josiah Gilbert Holland.
    1855. Republished in *History of Deerfield, Massachusetts*.

George Sheldon. 2 Vols. Deerfield, MA: Press of E. M. Hall, 1895–1896. 1: 545–49.

Hughes, Langston, and Arna Bontemps, eds. *The Poetry of the Negro: 1746–1949*. Garden City, NY: Doubleday, 1949.

Patterson, Lindsay, ed. *An Introduction to Black Literature in America from 1746 to the Present*. New York: Publishers Co., 1968.

Randall, Dudley, ed. *The Black Poets*. New York: Bantam Books, 1971.

Robinson, William H., Jr., ed. *Early Black American Poetry*. Dubuque, IA: William C. Brown Company Publishers, 1969. 3–4.

Shockley, 15.

Stetson, Erlene, ed. *Black Sister: Poetry by Black American Women, 1746–1980*. Bloomington: Indiana University Press, 1981. 12.

Writings about

Baskin, Wade, and Richard N. Runes. *A Dictionary of Black Culture*. New York: Philosophical Library, 1973. 430.

Dannett, 1: 30–31.

Garrett, Romeo B. *Famous First Facts about Negroes*. New York: Arno Press, 1972. 98.

Greene, Lorenzo Johnston. *The Negro in Colonial New England, 1620–1776*. New York: Columbia University Press, 1959.

Hughes, Langston, and Milton Meltzer. *A Pictorial History of the Negro in America*. New York: Crown, [1956]. 36.

Jackson, Blyden. *The Waiting Years: Essays in American Negro Literature*. Baton Rouge: Louisiana State University Press, 1976.

Kaplan, Sidney. *The Black Presence in the Era of the American Revolution, 1770–1800*. New York: New York Graphic Society in association with the Smithsonian Institution Press, 1973.

Katz, Bernard. *Black Woman*. New York: Pantheon Books, 1973.

———. "A Second Version of Lucy Terry's Early Ballad." *Negro History Bulletin* (Fall 1966): 183–84.

Katz, William Loren. *Eyewitness: The Negro in American History*. New York: Pitman, 1967. 24, 37.

Merriam, Robert L. *Lucy Terry Prince*. Conway, MA: the Author, 1983.

Rubin, Louis D. "The Search for a Language, 1746–1923." In *Black Poetry in America: Two Essays in Historical Interpretation*. Blyden Jackson and Louis D. Rubin, Jr. Baton Rouge: Louisiana State University Press, 1974. 1–35.

Rush, 691.

Sheldon, George. "Negro Slavery in Old Deerfield." *New England Magazine* (March–Aug. 1893): 49–60.

Shockley, 13–15.

Toppin, Edgar A. *A Biographical History of Blacks in America Since 1528*. New York: David McKay, 1971. 58.

Wright, Martha R. "Bijah's Luce of Guilford, Vermont." *Negro History Bulletin* (Apr. 1965): 152–53, 159.

Josephine St. Pierre Ruffin [Mrs. George L. Ruffin] (1842–1924)

Writings by

"Address of Josephine St. Pierre Ruffin, President of Conference." *Woman's Era* (Aug. 1895): 13–15.

Anthologies

Dunbar, Alice Moore, ed. *Masterpieces of Negro Eloquence.* New York: The Bookery, 1914; The Basic Afro-American Reprint Library, 1970; Johnson Reprints, 1970.

Writings about

Brawley, *NBH*, 261.

Brown, 151–53.

Bullock, 169–70, 189–94, 215.

DANB, 535–36.

Dannett, 1: 309.

Davis, 236–39.

[Editorial.] *Woman's Journal* (16 June 1900).

Flexner, Eleanor. *Century of Struggle: The Woman's Rights Movement in the United States.* Cambridge, MA: Belknap Press of Harvard University Press, 1959. 189–91.

Hall, Mrs. Walter A., Mrs. Joseph S. Leach, and Mrs. Frederick G. Smith, comps. *Progress and Achievement: A History of the Massachusetts State Federation of Women's Clubs, 1893–1931.* Boston: Massachusetts State Federation of Women's Clubs, 1932. 27.

Hopkins, Pauline E. "Josephine St. Pierre Ruffin at Milwaukee, 1900." *Colored American Magazine* (July 1902): 210–13.

———. "Some Famous Women." *Colored American Magazine* (Aug. 1902): 273–77.

Howe, Julia Ward. *Sketches of Representative Women of New England.* Boston: New England Historical Publishing Co., 1904.

Leonard, John William, ed. *Woman's Who's Who of America: A Biographical Dictionary of Contemporary Women of the*

United States and Canada, 1914–15. New York: American Commonwealth Co.; Detroit: Gale Research Co., 1976.

Logan, Rayford W. *The Betrayal of the Negro from Rutherford B. Hayes to Woodrow Wilson*. New York: Collier Books, 1965. 238–41.

Lord, Myra B. *History of the Northeast Woman's Press Association, 1885–1931*. Newton, MA: The Graphic Press, 1932.

Mossell, 15, 34.

NAW, 3: 206–8.

[Photograph.] *Woman's Era* (Apr. 1895): 1.

Porter, Dorothy B. "Women Activists, Wives, Intellectuals, Mothers, and Artists." In *Candidates for Rediscovery: The Boston Version*. Proceedings of a Symposium at the Afro-American Studies Center, Boston University, 12 Apr. 1975. Boston: Afro-American Studies Center, Boston University, 1975. 76–84.

Richings, B. F. *Evidence of Progress among Colored People*. 3rd Edition. Philadelphia: Geo. S. Ferguson Co., 1897.

Scruggs, 144.

Wesley, 13, 32, 47, 49, 108, 212, 311.

Woman's Journal (23 June 1900; 30 June 1900).

Wood, Mary I. *History of the General Federation of Women's Clubs*. New York: General Federation of Women's Clubs, 1912. 129–31.

Papers in Collections

Fields, Emma L. "The Women's Club Movement in the U.S., 1877–1900." M.A. Thesis, Howard University, 1948.

Papers in Amistad Research Center, Tulane University.

Photograph and *Los Angeles Herald* article. [N.d.] Sophia
  Smith Collection, Smith College.
Ruffin Papers and incomplete files of the New Era Club,
  Moorland-Spingarn Research Center, Howard Univer-
  sity.

*Anne Bethel Scales

Writings By

"Beth's Triumph (A Two-Part Story)." *Colored American
  Magazine* (Aug. 1900): 152–59; (Sept. 1900): 238–44.

Anthologies

Ammons, Elizabeth, comp. *Short Fiction by Black Women,
  1900–1920*. New York: Oxford University Press, 1991.

Josephine Silone-Yates (1852–1912)

Writings by

"Afro-American Women as Educators." Scruggs, 309–19.
"Did the American Negro Make, in the Nineteenth Century,
  Achievements Along the Lines of Wealth, Morality,
  Education, etc., Commensurate with His Opportunities?
  If so, What Achievements Did He Make?" Second Paper.
  Culp, 21–28.
"Education and Genetic Psychology." *Colored American Mag-
  azine* (May 1906): 292–97.
"Educational Department." *Colored American Magazine* (June
  1907): 441–42.
"Educational Work at Lincoln Institute." *Colored American
  Magazine* (Aug. 1907): 140–43.

"The Equipment of the Teacher." *Voice of the Negro* (June 1904): 248.

"French Literature in the Seventeenth Century—Poetry and Drama." *A.M.E. Church Review* (Jan. 1901): 204–12.

"An Indian Summer Day." *Colored American Magazine* (Dec. 1900): 11.

"The Influence of Woman in the Amelioration of African Slavery." *Colored American Magazine* (May 1907): 377–81.

"Kansas City Letter." *Woman's Era* (1 May 1894): 2; (Aug. 1894): 9; (Sept. 1894): 4.

"Kindergartens and Mother's Clubs." *Colored American Magazine* (June 1905): 304–11.

"Lincoln Institute." *Colored American Magazine* (Jan. 1907): 25–32.

"Missouri." *Woman's Era* (June 1895): 10–12; (July 1895): 6–7.

"The National Association of Colored Women." *Voice of the Negro* (July 1904): 283–87.

"Parental Obligation." *Colored American Magazine* (Apr. 1907): 285–90.

"Report of the National Federation of Colored Women's Clubs." *Colored American Magazine* (May 1905): 258–62.

"Shall We Have a Convention of the Colored Women's Clubs, Leagues and Societies?" *Woman's Era* (1 May 1894): 3–4.

"Thought Power in Education." *Voice of the Negro* (Apr. 1905): 242.

"The Twentieth Century Negro—His Opportunities for Success." *Colored American Magazine* (Oct. 1906): 227–42.

"Women as a Factor in the Solution of Race Problems." *Colored American Magazine* (Feb. 1907): 126–35.

Writings about

Brown, 178–81.

Bullock. 97, 115, 127, 159, 192.

Culp, 20.

Dannett, 1: 333.

Davis, 166–68.

Hunton, Addie W. "The Southern Federation of Colored Women." *Voice of the Negro* (Dec. 1905): 850–54.

Majors, 44–50.

Mossell, 16.

"The National Association of Colored Women." *Voice of the Negro* (July 1904): 310.

Scruggs, 340.

Voice of the Negro (Aug. 1906): frontispiece.

*Albreta Moore Smith

Writings by

"An Answer to 'Mr. Roosevelt's Negro Policy.' " *Colored American Magazine* (March 1903): 360.

"Catering, and Charles H. Smiley of Chicago." *Colored American Magazine* (July 1901): 222–27.

"Chicago Notes." *Colored American Magazine* (Dec. 1900): 147; (June 1901): 149; (Aug. 1901): 306.

"Comment." *Colored American Magazine* (Oct. 1901): 479.

"Editorial and Publishers Announcements." *Colored American Magazine* (Oct. 1901): 478.

"A Few Essential Business Qualities." *Colored American Magazine* (May 1902): 26–28.

"L. M. Lawson Guild, No. 2." *Colored American Magazine* (Aug. 1901): 306–7.

"Noted Business Women of Chicago. Mrs. Hattie M. Hicks."
Colored American Magazine (July 1903): 507–9.

"A Plea for Missionary Work and Workers." *Colored American Magazine* (Feb. 1903): 275–79.

"Why?" *Colored American Magazine* (Oct. 1901): 467–70.

"Woman's Development in Business." *Colored American Magazine* (March 1902): 323–26.

Writings about

"Editors and Publishers Announcements." *Colored American Magazine* (Nov. 1900): 73.

Lewis, Frances A. [Article.] *Woman's Era* (July 1894): 1.

"Mrs. Albreta Moore Smith." *Colored American Magazine* (May 1901): 47.

[Photograph.] *Colored American Magazine* (May 1901): 52.

Wesley, 58.

Lucy Wilmot Smith

Writings by

"Women as Journalists: Portraits and Sketches of a Few of the Women Journalists of the Race." *Indianapolis Freeman* (23 Feb. 1889). Reprinted in Dann, 61–67.

Writings about

Bullock, 168.

Dunnigan, Alice E. "Early History of Negro Women in Journalism." *Negro History Bulletin* 28 (Summer 1965): 178.

Majors, 202–3.

Mossell, 12.

Penn, 376, 379 [portrait].

Scruggs, 165.

Mary E. C. Smith

Writings by

"Is the Negro as Morally Depraved as He Is Reputed to Be?" Culp, 246–53.

Writings about

Culp, 246.

*Georgia F. Stewart

Writings by

"Aunt 'Ria's Ten Dollars." *Colored American Magazine* (June 1901): 105–8.

"The Wooing of Pastor Cummings." *Colored American Magazine* (Aug. 1901): 273–76.

Anthologies

Ammons, Elizabeth, comp. *Short Fiction by Black Women, 1900–1920*. New York: Oxford University Press, 1991.

*Kate D. Sweetser

Writings by

"Marjorie's Scheme." *Colored American Magazine* (Dec. 1903): 879–81.

Anthologies

Ammons, Elizabeth, comp. *Short Fiction by Black Women, 1900–1920*. New York: Oxford University Press, 1991.

Mary Burnett Talbert (1866–1923)

Writings by

"Did the American Negro Make, in the Nineteenth Century, Achievements Along the Lines of Wealth, Morality, Education, etc., Commensurate with His Opportunities? If so, What Achievements Did He Make?" Topic 1. Culp, 17–21.

Writings about

Brawley, *NBH*, 261.
Brown, 217–19.
Crisis (Feb. 1917): 174–76; (Aug. 1917): 167–68; (July 1921): 130; (July 1922): 125; (Aug. 1922): 171; (Dec. 1923): 56–57.
Culp, 16.
DANB, 576–77.
Dannett, 1: 317.
Davis, 40.
Robinson, 127–28.
Wesley, 70, 72, 78, 83–86, 87, 89–90, 93, 107, 177, 201, 357, 413.

Papers in Collections

Papers in Charlotte Hawkins Brown manuscript collection, Schlesinger Library, Radcliffe College.

Clarissa Minnie Thompson

Writings by

"Humane Education." In *Afro-American Encyclopedia*. . . . James T. Haley, comp. Nashville: Haley & Florida, 1895. 267–70.

"In Memoriam—The Grand Old Man." In *Afro-American Encyclopedia*. . . . James T. Haley, comp. Nashville: Haley & Florida, 1895. 549.

"Only a Flirtation" [Not Located].

"A Simple Tale of Simple Trust." *Christian Review* (8 Oct. 1885).

"Treading the Winepress; or, A Mountain of Misfortune" [Serial]. *Boston Advocate* (26 Sept. 1885–25 Dec. 1886).

Anthologies
Shockley, 146.

Writings about
"Clarissa M. Thompson." In *Afro-American Encyclopedia*. . . . James T. Haley, comp. Nashville: Haley & Florida, 1895. 566–70.

Majors, 64–71.

"Our Literary Women." *Lancet* 10 (Oct. 1885): 1.

Sherman, 246.

Shockley, 144–46.

Lillian V. Thompson

Writings by
"The Slave Girl's Prophecy." *A.M.E. Church Review* (July 1891).

Writings about
[Notice Regarding "The Slave Girl's Prophecy."] *Christian Recorder* (23 July 1891): 4.

Sherman, 246.

*Ruth D. Todd

Writings by

"Florence Grey, A Three-Part Story." *Colored American Magazine* (Aug. 1902): 307–13; (Sept. 1902): 391–97; (Oct. 1902): 469–77.

"The Folly of Mildred, A Race Story with a Moral." *Colored American Magazine* (March 1903): 364–70.

"The Octoroon's Revenge." *Colored American Magazine* (March 1902): 291–95.

"The Taming of a Modern Shrew." *Colored American Magazine* (March 1904): 191–95.

Anthologies

Ammons, Elizabeth, comp. *Short Fiction by Black Women, 1900–1920.* New York: Oxford University Press, 1991.

*Grace Ellsworth Tompkins

Writings by

"The Luck of Lazarus." *Colored American Magazine* (Apr. 1907): 283–84.

Anthologies

Ammons, Elizabeth, comp. *Short Fiction by Black Women, 1900–1920.* New York: Oxford University Press, 1991.

Josephine Turpin Washington [Mrs. S.S.H. Washington]

Writings by

"Cedar Hill Saved." *Crisis* (Feb. 1919): 179.

"Child Saving in Alabama." *Colored American Magazine* (Jan. 1908): 48–51.

Foreword. Brown, v.

"Higher Education for Women." Scruggs, 365–72.

"Impressions of a Southern Federation." *Colored American Magazine* (Nov. 1904): 676–80.

Introduction. Scruggs, ix–xx.

"A Poet of Promise." *Voice of the Negro* (Oct. 1905): 700.

"The Province of Poetry." *A.M.E. Church Review* (Oct. 1889): 137.

"To Elizabeth." *Colored American Magazine* (Aug. 1907): 139.

"What the Club Does for the Club-Woman." *Colored American Magazine* (Feb. 1907): 122–25.

Writings about

Bullock, 115, 129.

Dannett, 1: 321.

Dunnigan, Alice E. "Early History of Negro Women in Journalism." *Negro History Bulletin* 28 (Summer 1965): 178.

Majors, 199.

Mossell, 16.

"Our Literary Women." *Lancet* 10 (Oct. 1885): 1.

Penn, 393–96.

Scruggs, 89.

Suggs, Henry Lewis. *The Black Press in the South, 1865–1979.* Westport, CT: Greenwood Press, 1983.

Wesley, 261, 283.

Frankie E. Harris Wassom

Writings by

"Life's Struggle." In *Afro-American Encyclopedia. . . .* James T. Haley, comp. Nashville: Haley & Florida, 1895. 548.

Writings about

Majors, 71–74, 328.
Mossell, 14.
Sherman, 246.

Virginia Whitsett [Virgie Whitsett]

Writings by

"The Church." *Christian Recorder* (14 Jan. 1897): 1.
"Idle Dreamer." *Christian Recorder* (18 Aug. 1898): 1.
"Life Is a Dream." *Christian Recorder* (20 Jan. 1898): 1.
"When the Dinner Bell Rings." *Colored American* (23 July 1898): 4.

Writings about

Mossell, 16.
Sherman, 246.

Sylvanie Fancaz Williams

Writings by

[Letter to the N.A.C.W. Convention.] *Woman's Journal* (18 Apr. 1903).
"The Phillis Wheatley Club." *Woman's Era* (Nov. 1895): 14.
"The Social Status of the Negro Woman." *Voice of the Negro* (July 1904): 298–300.

Writings about

Hunton, Addie W. "The Southern Federation of Colored Women." *Voice of the Negro* (Dec. 1905): 850–54.
Wesley, 35, 42, 43, 45.

PART IV

*Notable African-American
Women Who Were Not Writers but Who Were
the Subjects of Published Writings
before the End of 1910*

Note: Asterisk indicates writers identified in the process of compiling this listing, hence not searched in all the resources listed at the end of this volume.

*Catherine S. Campbell Beckett

Writings about

Coppin, Levi Jenkins, ed. *In Memoriam, Catherine S. Campbell Beckett.* N.p.: n.p., 1888.

Flora Batson Bergen

Writings about

Black Perspective in Music 7 1: 95–106.

Brawley, *NBH*, 245.

Brawley, *NG*, 137–39.

Brawley, *NLA*, 137–38.

Majors, 92–94.

Millar, Gerard. *Life, Travels and Works of Miss Flora Batson, Deceased Queen of Song.* N.p.: T.M.R.M. Company, n.d.

Mossell, 22, 67.

["Mrs. Flora Batson-Bergen, the Celebrated. . . ."] *Weekly Call* (12 Oct. 1895): 1.

["Mrs. Flora Batson-Bergen gave a return. . . ."] *Weekly Call* (20 March 1896): 2.

["Mrs. Flora Batson-Bergen sang. . . ."] *Weekly Call* (21 March 1896): 8.

[Notice.] *Christian Recorder* (9 Apr. 1891): 4.

Richings, B. F. *Evidences of Progress among Colored People.* 3rd Edition. Philadelphia: Geo. S. Ferguson Company, 1897.

Scruggs, 26.
Wesley, 9.

Hannah Tranks Carson (1808–1864)

Writings about

*Glorying in Tribulation: A Brief Memoir of Hannah Carson,
    for Thirteen Years Deprived of the Use of All Her Limbs.*
    Philadelphia: Protestant Episcopal Book Society, 1864.

Catherine Ferguson (1779?–1854)

Writings about

Boyd, R. H., and J. T. Brown. *The National Baptist Sunday
    School Lesson Commentary for 1905.* Nashville: National
    Baptist Publication Board, n.d.

Brown, 3–4.

DANB, 220.

Hartnick, Allen. "Catherine Ferguson, Black Founder of a
    Sunday School." *Negro History Bulletin* (Dec. 1972):
    176–77.

Katy Ferguson; or, What a Poor Colored Woman May Do.
    Boston: American Tract Society Publication, n.d.

"Katy Ferguson; or What a Poor Colored Woman May Do."
    Christian Recorder (25 May 1861): 1.

Latimer, Catherine. "Catherine Ferguson." *Negro History
    Bulletin* (Nov. 1941): 38–39.

Lossing, Benson John. *Eminent Americans.* New York: Hov-
    endon Co., [c.1855–1890]; Mason Bros., [c.1856].
    404–7.

Mossell, 26.

Robinson, 79–80.

Papers in Collections

Writers' Program of the Work Projects Administration. *Negroes of New York*. New York, 1938–1941. [Microfilm.] Schomburg Center, New York Public Library.

Meta Vaux Warrick Fuller (1877–1968)

Writings about

Bentley, Florence L. "Meta Warrick, Promising Sculptor." *Voice of the Negro* (March 1907): 116.

Bontemps, Arna Alexander, ed. *Forever Free: Art by African-American Women, 1862–1980*. Alexandria, VA: Stephenson, 1980. 76–77.

Brawley, *NBH*, 248.

Brawley, *NG*, 184–89.

Brawley, *NLA*, 4, 112–24.

Brawley, Benjamin. *Women of Achievement*. Chicago: Women's American Baptist Home Mission Society, [c.1919].

Bullock, 82, 111, 116, 127, 219.

Cederholm, Theresa D. *Afro-American Artists: A Bio-Bibliographical Directory*. Boston: Trustees of the Boston Public Library, 1973.

DANB, 245–47.

Dannett, 2: 31–46.

The Evolution of Afro-American Artists: 1800–1950. New York: New York City College, 1967.

Fauset, Arthur Huff. *For Freedom: A Biographical Story of the American Negro*. Philadelphia: Franklin Publishing & Supply Co., 1928.

Fine, Elsa Honig. *The Afro-American Artist*. New York: Holt, Rinehart and Winston, n.d. 75–76, 91.

Hoover, Velma J. "Meta Vaux Warrick Fuller: Her Life

and Her Art." *Negro History Bulletin* 40.2 (1977): 678–81.

Igoe, Lynn Moody. *250 Years of Afro-American Art: An Annotated Bibliography.* New York: R. R. Bowker, 1981. 686–90.

Lewis, Samella. *Art: African American.* New York: Harcourt Brace Jovanovich, 1978. 53–55.

Locke, Alain. *The Negro in Art.* Chicago: Afro-American Press, 1969. 30–31.

Ovington, Mary White. *Portraits in Color.* New York: Viking Press, 1927.

Porter, James A. *Modern Negro Art.* New York: Dryden Press, 1943; Arno Press and the *New York Times,* 1969.

Terrell, Mary C. "The Social Functions During Inauguration Week." *Voice of the Negro* (Apr. 1905): 237.

Thompson, W. O. "Collins and Devellis—Two Promising Painters." *Voice of the Negro* (Oct. 1905): 690.

Wayman, H. Harrison. "Meta Vaux Warrick: Sculptress." *Colored American Magazine* (March 1903): 325.

Sarah J. Smith Garnet (1831–1911)

Writings about

Brown, 110–16.

DANB, 253–54.

Dannett, 1: 257.

Davis, 226–27.

Frazier, Susan Elizabeth. "Some Afro-American Women of Mark." *A.M.E. Church Review* (Apr. 1892): 378–86.

NAW, 2: 18–19.

New York Age (30 June 1888).

Scruggs, 226–30.

Wesley, 70, 77.

Elizabeth Taylor Greenfield ["The Black Swan"] (1809–1876)

Writings by

Letters

Letter to J.W.C. Pennington et al. *National Anti-Slavery Standard* (7 Apr. 1853). *(BAP)*.

Writings about

The Black Swan at Home and Abroad: or, A Biographical Sketch of Miss Elizabeth Taylor Greenfield, The American Vocalist. Philadelphia: Wm. S. Young, Printer, 1855.

Brawley, *NBH*, 245.

Brawley, *NG*, 46–49.

Brawley, *NLA*, 136–37.

A Brief Memoir of the "Black Swan", Miss E. T. Greenfield, the American Vocalist. London: n.p., 1853.

Bullock, 116, 195.

Cary, M. A. Shadd. "Miss E. T. Greenfield: 'The Black Swan.' " *Weekly Anglo–African* (9 Feb. 1861). *(BAP)*.

[Concert Announcement.] *Weekly Anglo-African* (9 Feb. 1861). *(BAP)*.

DANB, 268–70.

Dannett, 1: 115–17.

Delany, Martin Robinson. *The Condition, Elevation, Immigration, and Destiny of the Colored People of the United States.* Philadelphia: the Author, 1852; New York: Arno Press, 1968.

Douglass, Frederick. "Miss Elizabeth T. Greenfield: 'The Black Swan.' " *Frederick Douglass' Paper* (26 Feb. 1852): 3.

Hare, Maud Cuney. *Negro Musicians and Their Music.* Washington, DC: Associated Publishers, 1936.

Majors, 155–78.

NAW, 2: 87–89.

Noyes, Edward. "The Black Swan." *Milwaukee History* 6.4 (1983): 102–6.

[Obituary.] *New York Times* (2 Apr. 1876).

[Obituary.] *Philadelphia Public Ledger* (3 Apr. 1876).

Quarles, Benjamin. *Black Abolitionists*. New York: Oxford University Press, 1969. 86, 218.

Richards, Agnes. "The Black Swan." *Negro Digest* (Nov. 1950): 73–75.

Robinson, 84–85.

Ryder, Georgia A. "Black Women in Song: Some Socio-Cultural Images." *Negro History Bulletin* 39.5 (1976): 601–3.

Scruggs, 78.

Stowe, Harriet Beecher. *Sunny Memories of Foreign Lands*. Boston: Phillips, Sampson, 1854.

Trotter, James Monroe. *Music and Some Highly Musical People*. Boston: Lee and Shepard; New York: Charles T. Dillingham, 1878. 66.

Wesley, 9.

Letters

Letter from J.W.C. Pennington. *National Anti-Slavery Standard* (7 Apr. 1853). *(BAP)*.

Anna and Emma Hyers

Writings about

Brawley, *NG*, 133–36.

Brawley, *NLA*, 137.

Dannett, 1: 273.

["George Bailey will not. . . ."] *Topeka Call* (8 Nov. 1891):
4.

["Hyers Sisters are. . . ."] *Topeka Call* (4 Oct. 1891): 3.

["The Hyers sisters are no longer. . . ."] *Topeka Call* (7
May 1893): 1.

Majors, 108–11.

["Mr. Hyers, father. . . ."] *Topeka Call* (13 Dec. 1891):
2.

Scruggs, 105.

Trotter, James Monroe. *Music and Some Highly Musical
People*. Boston: Lee and Shepard; New York: Charles T.
Dillingham, 1878.

[Matilda] Sissieretta Jones [Matilda Joyner; "The Black Patti"] (1869–1933)

Writings about

Brawley, *NBH*, 245.

Brawley, *NG*, 139–42.

Brawley, *NLA*, 138.

DANB, 367–68.

Dannett, 1: 279; 2: 306.

*Farewell Appearance of Sissieretta Jones: Known as the Black
Patti*. Chicago: Star Lecture Course, 1893.

Haley, James T., comp. *Sparkling Gems of Race Knowledge
Worth Reading*. . . . Nashville: J. T. Haley and Co.,
1897. 88 [portrait].

Johnson, James Weldon. *Black Manhattan*. New York: Knopf,
1930. 99.

"Madam Sissiretta [*sic*] Jones." In *Afro-American Encyclopedia*. . . . James T. Haley, comp. Nashville: Haley &
Florida, 1895. 575–76.

["Madame Sissieretta Jones appeared. . . ."] *Weekly Call* (15 Feb. 1896): 1.

["Madame Sissieretta Jones, Black Patti, . . ."] *Weekly Call* (21 Dec. 1895): 1.

["Madame Sissieretta Jones, the colored. . . ."] *Weekly Call* (17 Nov. 1894): 1.

["Madame Sissieretta Jones sang. . . ."] *Topeka Call* (18 Sept. 1892): 1.

["Madame Sissieretta Jones sang before. . . ."] *Topeka Call* (3 Apr. 1892): 1.

["Madame Sissieretta Jones was recently. . . ."] *Topeka Call* (3 Apr. 1892): 4.

["Madame Sissieretta Jones will make. . . ."] *Weekly Call* (14 Dec. 1895): 1.

Miller, Kelly. "The Artistic Gifts of the Negro." *Voice of the Negro* (Apr. 1906): 252.

Mossell, 22, 67.

["Mrs. Sissieretta Jones, . . ."] *Weekly Call* (19 Jan. 1895): 1.

National Encyclopedia of American Biography. Vol. 13. New York: J. T. White, 1898. 424.

NAW, 2: 288–90.

Norfolk Journal and Guide (8 July 1933; 15 July 1933).

Northrop, Henry Davenport, J. R. Gay, and I. Garland Penn. *The College of Life or Practical Self Educator*. Denver: The Western Book Co., 1896.

Scruggs, 325.

Terry, F. C. "The Closing Chapters in the Life of 'Black Patti.' " *Providence Sunday Journal* (16 July 1933).

Wesley, 9.

Papers in Collections

Carl R. Gross manuscript collection, Moorland-Spingarn Research Center, Howard University.

Daughtry, Willa E. "Sissieretta Jones: A Study of the Negro's Contribution to Nineteenth Century Américan Concert and Theatrical Life." Diss., Syracuse University, 1968.

Mary Edmonia Lewis (1845–1909?)

Writings about

American Art Journal (May 1978).

Athenaeum [London] (3 March 1866): 302.

Blodgett, Geoffrey. "John Mercer Langston and the Case of Edmonia Lewis: Oberlin, 1862." *Journal of Negro History* 53.3 (1968): 201–18.

―――. "Spiced Wine: An Oberlin Scandal of 1862." *Oberlin Alumni Magazine* (Feb. 1970).

Bontemps, Arna Alexander, ed. *Forever Free: Art by African-American Women, 1862–1980*. Alexandria, VA: Stephenson, 1980. 98–99.

Brawley, *NG*, 126–27.

Brawley, *NLA*, 112–13.

Brown, Williams Wells. *The Rising Son; or, the Antecedents and Advancement of the Colored Race*. Boston: A. G. Brown & Co., 1874.

Bullard, Laura Curtis. "Edmonia Lewis." *The Revolution* (20 Apr. 1871).

―――. *New National Era* (May 1871).

Bullock, 116, 219.

Cederholm, Theresa D. *Afro-American Artists: A Bio-Bibliographical Directory*. Boston: Trustees of the Boston Public Library, 1973. 176–78.

Cheney, Ednah D. *Freedman's Record* (Apr. 1866): 69.

Child, Lydia Maria. *The Broken Fetter*. Detroit: Advertiser & Tribune Co., 3 March 1865.

DANB, 393–95.

Dannett, 1: 119–23.

Darcy, Cornelius P. "Edmonia Lewis Arrives in Rome." *Negro History Bulletin* 40.2 (1977): 688–89.

Dover, Cedric. *American Negro Art.* Greenwich, CT: New York Graphic Society, 1960. 26–68, 82.

Echoes. Columbus: Published by Ohio Historical Society, 1968.

"Edmonia Lewis." *New National Era* (4 May 1871): 1.

"Edmonia Lewis, Sculptress." In *Afro-American Encyclopedia.* . . . James T. Haley, comp. Nashville: Haley & Florida, 1895. 413.

The Evolution of Afro-American Artists: 1800–1950. New York: New York City College, 1967.

Faithful, Emily. *Three Visits to America.* Edinburgh: D. Douglas; New York: Fowler and Wells, 1884. 293–94.

Fine, Elsa H. *The Afro-American Artist.* New York: Holt, Rinehart and Winston, n.d. 3, 63–67.

———. *Women and Art: A History of Women Painters and Sculptors from the Renaissance to the 20th Century.* Montclair, NJ: Allanheld & Schram, 1978.

Frazier, Susan Elizabeth. "Some Afro-American Women of Mark." *A.M.E. Church Review* (Apr. 1892): 378–86.

Gerdts, William. Essay on Edmonia Lewis. In *Ten Afro-American Artists of the Nineteenth Century.* James A. Porter. Catalog. Washington DC: Howard University Gallery of Art, 1967. 17–19.

———. *The White, Marmorean Flock.* Poughkeepsie, NY: Vassar College, 1972. 12–13, 19, 30–32.

Goldberg, Marcia, and W. E. Bigglestone. "A Wedding Gift of 1862." *Oberlin Alumni Magazine* (Jan./Feb. 1977): 20–21.

Harley, Ralph L. "A Checklist of Afro-American Art and Artists." *Serif* 7.4 (1970): 3–63.

Hartigan, Lynda Roscoe. *Sharing Tradition: Five Black Artists*

in Nineteenth Century America. Washington, DC: Smithsonian Institution Press, 1985. 85–98.

Holland, Patricia G., and Milton Meltzer, eds. *Collected
Correspondence of Lydia Maria Child, 1817–1880*. Mill-
wood, NY: Kraus Microform, 1980.

How Edmonia Lewis Became an Artist. N.p.: n.p., [c.1868].

Igoe, Lynn Moody. *250 Years of Afro-American Art: An
Annotated Bibliography*. New York: R. R. Bowker, 1981.
899–905.

Johnson, William Henry. *Autobiography of Dr. William Johnson*. Albany, NY: The Argus Co., 1900.

Johnston, Robert P. "Six Major Figures in Afro-American
Art." *Michigan Academician* 3.4 (1971): 51–58.

Langston, John Mercer. *From the Virginia Plantation to The
National Capitol: or, the First and Only Negro Represen-
tative in Congress from the Old Dominion*. Hartford, CT:
American Publishing Co., 1874.

Leach, Joseph. *Bright and Particular Star, The Life and
Times of Charlotte Cushman*. New Haven: Yale University
Press, 1970. 335.

Lewis, Samella. *Art: African American*. New York: Harcourt
Brace Jovanovich, 1978. 39–43.

Liberator (29 Jan. 1864): 19; (9 Dec. 1864): 199; (20 Jan.
1865): 12.

Locke, Alain. *The Negro in Art*. Washington, DC: Associates
in Negro Folk Education, 1940; Chicago: Afro-American
Press, 1969.

Majors, 27–30.

Montesano, Philip M. "The Mystery of the San Jose Statues."
Urban West (March–Apr. 1968): 25–27.

Mossell, 22.

Murray, Freeman H. M. *Emancipation and the Freed in
American Sculpture*. Washington, DC: n.p., 1916. 21.

National Anti-Slavery Standard (20 Nov. 1869): 2.

National Cyclopedia of American Biography. New York: J. T. White, 1898. 5: 173.

NAW, 2: 397–99.

Nickerson, Cynthia D. "Artistic Interpretations of Henry Wadsworth Longfellow's 'The Song of Hiawatha,' 1885–1900." *American Art Journal* 16.3 (1984): 49–77.

O'Neill, Scannell. "The Catholic Who's Who." *Rosary Magazine* (Feb. 1909): 322–23.

Our Colored Missions. New York: The Catholic Board for Mission Work Among the Colored People. Vol. 7. (Nov. 1931): 164.

Petersen, Karen, and J. J. Wilson. *Women Artists: Recognition and Reappraisal from the Middle Ages to the 20th Century*. New York: Harper & Row, 1976.

Porter, James A. *Modern Negro Art*. New York: Dryden Press, 1943; Arno Press and the *New York Times*, 1969.

———. "Versatile Interests of Early Negro Artists." *Art in America* (24 Jan. 1936): 16–27.

Richardson, Marilyn. "Vita: Edmonia Lewis." *Harvard Magazine* 88.4 (1986): 40–41.

Robinson, 95–96.

Rollins, Charlemae Hill. *They Showed the Way: Forty American Negro Leaders*. New York: Thomas Y. Crowell, 1964.

Scruggs, 69.

"A Sidelight on Edmonia Lewis." *Journal of Negro History* (Jan. 1945).

Taft, Lorado. *The History of American Sculpture*. New York and London: Macmillan, 1903. 212.

Thompson, W. O. "Collins and Devellis—Two Promising Painters." *Voice of the Negro* (Oct. 1905): 690.

Thorp, Margaret (Farrand). "The White, Marmorean Flock." *New England Quarterly* (June 1959): 147–70.

Toppin, Edgar A. *A Biographical History of Blacks in America Since 1528*. New York: David McKay, 1971.

Tuckerman, Henry T. *Book of the Artists*. New York: Putnam & Sons, 1867. 603–4.

Tufts, Eleanor. "Edmonia Lewis: Afro-Indian Neo-Classicist." *Art in America* 62.4 (1974): 71–72.

———. *Our Hidden Heritage*. New York, London, and Toronto: Paddington Press, 1974.

Waters, Clara (Erskine) Clement, and Laurence B. Hutton. *Artists of the 19th Century and Their Works*. Boston: Houghton Osgood and Co., 1879.

Woman's Journal (16 Aug. 1873): 257; (4 Oct. 1873): 313; (12 Oct. 1873): 321; (21 Dec. 1878): 401; (4 Jan. 1879): 1; (10 March 1883): 73.

Wyman, Lillie Buffum Chace, and Arthur Crawford Wyman. *Elizabeth Buffum Chace*. Boston: W. B. Clarke Co., 1914. 2: 37–38.

Letters

Child, Lydia Maria. Letter to Harriet Sewell. 10 July 1868. In *Lydia Maria Child, Selected Letters, 1817–1880*. Milton Meltzer and Patricia G. Holland, eds. Amherst: University of Massachusetts Press, 1982. 480–81.

———. Letter to Sarah Shaw. 3 Nov. 1864. In *Lydia Maria Child, Selected Letters, 1817–1880*. Milton Meltzer and Patricia G. Holland, eds. Amherst: University of Massachusetts Press, 1982. 447–48.

Papers in Collections

Collected correspondence, Anti-Slavery Collections, Boston Public Library.

Correspondence with Lydia Maria Child, Lydia Maria Child Manuscript Collection, Schlesinger Library, Radcliffe College.

Letter from Marianna Mott to Thomas Mott. 29 Feb. 1868.
Sophia Smith Collection, Smith College.

Ethel Hedgeman Lyle

Writings about

Noyer, Sallie C. "Visit with Ethel Hedgeman Lyle: Founder
of Alpha Kappa Alpha Sorority." *Brown American* (Nov.–
Dec. 1941): 18–19.

Papers in Collections

Papers in the Notable American Women manuscript collection, Schlesinger Library, Radcliffe College.

Mary Eliza Mahoney (1845–1926)

Writings about

Chayer, Mary Ella. "Mary Eliza Mahoney." *American Jour-
nal of Nursing* (Apr. 1954): 424–31.
DANB, 420–21.
NAW, 2: 486–87.
New England Hospital for Women and Children, *Annual
Report*. Vols. 13, 14. Boston: n.p., 1878, 1879.
Staupers, Mabel Keaton. *No Time for Prejudice: A Story of
the Integration of Negroes in Nursing in the U.S.* New
York: Macmillan, 1961.
Thoms, Adah B., comp. *Pathfinders, A History of the Progress
of Colored Graduate Nurses*. New York: Kay Printing
House, 1929.

Papers in Collections

Biographical magazine article, Sophia Smith Collection, Smith
College.

Nellie Brown Mitchell

Writings about

Brawley, *NG*, 125–26.
Dannett, 1: 293.
Majors, 176.
["Mme. Nellie Brown Mitchell will appear. . . ."] *Topeka Call* (3 Apr. 1892): 1.
Mossell, 22, 67.

Lucy Ellen Moten (1851–1933)

Writings about

Carrothers, Thomasine. "Lucy Ellen Moten, 1851–1933." *Journal of Negro History* (Jan. 1934): 102–6.
Dabney, Lillian J. *The History of Schools for Negroes in the District of Columbia, 1807–47*. Washington, DC: Catholic University of America Press, 1949.
DANB, 458–59.
"Lucy Ellen Moten, 1851–1933." *Journal of Negro History* (Jan. 1932): 124–40.
Majors, 318–19.
Mossell, 11.
NAW, 2: 591–92.
Wormly, G. Smith. "Educators of the First Half Century of the Public Schools of the District of Columbia." *Journal of Negro History* (Apr. 1932).

Papers in Collections

Hatter, Henrietta R. "History of Miner Teacher's College." Master's thesis, Howard University, 1939.
Peterson, Gladys T. Typescript of a biography. Manuscript

Collection, Library of the University of the District of Columbia.

Mary Smith Kelsey Peake (1823–1862)

Writings about

DANB, 486.

Dannett, 1: 159–63.

Fen, Sing-Nan. "Charles P. Day, the Successor to Mary S. Peake." *Phylon* 24.4 (1963): 388–91.

Hannaford, Phebe. *Daughters of America*. Augusta, ME: True and Co., 1882.

Lockwood, Lewis C. *Mary S. Peake, the Colored Teacher at Fortress Monroe*. Boston: American Tract Society, [1863?].

Majors, 183.

Mary Ellen Pleasant ["Mammy Pleasant"] (c.1814–1904)

Writings about

Beasley, Delilah L. *The Negro Trail Blazers of California*. Los Angeles: Times Mirror Printing and Binding House, 1919; New York: Negro Universities Press, 1969. 95–97.

Burt, Olive W. *Negroes in the Early West*. New York: Julian Messner, 1969.

City Argus [San Francisco] (18 Sept. 1897): 23.

DANB, 495–96.

Davis, Sam P. "Memoirs and Autobiography." *Pandex of the Press* [San Francisco] (Jan. 1902).

Dobie, Charles C. *San Francisco, a Pageant*. New York: Appleton-Century, 1933.

Drago, Harry Sinclair. *Notorious Ladies of the Frontier*. New York: Dodd, Mead, [c.1969].

Field, Stephen J. *Personal Reminiscences of Early Days in California*. Washington, DC: Privately printed, 1893. 282.

Holdredge, Helen. *Mammy Pleasant*. New York: G. P. Putnam, 1953.

―――. *Mammy Pleasant's Partner*. New York: G. P. Putnam, 1954.

―――, comp., ed. *Mammy Pleasant's Cookbook*. San Francisco: 101 Productions, [c.1970].

Katz, William L. *The Black West*. Garden City, NY: Anchor Press, Doubleday, 1973.

Lewis, Oscar, and Carroll D. Hall. *Bonanza Inn*. New York: Knopf, 1939.

NAW, 3: 75–77.

Robinson, 109–10.

Thurman, Sue Bailey. *Pioneers of Negro Origin in California*. San Francisco: Acme Publishing Co., 1952. 47–50.

Young, John P. *San Francisco*. Vol. 2. San Francisco and Chicago: S. J. Clarke, 1912. 811.

Papers in Collections

Conrich, J. Lloyd. "The Mammy Pleasant Legend." Typescript of unpublished manuscript. N.d. California State Historical Society, San Francisco.

Miscellaneous documents, papers, and photographs, California State Historical Society, San Francisco.

Pleasants, Respondents vs. the North Beach and Mission Railroad Co., Appellant. 1868. Broadside. California State Archives, Sacramento.

Two letters to James Grasses with calling card. San Francisco,

1896. Bancroft Library, University of California, Berkeley.

Fannie Moore Richards (1840–1923)

Writings about

DANB, 524–25.

Hartgrave, W. B. "The Story of Marie Louise Moore Richards and Fannie M. Richards." *Journal of Negro History* (Jan. 1916): 23–33.

Jackson, Harvey C. "Pioneers and Builders in Michigan: Fannie M. Richards." *Negro History Bulletin* (May 1942).

Robinson, 116–17.

"Tea at Museum Honors First Negro Teacher." *Detroit Historical Society Bulletin* (Jan. 1971).

Wesley, 357.

Marie Louise Moore Richards

Writings about

Hartgrave, W. B. "The Story of Marie Louise Moore Richards and Fannie M. Richards." *Journal of Negro History* (Jan. 1916): 23–33.

Robinson, 116–17.

Madame Marie Selika [Sampson Williams]

Writings about

Brawley, *NBH*, 245.

Brawley, *NG*, 136–37.

Brawley, *NLA*, 137.

Bullock, 116.

Dannett, 1: 331.

"Madame Selika." *Topeka Call* (15 Apr. 1893): 3.

["Madame Selika sang. . . ."] *Weekly Call* (7 Dec. 1895): 1.

Majors, 307–9.

Mossell, 22, 67.

"Musical and Dramatic." *Lancet* 10 (Oct. 1885): 1.

Scruggs, 361.

Charlotte Stephens (1854–1951)

Writings about

Anthony, Mary. "Dean of the School Marms." *Negro Digest* (May 1951): 31–32.

Dillard, Tom W., and Adolphine F. Terry. *Charlotte Stephens: Little Rock's First Black Teacher*. Little Rock: Academic Press of Arkansas, 1973.

Rebecca Steward

Writings about

"Memoirs of Mrs. Rebecca Steward" [Review]. *Christian Recorder* (24 Jan. 1878): 2.

Steward, Theophilus Gould. *Memoirs of Mrs. Rebecca Steward, Containing: A Full Sketch of Her Life, with Various Selections from Her Writings and Letters; Also Contributions from Bishop Campbell and Others*. Philadelphia: Publication Department of the A.M.E. Church, 1877; Ann Arbor: University Microfilms, 1972.

*Annie E. Walker (1855–1929)

Writings about

Cederholm, Theresa D. *Afro-American Artists: A Bio-Bibliographical Directory*. Boston: Trustees of the Boston Public Library, 1973. 290.

Crisis (Apr. 1942): 117.

Exhibition of Graphic Arts and Drawings by Negro Artists. Catalog. Washington, DC: Howard University Gallery of Art, 1950.

Igoe, Lynn Moody. *250 Years of Afro-American Art: An Annotated Bibliography*. New York: R. R. Bowker, 1981. 899–905.

Porter, James A. *Ten Afro-American Artists of the Nineteenth Century*. Catalog. Washington DC: Howard University Gallery of Art, 1967. 21, 29, 33.

Trends in American Drawings. Catalog. Washington, DC: Howard University Gallery of Art, 1952.

Maggie Lena Mitchell Walker
[Mrs. Armistead Walker] (1867–1934)

Writings about

Baker, Houston, Jr. *Long Black Song: Essays in Black American Literature and Culture*. Charlottesville: University Press of Virginia, 1972.

Bowles, Eva. "Opportunities for Colored Women." *Opportunity* (March 1923): 8–10.

Brawley, *NBH*, 265, 267–72.

Dabney, Wendell Phillips. "Maggie L. Walker: A Tribute to a Friend." *Opportunity* (July 1935): 216.

———. *Maggie L. Walker and the I.O. of Saint Luke, the*

Woman and Her Work. Cincinnati: Dabney Publishing Co., 1927.

DANB, 626–27.

Daniel, 28–52.

Dannett, 1: 191–97.

Fleming, Beatrice J. "America's First Woman Bank President." *Negro History Bulletin* (Jan. 1942): 75.

Hammond, Lily H. *In the Vanguard of a Race*. New York: Council of Women for Home Missions, and Missionary Education Movement of the United States and Canada, 1922.

Longwell, Marjorie R. *America and Women: Fictionized Biography*. Philadelphia: Dorrance, 1962. 185–205.

Marlow, Jean. *The Great Women*. New York: A & W Publishers, 1978.

Meier, August. *Negro Thought in America, 1880–1915: Racial Ideologies in the Age of Booker T. Washington*. Ann Arbor: University of Michigan Press, 1963. 138.

NAW, 3: 530–31.

[Obituary.] *Journal of Negro History* (Jan. 1935): 121–23.

Ovington, Mary White. *Portraits in Color*. New York: Viking Press, 1927. 127–34.

Robinson, 139.

Rollins, Charlemae Hill. *They Showed the Way: Forty American Negro Leaders*. New York: Thomas Y. Crowell, 1964.

Simmons, Charles Willis. "Maggie Lena Walker and the Consolidated Bank & Trust Company." *Negro History Bulletin* 38.2 (1975): 345–49.

Wesley, 90, 110, 276.

Papers in Collections

Writers' Program of the Work Projects Administration. *Negroes of New York*. New York, 1938–1941. [Microfilm.] Schomburg Center, New York Public Library.

Mary E. Webb [Mrs. Frank J. Webb] (?–1859)

Writings about

Hughes, Langston, and Milton Meltzer. *A Pictorial History of the Negro in America*. Third Revision by C. Eric Lincoln and Milton Meltzer. New York: Crown, 1968. 145 [portrait].

Liberator (19 Nov. 1855).

National Anti-Slavery Standard (13 Dec. 1855): 3; (23 Aug. 1856): 2; (13 March 1858): 3; (3 Sept. 1859).

Salem Register [Mass.] (19 Nov. 1855).

PART V

Selected Contemporary Writings
about but Not by African-American Women:
to the End of 1910

Note: Included in this section are writings by authors whom we have not identified as African-American women, although in several instances, they are women closely identified with black publications. For writings on the subjects listed below by women identified as African American, see Parts I–III.

General

Adams, John H., Jr. "Rough Sketches: A Study of the Features of the New Negro Woman." *Voice of the Negro* (Aug. 1904): 323–26.

Benjamin, Robert Charles O'Hara. *Don't: A Book for Girls.* N.p.: S. F., Valleau & Peterson, 1891.

Blauvelt, Mary Taylor. "The Race Problem, As Discussed by Negro Women." *American Journal of Sociology* (March 1901): 662–72.

Bourne, George. *Slavery Illustrated in Its Effects upon Women and Domestic Society.* Boston: I. Knapp, 1837; Freeport, NY: Books for Libraries Press, 1972.

Bradford, B. E. "Woman." *Colored American Magazine* (Aug. 1909): 103–4.

Chase, Calvin, "Our Women." *Bee* (17 Mar. 1894).

Child, Lydia Maria. *History of the Condition of Women.* Vol. 2. New York: C. S. Francis Co.; Boston: J. H. Francis, 1835, 1849. 213–21.

Clowes, William Laird. "Black America a Study of the Ex-Slave and His Late Master." Reprinted with additions from *Times.* London: Cassell & Co., 1891.

Cotter, Joseph S. "The Negro Woman." *Savannah Tribune* (27 Aug. 1910): 6.

Delany, Martin Robinson. *The Condition, Elevation, Immigration, and Destiny of the Colored People of the United*

States. Philadelphia: the Author, 1852; New York: Arno Press, 1968. 196–97, *passim*.

Drew, Benjamin. *A North-Side View of Slavery*. Boston: J. P. Jewett and Co.; New York: Sheldon, Lamport and Blakeman, 1856.

Du Bois, W.E.B., ed. *Some Efforts of American Negroes for Their Own Social Betterment*. Atlanta University Publications, no. 3. Atlanta: Atlanta University Press, 1898. 2nd Edition: *Efforts for Social Betterment among Negro Americans*. Atlanta University Publications, no. 14. Atlanta: Atlanta University Press, 1910; New York: Arno Press, 1968.

———. *The Souls of Black Folk*. Chicago: A. C. McClurg & Co., 1903.

Gibson, John Williams, and W. H. Crogman. *The Colored American, from Slavery to Honorable Citizenship by Prof. J. W. Gibson . . . and Prof. W. H. Crogman. . . .* Atlanta and Naperville, IL: Nichols & Co., 1901.

Haley, James T., comp. "Opportunities and Responsibilities of Colored Women." In *Afro-American Encyclopedia. . . .* Nashville: Haley & Florida, 1895.

———. *Sparkling Gems of Race Knowledge Worth Reading. . . .* Nashville: J. T. Haley and Co., 1897.

Harris, Mrs. L. H. "Negro Womanhood." *Independent* (June 1899): 1687–90.

———. "A Southern Woman's View [of the Negro]." *Independent* (18 May 1899): 1354–55.

Isabelle, Lizzie. "The Women of Our Race Worthy of Imitation" [Literary Notice]. *Christian Recorder* (3 Oct. 1889): 3.

Joyce, Thomas Athol, and N. W. Thomas, eds. *Women of All Nations: A Record of Their Characteristics, Habits,*

Manner, Customs and Influence. London and New York: Cassell and Company, 1908; New York: Metro Publications, 1942.

Kellor, Frances A. "To Help Negro Women." *Boston Traveler* (31 May 1905).

Kletzing, H. F., and W. H. Crogman. "The Colored Woman of Today." In *Progress of a Race or the Remarkable Advancement of the Afro-American*. Atlanta: Nichols & Co., 1897.

Miller, Kelly. "Surplus Negro Women." *Southern Workman* (Oct. 1905): 222. Republished in *Race Adjustment: Essays on the Negro in America*. New York: Neale Publishing Co., 1908.

Murray, Anna E. "The Negro Woman." *Southern Workman* (Apr. 1904): 232.

Narrative of the Facts in the Case of Passimore Williamson [Re: Fugitive Jane Johnson]. Philadelphia: Pennsylvania Anti-Slavery Society, 1855.

"Negro Problem, by a Colored Woman and Two White Women." *Independent* (17 March 1904): 586–89.

"Problem as Viewed by a Southern Colored Woman." *Independent* (18 Sept. 1902): 2221–24.

"Problem as Viewed by a Southern White Woman." *Independent* (18 Sept. 1902): 2224–28.

Redpath, James. *Echoes of Harper's Ferry*. Boston: Thayer and Eldridge, 1860; Westport, CT: Negro Universities Press, 1970.

Stowe, Harriet Beecher. *The Edmondson Family and the Capture of the Schooner 'Pearl.'* Cincinnati: American Reform Tract and Book Society, 1854.

Tayleur, Eleanor. "Negro Woman." *Outlook* (30 Jan. 1804): 266–71.

Washington, Booker T. "Negro Women and Their Work." *The Story of the Negro*. New York: Doubleday, Page & Co., 1909; Negro Universities Press, 1969.

————. "The New Negro Woman." *Lend a Hand* 15 (1895): 254.

Washington, Forrester B. "Reconstruction and the Colored Woman." *Life and Labor* 9.1: 3–7.

Antislavery Publications

Also see Part I, for example, Mary Ann Shadd Cary, Charlotte L. Forten, Frances Ellen Watkins Harper, Harriet Ann Jacobs, Susan Paul, and Sarah Parker Remond. See as well all items in Part II (particularly Sojourner Truth and Harriet Tubman), presenting the dictated narratives and biographies of women who had been held in slavery.

Black and white abolitionists routinely addressed the condition of women in slavery. With the establishment, in 1825, of *Genius of Universal Emancipation*, Benjamin Lundy, and later his protégés Elizabeth Margaret Chandler and William Lloyd Garrison, wrote about this subject, often addressing themselves directly to female readers of the antislavery press—many of whom were black. Later, as the Garrisonian movement developed, female antislavery societies were organized. These included groups that were all black and all white, as well as groups that were racially integrated. Like local, state, and national antislavery societies, female antislavery societies concerned themselves with women in slavery. Many, like the Boston Society, issued annual reports. In addition, they published numerous children's books featuring black women and children—such as McDougall's *The Envoy*, listed below. Further, the women's organizations invited speakers who, like James Forten, Jr. (listed below), discussed the condition of female slaves. The items included in this list only hint at the materials in official abolitionist publications that concern women in slavery. For a standard listing, see Dwight L. Dumond, *A Bibliography of Anti-Slavery in America* (Ann Arbor: University of Michigan Press, 1961). In addition, see colonizationist publications, such as American Colonization Society *Annual Reports, 1818–1910.*

"Address of the Anti-Slavery Women of Western New York." *North Star* (24 March–11 Aug. 1848).

American Anti-Slavery Society. *Annual Reports, 1834–1861.* New York: American Anti-Slavery Society, 1834–1861.

———. *Proceedings at Its Second Decade, Held in the City of Philadelphia, December 3rd, 4th and 5th, 1853.* New York: American Anti-Slavery Society, 1854.

———. *Proceedings at Its Third Decade, Held in the City of Philadelphia, December 3rd and 4th, 1864.* New York: American Anti-Slavery Society, 1864.

Anti-Slavery Convention of American Women. *Address to Anti-Slavery Societies.* Philadelphia: Merrihew and Gunn, 1838.

———. *An Address to Free Colored Americans.* . . . New York: William S. Dorr, 1837.

———. *Address to the Senators and Representatives of the Free States in the Congress of the United States.* Philadelphia: Merrihew and Gunn, 1838.

Anti-Slavery Convention of American Women [Angelina E. Grimké Weld]. *An Address from the Convention of American Women, to the Society of Friends.* . . . Philadelphia: Merrihew and Thompson, 1839; Bristol, England: J. Wright, 1840.

Anti-Slavery Convention of American Women [Angelina E. Grimké Weld] *An Appeal to the Women of the Nominally Free States, Issued by an Anti-Slavery Convention of American Women. . . .* New York: W. S. Dorr, 1837.

————. *Proceedings of the Anti-Slavery Convention of American Women . . . 1837.* New York: William S. Dorr, 1837.

————. *Proceedings of the Anti-Slavery Convention of American Women . . . 1838.* Philadelphia: Merrihew and Gunn, 1838.

————. *Proceedings of the Third Anti-Slavery Convention of American Women . . . 1839.* Philadelphia: Merrihew and Thompson, 1839.

Forten, James, Jr. *An Address Delivered before the Ladies Anti-Slavery Society of Philadelphia.* Philadelphia: Merrihew and Gunn, 1836.

McDougall, Frances Harriet (Whipple) Greene. *The Envoy, from Free Hearts to the Free.* Pawtucket, RI: Juvenile Emancipation Society, 1840.

[Weld, Theodore D.] *American Slavery as It Is: Testimony of a Thousand Witnesses.* New York: American Anti-Slavery Society, 1839.

The Arts

Also see Part IV, which lists publications about Meta Vaux Warrick Fuller and Mary Edmonia Lewis, sculptors; Flora Batson Bergen, Elizabeth Taylor Greenfield, and [Matilda] Sissieretta Jones, singers; Anna and Emma Hyers, actresses; and Mary E. Webb, elocutionist.

Allen, William Francis, Charles P. Ware, and Lucy McKim Garrison, eds. *Slave Songs of the United States.* New York:

A. Simpson & Co., 1867; Freeport, NY: Books for Libraries Press, 1971.

"Ladies of the Fisk Jubilee Singers." Scruggs, 130–34.

McKim, Lucy. "Songs of the Port Royal Contraband." *Dwight's Journal of Music* (8 Nov. 1862): 254–55.

Waters, Clara Erskine Clements. *Women in the Fine Arts.* Boston: Houghton Mifflin, 1904; New York: Hacker Art Books, 1974.

Collective Biographies

Also see Part I (Hallie Quinn Brown, Gertrude E. H. Bustill Mossell, and Susan Isabella Lankford Shorter), and Part III (Susan Elizabeth Frazier).

Black and white abolitionists like William C. Nell, Wilson A. Armistead, and Abigail F. Mott early included women in their collective biographies of African Americans. By the end of the nineteenth century, women were included in a number of collective biographies celebrating the advances made since emancipation. As far as black women were concerned, however, collective biographies were transformed into a genre in which black women became the subjects of their own writings when in 1894 Mrs. N. F. Mossell (Gertrude E. H. Bustill Mossell) published *The Work of the Afro-American Woman.*

The discourse that women like Hallie Q. Brown and others later structured testifies to a spirit of self-conscious celebration of a black female culture. But turn-of-the-century collective biographies of black women also testify to the segregationism of the contemporary women's movement: Frances E. Willard and Mary A. Livermore included not a single black woman among 1,500 entries in their (misnamed) *American Women . . . A Comprehensive Encyclopedia of the Lives and Achieve-*

ments of American Women During the Nineteenth Century, 2 vols. (New York: Mast, Crowell, & Kirkpatrick, [1897]).

Armistead, Wilson A. *A Tribute for the Negro*. Connecticut: Irwin Manchester, 1848.

Bruce, John Edward. *Short Biographical Sketches of Eminent Negro Men and Women in Europe and the United States*. Yonkers, NY: Gazette Press, 1910.

Culp.

Majors.

Mott, Abigail F. *Biographical Sketches and Interesting Anecdotes of Persons of Color*. New York: M. Day, 1826. 2nd Edition. York, England: W. Alexander & Son, 1828. Revised and Enlarged, New York: M. Day, 1839, 1850.

————, comp. *Narratives of Colored Americans*. New York: William Wood and Co., 1875.

Nell, William C. *The Colored Patriots of the American Revolution*. Boston: Robert F. Wallcut, 1855; New York: Arno Press, 1969.

Richings, G. F. "Prominent Colored Women." In *Evidences of Progress Among Colored People*. Philadelphia: Geo. S. Ferguson, 1909.

Scruggs.

Thompson, Mary W. *Sketches of the History, Character, and Dying Testimony of Beneficiaries of the Colored Home, in the City of New York*. New York: John F. Trow, 1851.

Education

Also see listings under the names of such educators as those in Part I: Hallie Quinn Brown, Mary Ann Shadd Cary, Anna Julia Haywood Cooper, Frances Jackson Coppin, Alice Ruth Moore Dunbar-Nelson, Charlotte L. Forten, Maria

W. Miller Stewart, and Susie Baker King Taylor; Part III: Maria Louise Baldwin, Sarah Mapps Douglass Douglass, and Lucy Craft Laney; and Part IV: Sarah J. Smith Garnet and Lucy Ellen Moten.

Since before emancipation slaves were forbidden literacy and free women generally received minimal formal education, and since at the end of the nineteenth century, racism was institutionalized in American schools, it is not surprising that the education of African-American women sometimes triggered antiblack violence. Some of the items listed below refer to the Prudence Crandall case, in which violence was directed against a school that admitted black girls in the North; the item by Margaret Douglass reports the jailing of a white woman for teaching free children in the South. With the exception of Lydia Maria Child's *The Freedmen's Book*, textbooks designed for the freed people's schools are not included in this listing.

Alexander, William T. "Woman's Higher Education." *History of the Colored Race in America*. Kansas City, MO: Palmetto Publishing Co., 1887.

"Bethune School for Girls." *Woman's Journal* (27 July 1907).

Brawley, Benjamin Griffith. "Women Who Have Led in Education." Brawley, *NBH*, 273–88.

Child, Lydia Maria. *The Freedmen's Book*. Boston: Ticknor and Fields, 1865.

The College-Bred American Negro. Atlanta University Studies, no. 15. Atlanta, 1910.

The College-Bred Negro. Atlanta University Studies, no. 5. Atlanta, 1900.

"Colored Women's Good Work." *Woman's Journal* (4 Aug. 1906).

Douglass, Margaret. *Educational Laws of Virginia*. Boston:

J. P. Jewett & Co.; Cleveland: Jewett, Proctor & Worthington, 1854.

"The First Colored Woman to Receive the Degree of M.A." *Woman's Journal* (5 Jan. 1895).

Holmes, Josephine E. "A Study of Education's Triumph." *Colored American Magazine* (Jan. 1908): 35–44.

Mayo, Amory Dwight. *Southern Women in the Recent Educational Movement in the South*. Washington, DC: Government Printing Office, 1892.

Parsons, M. "Mount Holyoke of the South." *Home Mission Monthly* (1908).

"Prudence Crandall School for Young Colored Women, 1803–1891." *Barnard's American Journal of Education* 11: 328.

Report of the Arguments of Counsel in the Case of Prudence Crandall Plaintiff in Error vs. State of Connecticut. Boston: Garrison and Knapp, 1834.

Soch, Emma. "Gardening for Girls." *Southern Workman* (Dec. 1907): 661–64.

Twenty-Two Years Work of the Hampton, Virginia Normal and Agricultural Institute. Hampton, VA: n.p., 1893.

Employment

Also see Part I: lawyers Mary Ann Shadd Cary and Charlotte E. Ray, and physician Sarah Parker Remond, as well as Part IV: nurse Mary Eliza Mahoney and businesswoman Maggie Lena Mitchell Walker.

Bishop, S. H. "Industrial Conditions of the Negro Women in New York." *Southern Workman* (Sept. 1910): 525–28.

Butler, H. R. "What Negro Women Are Doing." In *Sparkling Gems of Race Knowledge Worth Reading. . . .* James T. Haley, comp. Nashville: J. T. Haley and Co., 1897. 61–62.

Du Bois, W.E.B. *Economic Cooperation among Negro Americans.* Atlanta: Atlanta University Press, 1907.

Easton, Hosea. *A Treatise on the Intellectual Character, and Civil and Political Conditions of the Colored People of the United States.* Boston: I. Knapp, 1837.

Fleming, Walter Lynwood. "The Servant Problem in a Black Belt Village." *Sewanee Review* (13 Jan. 1905): 1–17.

Jackson, Giles B., and D. Webster Davis. *The Industrial History of the Negro Race in the United States.* Richmond: Virginia Press, 1908; Freeport, NY: Books for Libraries Press, 1971.

Langhorne, Ora. "Domestic Service in the South." *American Journal of Social Science* 39 (1901): 169.

Layten, W. S. "The Servant Problem." *Colored American Magazine* 12.1 (1907): 13–15.

Miller, Kelly. "Surplus Negro Women." *Southern Workman* (10 Oct. 1905): 522–28. Reprinted in *Race Adjustment: Essays.* New York and Washington: Neale Publishing Co., 1908, 1968; Freeport, NY: Books for Libraries Press, 1971.

The Negro Labor Question, by a New York Merchant. New York: John A. Gray, 1858.

Salmon, Lucy Maynard. *Domestic Service.* New York and London: Macmillan, 1897.

Small, [Mrs.] Sam. "Club Girls and Working Girls." *Savannah Tribune* (29 Feb. 1908): 8.

United States Bureau of the Census Special Reports. *Occupations at the Twelfth Census.* Washington, D.C.: Government Printing Office, 1904.

Geographical and Regional Discussions

Abbott, Edith A. "The Negro Woman and the South."
Outlook (21 May 1904): 165–68.

Crummell, Alexander. *The Black Woman of the South: Her
Neglects and Her Needs*. Washington, DC: B. S. Adams,
1883.

Du Bois, W.E.B. *The Philadelphia Negro: A Social Study*.
Philadelphia: University of Pennsylvania, 1899; New
York: Schocken Books, 1967.

Hobson, Elizabeth Christopher, and [Mrs.] C. E. Hopkins.
A Report Concerning the Colored Women of the South.
Baltimore: The Trustees of the John F. Slater Fund.
Occasional Papers, no. 9. J. Murphy & Co., 1896.

Jefferson, Olive R. "Southern Negro Women." *Chautauquan*
18 (1894): 91.

Orrick, L. S. "Advance of Negro Women in the South."
Boston National Magazine 21 (1905): 172.

Raymond, Rev. W. O. "The Negro in New Brunswick."
Neith (Feb. 1903).

*Report of the Merchants Committee for the Relief of Colored
People Suffering from the Riots in the City of New York,
July, 1863*. New York: G. A. Whitehorn, Printer, 1863.

Thompson, Mary W. *Sketches of the History, Character, and
Dying Testimony of Beneficiaries of the Colored Home, in
the City of New York*. New York: John F. Trow, Printer,
1851.

Towne, Laura M. "Pioneer Work on the Sea Islands."
Southern Workman (July 1901).

Health and Medicine

Also see Part I: Sarah Parker Remond, physician; and Part
IV: Mary Eliza Mahoney, nurse.

Williams, Daniel H. "Cancer in the Breast in the Afro-American Women." *A.M.E. Church Review* (Jan. 1897): 297.
———. "Ovarian Cysts in Colored Women." *Philadelphia Medical Journal* (29 Dec. 1900).

Literature and Journalism

Also see Part I: poets Christina Moody Briggs, Alice Ruth Moore Dunbar-Nelson, Mary Weston Fordham, Charlotte L. Forten, Frances Ellen Watkins Harper, Josephine Delphine Henderson Heard, Adah Isaacs Menken, Lizelia Augusta Jenkins Moorer, Ann Plato, Henrietta Cordelia Ray, Effie Waller Smith, and Eloise Bibb Thompson; and journalists Mary Ann Shadd Cary, Lucretia H. Newman Coleman, and Ida Bell Wells-Barnett. See as well Part III: poet Mamie Eloise Fox, and journalists Mary V. Cook [Grace Ermine] and Lucy Wilmot Smith.

Haley, James T., comp. *Sparkling Gems of Race Knowledge Worth Reading.* . . . Nashville: J. T. Haley and Co., 1897.
Mann, C. A. "Our Early Women Writers." *A.M.E. Church Review* (Apr. 1900): 479.
McClellan, J. M. "The Negro as a Writer." In *20th Century Negro Literature.* D. W. Culp, ed. Naperville, IL: J. L. Nichols & Co., 1902; New York: Arno Press, 1969; Miami: Mnemosyne Publishing Co., 1969.
Penn, Irvine G. "Afro-American Women in Journalism." Penn, 367–427.
Penn, Irvine G., and Henry D. Northrop. "Rise and Progress of Afro-American Literature." In *The College of Life; or, Practical Self-Educator.* Chicago: Chicago Publication and Lithograph Co., 1895. 86–102.

Wilson, Joseph T. "Some Negro Poets." *A.M.E. Church Review* 4 (1888): 236–45.

Marriage, Family, and the Home

In a number of articles cited, traditional notions of "true womanhood" are interpreted in relation to black women. For a short story that questions the appropriateness of these notions, see Frances Ellen Watkins Harper's innovative "The Two Offers," cited in Part I.

Arnett, Bishop. "Married Life—Its Joys and Sorrows." In *Sparkling Gems of Race Knowledge Worth Reading*. . . . James T. Haley, comp. Nashville: J. T. Haley and Co., 1897. 157–60.

Banks, Frank D., and Portia Smiley. "Old-Time Courtship Conversation." *Southern Workman* (1895): 251–57.

Burrell, Ida K. "The Value of Domestic Science." *Colored American Magazine* (July 1907): 59–60.

Fortune, T. Thomas. "Intermarriage and Natural Selection." *Colored American Magazine* (June 1909): 380–81.

Gibbs, Ione E. "Women's Part in the Uplift of the Negro Race." *Colored American Magazine* (Apr. 1907): 264–67.

Murray, Daniel. "Race Integrity—How to Preserve It in the South." *Colored American Magazine* (Dec. 1906): 369–77.

"Qualities of a Colored Man's Wife." *Colored American Magazine* (Sept. 1907): 169–70.

Scruggs, Lawson A. "The Influence of Negro Women in the Home." Scruggs, 372–82.

Shadrach, J. Shirley. "Furnace Blasts. 11. Black or White— Which Should Be the Young Afro-American's Choice in

Marriage?" *Colored American Magazine* (March 1903): 348–52.

"Shall Women Propose to the Men?" *Colored American Magazine* (July 1907): 10.

"The Successful Negro Mother." *Colored American Magazine* (July 1908): 396.

"A Talk about Marriage." *Repository of Religion and Literature and of Science and Art* (July 1861): 118–22.

"Why the Men Don't Marry." *Colored American Magazine* (Nov. 1907): 328–29.

Organizations

Also see Part I: Ida Bell Wells-Barnett and Fannie Barrier Williams; Part III: Josephine St. Pierre Ruffin and Josephine Silone-Yates; and in this section of the bibliography, *Antislavery Publications* and *Women's Suffrage and Feminism.*

[Announcement of Colored Woman's Club meetings in Boston.] *Woman's Journal* (3 Aug. 1895).

Barrett, [Mrs.] Harris. "Negro Women's Clubs and the Community." *Southern Workman* (Jan. 1910): 33–34.

Forten, James, Jr. Speech to the American Moral Reform Society. *The Minutes and Proceedings of the First Annual Meeting of the American Reform Society.* Philadelphia, 1837. 42–43.

"General Federation of Women's Clubs Effectively Bars Colored Women's Clubs." *Woman's Journal* (17 May 1902).

Gibson, William H. *History of the United States of Friendship and Sisters of the Mysterious Ten, in Two Parts. A Negro Order.* Louisville, KY: Bradley and Gilbert Co., 1897.

[Letter from Interracial Woman's Era Club of Boston.] *Woman's Journal* (10 June 1893).

"The National Association of Colored Women." *Voice of the Negro* (July 1904): 310.

[Re: Alabama State Association of Colored Women.] *Woman's Journal* (28 Dec. 1901).

[Re: Negro Conference at Hampton.] *Woman's Journal* (29 June 1899).

[Re: New England Federation of Colored Women's Clubs.] *Woman's Journal* (25 Aug. 1900).

[Re: New England Federation of Colored Women's Clubs as part of National Federation of Colored Women's Clubs; Conference in Brooklyn.] *Woman's Journal* (26 July 1902).

Women's Baptist Home Mission Society. *Twenty-Nine Years' Work among Negroes*. Chicago: Women's Baptist Home Mission Society, 1906.

Religion

Also see Part I, especially Frances Jackson Coppin, a foreign missionary, and Amanda Berry Smith, an evangelist and missionary.

American Missionary Association. *History of the A.M.A.: Its Churches and Educational Institutions among the Freedmen, Indians and Chinese*. New York: n.p., 1874.

Bassett, William. *Letter to a Member of the Society of Friends in Reply to Objections against Joining Anti-Slavery Societies*. Boston: I. Knapp, 1837.

Burdette, M. G. "Woman and the American Negro: Woman's Work for the Afro-American." In *Women in Missions:*

Papers and Addresses Presented at the Women's Congress of Missions, October 2–4, 1893. New York: American Tract Society, 1894. 125–44.

Helm, Mary. "Work of the Woman's Home Missionary Societies." In *From Darkness to Light: The Story of Negro Progress.* New York and Chicago: F. H. Revell, 1909; New York: Negro Universities Press, 1969; Westport, CT: Greenwood Press, 1969.

Stanford, Rev. A. L. "Extent of Female Influence and Importance of Exerting It in Favor of Christianity." *Repository of Religion and Literature and of Science and Art* (Jan. 1861): 6–8.

Reminiscences

A number of white Northern and black male reformers active in the antislavery movement before and during the Civil War and in civil rights efforts during Reconstruction later wrote memoirs discussing black women. Similarly, a number of Southern white men and women produced reminiscences presenting black women as subjects. What follows is a sampling of writings from these groupings.

Also see various listings in Parts I and II.

Ames, Mary. *From a New England Woman's Diary in Dixie in 1865.* Norwood, MA: Plimpton Press, 1906; New York: Negro Universities Press, 1969.

Banks, Mary Ross. *Bright Days in Old Plantation Times.* Boston: Lee and Shepard; New York: C. T. Dillingham, 1882.

Bothume, Elizabeth Hyde. *First Days amongst the Contrabands.* Boston: Lee and Shepard, 1893.

Burwell, Letitia M. *A Girl's Life in Virginia before the War*. New York: F. A. Stokes Co., 1895.

———— [Page Thacker, pseud.]. *Plantation Reminiscences*. Owensburg, KY: n.p., 1878.

Chace, Elizabeth Buffum. *Anti-Slavery Reminiscences*. Central Falls, RI: E. L. Freeman & Son, State Printers, 1891.

Clarke, James Freeman. *Anti-Slavery Days*. New York: J. W. Lovell Company, 1883; Westport, CT: Greenwood Press, 1970.

Coffin, Levi. *Reminiscences of Levi Coffin, the Reputed President of the Underground Railroad*. Cincinnati: Western Tract Society, 1876. 2nd Edition. Cincinnati: R. Clarke & Co., 1880; New York: AMS Press, 1971.

Colman [Mrs.] Lucy Newhall. *Reminiscences*. Buffalo, NY: H. L. Green, 1891.

De Saussure, Nancy. *Old Plantation Days, Being Recollections of Southern Life before the Civil War*. New York: Duffield, 1909.

Devereux, Margaret. *Plantation Sketches*. Cambridge, MA: Riverside Press, 1906.

Geilow, Martha. *Mammy's Reminiscence and Other Sketches*. New York: A. S. Barnes and Company, 1898.

————. *Old Plantation Days*. New York: R. H. Russell, 1902.

Hallowell, Anna Davis. *James and Lucretia Mott: Life and Letters*. Boston and New York: Houghton Mifflin, 1884.

Hammond, Natalie. *A Woman's Part in a Revolution*. New York and London: Longmans, Green and Co., 1897.

Haviland, Laura S. *A Woman's Life-Work: Labors and Experiences of Laura S. Haviland*. Cincinnati: Walden & Stowe, 1881, 1882; Chicago: C. V. Waite, 1887; Publishers Association of Friends, 1889; Miami: Mnemosyne Publishing Co., 1969.

Holley, Sallie. *A Life for Liberty*. John White Chadwick, ed. New York and London: G. P. Putnam, 1899.

Kearney, Belle. *A Slaveholder's Daughter*. London and New York: Abbey Press, 1900.

Livermore, Mary A. *The Story of My Life; or, the Sunshine and Shadow of Seventy Years*. Hartford, CT: A. D. Worthington, 1897.

————. *My Story of the War; A Woman's Narrative of Four Years Personal Experience as Nurse in the Union Army, and in Relief Work at Home, in Hospitals, Camps and at the Front, During the War of the Rebellion*. Hartford, CT: A. D. Worthington, 1887.

May, Samuel J. *Some Recollections of Our Anti-Slavery Conflict*. 1869. New York: Arno Press, 1969.

Pillsbury, Parker. *Acts of the Anti-Slavery Apostles*. Concord, NH: Clague, Wegman, Schlicht & Co., Printers, 1883.

Southwick, Sarah H. *Reminiscences of Early Anti-Slavery Days*. Cambridge, MA: Riverside Press, 1893.

Still, William. *Underground Railroad Records*. . . . Philadelphia: Porter & Coates, 1872.

Swisshelm, Jane. *Half a Century*. Chicago: Jansen, McClurg & Company, 1880.

Towne, Laura M. *Letters and Diary of Laura M. Towne, Written from the Sea Islands of S.C.* Rupert S. Holland, ed. Cambridge, MA: Riverside Press, 1912; Westport, CT: Greenwood Press, 1970.

Washington, Amanda. *How Beauty Was Saved and Other Memories of the Sixties*. New York and Washington: Neale Publishing Co., 1907.

Wilkinson, Eliza. *Letters of Eliza Wilkinson*. New York: Samuel Colman, 1829.

Travelers' Accounts

Kemble, Frances Ann. *Journal of a Residence on a Georgian Plantation in 1838–39*. London: Longman, Green, Longman, Roberts and Green, 1863; New York: Harper & Brothers, 1863.

Martineau, Harriet. *Society in America*. Vol. 3. London: Saunders and Otley, 1837, 3 vols. New York: Saunders and Otley, 1837, 2 vols.

Redpath, James. *The Roving Editor; or Talks with Slaves in the Southern States*. New York: A. B. Burdick, 1859; Negro Universities Press, 1968.

Urban Issues

Du Bois, W.E.B. *Mortality among Negroes in Cities*. Atlanta: Atlanta University Press, 1896.

———. *Social and Physical Conditions of Negroes in Cities*. Atlanta: Atlanta University Press, 1897.

Kellor, Frances A. "Associations for the Protection of Colored Women." *Colored American* (Dec. 1905): 695–99.

———. "Opportunities for Southern Negro Women in Northern Cities." *Voice of the Negro* (July 1905): 470–73.

———. "Southern Colored Girls in the North." *Charities* (18 March 1905).

National League for the Protection of Colored Women. *Annual Report* (Nov. 1910).

Women's Suffrage and Feminism

Also see suffragists listed in Part I (Frances Ellen Watkins Harper, Mary Eliza Church Terrell, and Ida Bell Wells-

Barnett), Part II (Sojourner Truth and Harriet Tubman), and Part III (Josephine St. Pierre Ruffin). Also in Parts I and II, see Maria W. Miller Stewart, the first female American public speaker, and orators Hallie Quinn Brown, Sarah Parker Remond, Sojourner Truth, and Fannie Barrier Williams.

[Re: Lottie Wilson Jackson of Michigan, Black Delegate to NAWSA Convention.] *Woman's Journal* (13 May 1899).

Stanton, Elizabeth C., et al., eds. *History of Woman Suffrage*. 6 vols. New York: Fowler and Wells, 1881. 1: 114–17, 220, 224, 276, 324, 325, 329, 332, 337, 384, 567–69, 668, 824. 2: 22, 171, 178, 182, 183, 193–94, 222, 391–92, 399. 3: 61, 72–73, 151, 268–69, 955. 4: 298, 358, 395, 398–99, 425, 572. 5: 60, 105, 203.

Straker, David Augustus. "Citizenship, Its Rights and Duties. Woman Suffrage." *New National Era* (1874).

SOURCES CONSULTED

Abajian, James de T., comp. *Blacks and Their Contributions to the American West: A Bibliography and Union List of Library Holdings Through 1970.* Boston: G. K. Hall, 1974.

———. *Blacks in Selected Newspapers, Censuses, and Other Sources: An Index to Names and Subjects.* 3 vols. and supplement. Boston: G. K. Hall, 1977.

Arata, Esther Spring, and Rotoli, Nicholas John. *Black American Playwrights, 1800 to the Present: A Bibliography.* Metuchen, NJ: Scarecrow Press, 1972.

The Black Family and the Black Woman. Indiana University Library, Bloomington, 1972.

Blassingame, John, Mae Henderson, and Jessica M. Dunn. *Anti-Slavery Newspapers and Periodicals.* 5 vols. Boston: G. K. Hall, 1980–1984.

Brawley, Benjamin Griffith. *Negro Builders and Heroes.* Chapel Hill: University of North Carolina Press, 1937

———. *The Negro Genius.* New York: Dodd, Mead, 1937; Biblo and Tannen, 1966.

———. *The Negro in Literature and Art in the United States.* New York: Duffield & Co., 1918.

Brignano, Russell Carl. *Black Americans in Autobiography.* Durham, NC: Duke University Press, 1974, 1984.

Brown, Hallie Q., comp., ed. *Homespun Heroines and Other Women of Distinction.* Xenia, OH.: Aldine Publishing Co., 1926; New York: Oxford University Press, 1988.

Bullock, Penelope L. *The Afro-American Periodical Press, 1838–*

1909. Baton Rouge and London: Louisiana State University Press, 1981.

Busacca, Basil. "Checklist of Black Playwrights: 1823–1970." *Black Scholar* 5 (Sept. 1973): 48–54.

Carter, George, and Peter C. Ripley, eds. *Black Abolitionist Papers, 1830–1865; A Guide to the Microfilm Edition*. New York: Microfilming Corporation of America, 1981.

Corrigan, Robert. "Afro-American Fiction: A Checklist, 1853–1970." *Midcontinent American Studies Journal* 2 (1970): 114–35.

———. "Afro-American Fiction: Errata and Additions." *American Studies Journal* 12 (1971): 69–74.

Culp, Daniel Wallace, ed. *Twentieth Century Negro Literature: or, A Cyclopedia of Thought on the Vital Topics Relating to the American Negro by One Hundred of America's Greatest Negroes*. Toronto, Naperville, IL, and Atlanta: J. L. Nichols & Co., [c.1902]; Miami: Mnemosyne Publishing Co., 1969.

"Current Sources on Women and Literature." *Concerns* 9 (1 Dec. 1979).

Daniel, Sadie Iola. *Woman Builders*. Washington, DC: The Associated Press, 1931; Associated Publishers, [c.1970].

Dann, Martin E. *The Black Press 1827–1890: The Quest for National Identity*. New York: G. P. Putnam's Sons, 1971.

Dannett, Sylvia. *Profiles of Negro Womanhood*. Vol. 1, *1619–1900*. Yonkers, NY: The Negro Heritage Library, 1964.

———. *Profiles of Negro Womanhood*. 2 vols. Yonkers, NY: Educational Heritage, 1964, 1966.

Davis, Elizabeth. *Lifting As They Climb*. Chicago: National Association of Colored Women, 1933.

Davis, John P., ed. *The American Negro Reference Book*. Englewood Cliffs, NJ: Prentice-Hall, 1966.

Davis, Lenwood G. *The Black Woman in American Society: A Selected Annotated Bibliography*. Boston: G. K. Hall, [c.1975].

———. *Black Women in the Cities, 1872–1972: A Bibliography on the Life and Achievements of Black Women in Cities in the United*

States. Monticello, IL: Council of Planning Libraries, 1972. 2nd Edition, 1975.

Dictionary Catalog of the Jesse E. Moorland Collection of Negro Life and History. Howard University Library. 9 vols., 1970; 1st supplement, 3 vols., 1976. Boston: G. K. Hall, 1970, 1976.

Dictionary Catalog of the Negro Collection of the Fisk University Library. 6 vols. Nashville and Boston: G. K. Hall, 1974.

Dictionary Catalog of the Schomburg Collection of Negro Literature and History. New York Public Library. 9 vols., 1962; 1st supplement, 2 vols., 1967; 2nd supplement, 4 vols., 1974. Boston: G. K, Hall, 1962, 1967, 1974.

Dictionary Catalog of the Arthur E. Spingarn Collection of Negro Authors. 2 vols. Boston: G. K. Hall, 1970.

Freedman, Frances S., ed. *The Black American Experience: A New Anthology of Black Literature*. Toronto and New York: Bantam Pathfinders, [c. 1970].

Green, Elizabeth Atkinson. *The Negro in Contemporary American Literature*. Chapel Hill: University of North Carolina Press, [c. 1928].

Griffin, Appleton Prentiss Clark, comp. *Library of Congress Select List of References on the Negro Question*. 2nd Issue with Additions. Washington, DC: Government Printing Office, 1906.

Gubert, Betty Kaplan. *Early Black Bibliographies, 1863–1918*. New York: Garland, 1982.

Homer, Dorothy R. *The Negro in the United States: A List of Significant Books*. 8th Edition. New York: New York Publishers Co., 1960.

Indexes and Abstracts to Periodicals and Other Printed Material. Sarah Lawrence Library, Sarah Lawrence College, Bronxville, NY, Sept. 1977.

Jacobs, Donald M., ed. *Antebellum Black Newspapers: Indices to New York Freedom's Journal (1827–1829), The Rights of All (1829), The Weekly Advocate (1837), and The Colored American (1837–1841)*. Westport, CT: Greenwood Press, 1976.

Jacobs, Sue Ellen. *Women in Cross Cultural Perspectives: A Prelim-*

inary Source Book. Urbana: University of Illinois, Department of Urban and Regional Planning, 1971.

———. *Women in Perspective: A Guide for Cross-Cultural Studies*. Urbana: University of Illinois Press, 1974.

Jahn, Janheinz. *Bibliography of Neo-African Literature from Africa, London, and the Caribbean*. New York: Praeger, 1965; Budapest: Center for Afro-Asian Research of the Hungarian Academy of Sciences, 1969.

James, Edward T., and Janet W. James, eds. *Notable American Women, 1607–1950: A Biographical Dictionary*. Cambridge, MA: Harvard University Press, 1971.

Krichmar, Albert. *The Woman's Rights Movement in the United States, 1848–1970: A Bibliography and Sourcebook*. Metuchen, NJ: Scarecrow Press, 1972.

Latimer, C., comp. "Bibliography on the Contribution of Negro Women to American Civilization." [Typescript]. February 1940; additions February 1952. Schomburg Center, New York Public Library.

Lerner, Gerda. *Bibliography in the History of American Women*. 2nd Edition. Bronxville, NY: Sarah Lawrence College, 1975.

———, ed. *Black Women in White America: A Documentary History*. New York: Vintage Books, 1973.

Lewinson, Paul. *A Guide to Documents in the National Archives for Negro Studies*. Washington, DC: American Council of Learned Societies, 1947.

Loewenberg, Bert J., and Ruth Bogin, eds. *Black Women in Nineteenth-Century American Life: Their Words, Their Thoughts, Their Feelings*. University Park: Pennsylvania State University Press, 1976.

Logan, Rayford W., and Michael R. Winston, eds. *Dictionary of American Negro Biography*. New York: W. W. Norton, 1982.

Loggins, Vernon. *The Negro Author, His Development in America to 1900*. New York: Columbia University Press, 1931, 1959; Port Washington, NY: Kennikat Press, 1964.

Majors, Monroe Alphus. *Noted Negro Women, Their Triumphs and Activities*. Chicago: Donohue and Henneberry, 1893.

Matthews, Geraldine, et al., comps. *Black American Writers, 1773–1949: A Bibliography and Union List.* Boston: G. K. Hall, 1975.

McPherson, James, et al. *Blacks in America: Bibliographical Essays.* Garden City, NY: Doubleday, 1971, 1972.

Miller, Elizabeth. *The Negro in America.* Cambridge, MA: Harvard University Press, 1966, 1970.

Miller, Wayne C. *A Comprehensive Bibliography for the Study of American Minorities.* New York: New York University Press, 1976.

Mossell, Mrs. N. F. [Gertrude Bustill]. *The Work of the Afro-American Woman.* Philadelphia: G. S. Ferguson Co., 1894; New York: Oxford University Press, 1988.

Newman, Richard. *Black Index: Afro-Americana in Selected Periodicals, 1907–1949.* New York and London: Garland, 1981.

Nolen, Anita. "The Feminine Presence: Women's Papers in the Manuscript Division." *Quarterly Journal of the Library of Congress* 32 (Oct. 1975): 348–65.

Penn, Irvine Garland. *The Afro-American Press and Its Editors.* Springfield, MA: Wiley and Co., 1891; New York: Arno Press and the *New York Times,* 1969.

Ploski, Harry A. *The Negro Almanac.* New York: Bellwether, 1971.

Porter, Dorothy. "Early American Negro Writing." In *Bibliographic Society of America Papers.* New York, 1945. 39: 192–268.

———. *The Negro in the United States: A Selected Bibliography.* Washington, DC: Library of Congress, 1970.

———. *North American Negro Poets: A Bibliographical Checklist of Their Writings, 1760–1944.* Hattiesburg, MS: The Book Farm, 1945; New York: Franklin, 1963.

———. "Selected Writings by Negro Women." *Women's Education* (Dec. 1968): 4–5.

Pride, Armistead Scott. *Negro Newspapers on Microfilm.* Washington, DC: Library of Congress, 1953.

Recent Acquisitions on the Subject of Women. Sarah Lawrence Library, Sarah Lawrence College, Bronxville, NY, 21 March, 1977.

Robinson, Wilhelmina S. *Historical Negro Biographies.* International

Library of Negro Life and History. New York: New York Publishers Co., 1967. 2nd Edition Rev. Washington, DC: New York Publishers Co., 1969.

Rose Bibliography. *Analytical Guide and Indexes to the Colored American Magazine 1900–1909*. Westport, CT: Greenwood Press, 1974.

Rush, Theressa G., Carol F. Meyers, and Esther S. Arata, eds. *Black American Writers Past and Present: A Biographical and Bibliographical Dictionary*. 2 vols. Metuchen, NJ: Scarecrow Press, 1975.

Schatz, Walter, ed. *Directory of Afro-American Resources*. New York and London: R. R. Bowker, 1970.

Scruggs, Lawson A. *Women of Distinction: Remarkable Works and Invincible Character*. Raleigh, NC: L. A. Scruggs, 1893.

Sherman, Joan R. *Invisible Poets: Afro-Americans of the Nineteenth Century*. Urbana: University of Illinois Press, 1974.

Shockley, Ann Allen. *Afro-American Women Writers, 1746–1933: An Anthology and Critical Guide*. Boston: G. K. Hall, 1988.

Sims, Janet L. *Black Women: A Selected Bibliography*. Reference Department, Moorland-Spingarn Research Center, Howard University, 1978.

Spradling, Mary Mace, ed. *In Black and White. A Guide to Magazine Articles, Newspaper Articles, and Books Concerning More Than 15,000 Black Individuals and Groups*. 3rd Edition. Detroit: Gale Research, [c.1980].

———. *In Black and White. Third Edition Supplement: A Guide to Magazine Articles, Newspaper Articles, and Books Concerning More Than 6,700 Black Individuals and Groups*. Detroit: Gale Research, [c.1985].

Stineman, Esther, Catherine Loeb, and Whitney Walton. "Women's Studies Bibliography." *Concerns* 9 (1 Sept. 1979).

Welsch, Erwin K. *The Negro in the United States: A Research Guide*. Bloomington: Indiana University Press, 1965.

Wesley, Charles Harris. *The History of the National Association of*

Colored Women's Clubs: A Legacy of Service. Washington, DC: National Association of Colored Women's Clubs, 1984.

West, Earl H. *A Bibliography of Doctoral Research on the Negro, 1933–1966*. [Washington, DC]: Xerox, 1969. *Supplement 1967–1969*, Ann Arbor: Xerox University Microfilms, 1970.

Whiteman, Maxwell. *A Century of Fiction by American Negroes, 1853–1952*. Philadelphia: Jacobs, 1955.

Willard, Frances. *American Women*. New York: Mast, Crowell and Kirkpatrick, 1897; Detroit: Gale Research, 1973.

Williams, Ora. *American Black Women in the Arts and Social Sciences*. Metuchen, NJ: Scarecrow Press, 1973.

———. "A Bibliography of Works Written by American Black Women." *CLA Journal* 15 (March 1972): 354–77.

Wilson, Greta S., comp. *Guide to Processed Collections in the Manuscript Division of the Moorland-Spingarn Research Center*. Washington, DC: Howard University, 1983.

Women in American Labor History, 1825–1935. East Lansing: School of Labor and Industrial Relations and Michigan State University Library, 1972.

Women: A Selected Bibliography. Springfield, OH: Wittenberg University, 1973.

Women's History Research Center. *Bibliographies on Women*. Berkeley: University of California, 1973.

———. *Female Artists, Past and Present*. Berkeley: University of California, 1974.

Women's Work and Women's Studies, 1971–1973/74. New York: The Women's Center, Barnard College, 1972–1975.

Work, Monroe N., comp. *Bibliography of the Negro in Africa and America*. New York: The H. W. Wilson Company, 1928. Reprint, 1965.

Yellin, Jean Fagan. "An Index of Literary Materials in *The Crisis*, 1910–1934: Articles, Belles Lettres, and Book Reviews." *CLA Journal* 14 (June 1971): 425–65; (Dec.1971): 197–234.

PERIODICALS AND
NEWSPAPERS SEARCHED

Alexander's Magazine 1905–1909
Anglo-African Magazine 1859–1860
Bee 1884–1916
Christian Recorder 1854–1902
Colored American (New York) 1837–1842
Colored American Magazine 1900–1909
Crisis 1910–1940
Frederick Douglass' Paper 1847–1863
Freedom's Journal 1827–1829
Grit 1883–1884
Lancet 1882–1886
New National Era 1870–1874
Opportunity 1923–1940
Provincial Freeman 1853–1857
Repository of Religion and Literature and of Science and Art
    1859–1863
Savannah Tribune 1875–1930
Southern Workman 1872–1939
Voice of the Negro 1904–1907
Weekly Anglo-African 1861–1865
Weekly Call / Topeka Call 1891–1898
Woman's Era 1894–1897

ACKNOWLEDGMENTS

Finally completing this listing, so long a "work in progress," we think it is appropriate to honor the memory of Peter Fagan: he once told his youngest daughter a cautionary tale about a little girl who wanted to read everything in the Library of Congress but who died an old woman, having read only as far as the Cs. It is appropriate also to recall the encouragement of the late Charles T. Davis and the help of the late Bruce Bergman, as well as to express thanks to Ruth Bogin, William R. Ferris, Ernest Kaiser, and Joan R. Sherman, who generously read sections of earlier versions of this manuscript.

We are especially grateful to Dr. Dorothy Porter Wesley, Emeritus Curator, Moorland-Spingarn Research Center, Howard University and 1988–1989 Visiting Scholar at the W.E.B. Du Bois Institute of Afro-American Research, Harvard University, and to Betty Gubert, Assistant Chief Librarian for General Research and Reference at the Schomburg Center for Research in Black Culture, New York Public Library, for their timely aid with the present version of the manuscript; to Henry Louis Gates, Jr., General Editor of this series; and to William Sisler of Oxford University Press.

We would also like to recognize with gratitude those institutions that generously donated their time and resources to report on their collections for our research: the California State Historical Society; James Weldon Johnson Collection and the Beinecke Library, Yale University; the Library Company of Philadelphia; Robert W.

Woodruff Library, Atlanta University; and the Heartman Collection at Texas Southern University.

Finally, we thank Schomburg Center research aide Georgia C. Lewis, and we thank and congratulate the entire staff of the Black Periodical Literature Project at Cornell University for its good efforts and assistance with this bibliography beyond the routine of normal duties. Special thanks to research assistant Ellen Rauch for her early diligence and enthusiasm; to research aide Shannon Minter for her unflappable efficiency; and to Patricia Stafford, who typed most of the book manuscript with assiduous genius.

INDEX

This index includes the names of all African-American women listed as main entries in Parts I–IV of this bibliography.